JOE LOUIS vs. MAX SCHMELING
FIGHT OF THE CENTURY

ALSO BY PATRICK MYLER

Gentleman Jim Corbett: The Truth Behind a Boxing Legend
A Century of Boxing Greats
The Fighting Irish
Regency Rogue: Dan Donnelly, His Life and Legends

JOE LOUIS vs. MAX SCHMELING

FIGHT OF THE CENTURY

PATRICK MYLER
Foreword by BERT RANDOLPH SUGAR

Arcade Publishing • New York

For my wife, Frances, with love and gratitude.

Arcade Publishing books may be purchased in bulk at special discounts for sales promotion, corporate gifts, fund-raising, or educational purposes. Special editions can also be created to specifications. For details, contact the Special Sales Department, Arcade Publishing, 307 West 36th Street, 11th Floor, New York, NY 10018 or arcade@skyhorsepublishing.com.

Arcade Publishing® is a registered trademark of Skyhorse Publishing, Inc.®, a Delaware corporation.

Visit our website at www.arcadepub.com.

10 9 8 7 6 5 4 3 2 1

Library of Congress Cataloging-in-Publication Data is available on file.

ISBN: 978-1-61145-645-5

Printed in the United States of America

"Joe Louis was more than a sports legend. His career was an indictment of racial bigotry and a source of pride and inspiration to millions of white and black people around the world."

— Ronald Reagan

"Max Schmeling is my idol. When you meet this guy, you can just feel the history."

— Vitali Klitschko, World Boxing Council
heavyweight champion, 2004–2005

CONTENTS

FOREWORD

Race is a four letter word that has ignited and incited people to war both inside the ring and out, across the earth. Joe Louis versus Max Schmeling was a matchmaker's dream, a promoter's nirvana, and America's euphoric answer to the Third Reich as they marched their hobnailed boots across Europe. In one corner, there was Joe Louis, the measure of the uncomplicated man they called the "Brown Bomber." His passion stood out even outside the ring, and, in a field devoted to fashioning halos, Joe Louis wore a special nimbus. Across from him was Max Schmeling, who was touted by the Nazi brigades as the ultimate representation of the Aryan race, the pride of German superiority, but whose own decency and courage belied the atrocities of those who supported him the most.

Louis dispersed his words as he did his punches, with a commendable economy of effort, saying a surprising number of things and saying them in a way we all wished we had. There was his evaluation of his country's chances in the global confrontation with the Axis powers. "We'll win 'cause we're on God's side." Dignity. And then there was his enunciation of Billy Conn's chances in their second fight: "He can run, but he can't hide." Guts.

Reporters believed Joe Louis was the most dependable story in sports. To the public, he was all but invincible. But during their first fight in 1936, Max Schmeling, brought out of near retirement as yet another sacrificial lamb, derailed the Louis bandwagon, hitting him with a right hand over a lazy left no fewer than fifty-four times and finally knocking him out of myth and into reality in the twelfth round.

For most fighters, such a defeat was devastating. Their confidence—the essential property for success—took an enormous and sometimes unrecoverable jolt. But Joe Louis came back within two months to knockout another ex-champion, Jack Sharkey. Almost one year to the day after his destruction at the gloves of Schmeling, Louis won the heavyweight championship of the world from Jim Braddock.

In the true American spirit, Louis went on to avenge his loss to Schmeling with a 124-second annihilation that set back the cause of the "master race" and brought joy to millions of Americans. This was 1938, when the world sat on the brink of a war that would result in unimaginable crimes committed in the name of such a cause. Joe Louis versus Max Schmeling is rightfully touted as a symbolic victory that took the sport into the arena of global consequence.

Thirty-three years later, there was another so-called "fight of the century" when Muhammad Ali raged in his first war against Joe Frazier at Madison Square Garden. While the Louis-Schmeling bout was categorized as a fight for racial superiority, Ali-Frazier was a war of racial degradation. When Muhammad Ali called Joe Frazier an "Uncle Tom," the phrase cut through the Black community like a hot knife through butter. White America sat confused. Some praised Ali as a man who fought for his beliefs while others castigated him as a draft dodger. From the pulpit to the penitentiary, the most ardent Ali followers shuddered, and believed that he had gone too far in his verbal abuse of Frazier.

When the result came early in Round 15, as Frazier landed a left hook that put Ali on his back, many called it retribution for calumny. And in a decision, Ali lost his title.

Since Ali's retirement, there has been a plethora of heavyweight champions, among them: Larry Holmes, Mike Tyson, and Lenox Lewis—the last undisputed champion. Several have had success in the ring but could not master the demons outside the ropes. The new millennium has presented the public with a series of heavyweight champions who are about as distinct as a loaf of bread. It's been said of the current four heavyweight title holders that if they were placed in a line-up with the Maytag repairman, none would be recognized. National pride, and a hunger for a better way of life, has been replaced by a sad series of pretenders presenting themselves as contenders.

While our entrance into the twenty-first century appears to be filled with hyperbole, extravagant embellishments of facts, and a craving for fame, Patrick Myler's *Fight of the Century* is a book about a time when the term had substance and meaning. In each chapter, he brings to life an era and a mindset when ability and efficiency could grasp a nation by its jaws and remind us that faith and hard work still had power, that a cause bent on evil could be subverted by a single voice speaking up, that a good right served with might was convincing.

—Bert Randolph Sugar, 2011

ACKNOWLEDGMENTS

Writing a book, they say, is like having a baby. As a mere male, I am lost in my admiration for every woman who goes through that wondrous experience, but the comparison is not entirely frivolous. This particular offspring took me nine difficult months, from conception to birth. I would never have made it through the emotional strain, and the regular labor pains, without the unstinting nursing care of my family and good friends.

Tony Gee was available whenever help with research was needed. Niels Thorsen and Brian Doogan could always be relied on for advice and encouragement. John Exshaw generously offered to read the manuscript and provided useful information on Anny Ondra, Max Schmeling's film-star wife, Briana Cechova, of the Department of Film History, Czech National Film Archive, and Luke McKernan, head of information, British Universities Film and Video Council, were also helpful in this regard.

U.S. boxing historians Tracy Callis and Hank Kaplan provided expert analysis on Louis and Schmeling, as did Nigel Collins, editor in chief of *The Ring*. The professional records of both fighters were compiled by Tracy Callis, with input from Luckett Davis, for Cyber Boxing Zone.

I am grateful to Bonus Books/Volt Press for permission to use extracts from the American edition of Max Schmeling's autobiography and to Ullstein Verlag, Berlin, publishers of the original German version. I also thank Joe Louis Barrow Jr. for allowing me to quote from his biography of his father.

For expert translations of German material, I am indebted to Rinze van der Meer and Bernie O'Dwyer. *Danke sehr!*

Valuable help was also given by staff at the *Saturday Evening Post,* the *New York Post,* the Coca-Cola Company, Caesars Palace Hotel, Las Vegas, the U.S. National Archive, the British Library Newspaper Library, and the Irish National Library.

Hank Kaplan kindly provided some of the photographs used in this book. The rest are from the author's collection unless otherwise stated. Every effort has been made to ascertain the copyright holders of every photograph. We apologize for any omissions, which will be rectified in future editions.

INTRODUCTION

The day I discovered Joe Louis and Max Schmeling was the day I got my first boxing fix. I have never been able to shake off the addiction.

My father, an avid reader, had just two boxing books in his diverse collection, as far as I can remember. One was Nat Fleischer's biography of Jack Dempsey, the other a well-worn paperback copy of a 1937 American record book.

It was the latter that commanded my boyhood attention, especially the two-page picture spread bearing the heading "The Rise . . . and Fall of Joe Louis." On the left, the photos depicted the Brown Bomber's impressive knockouts of Primo Carnera, Max Baer, and King Levinsky. The right-hand side was entirely devoted to his sensational defeat by Max Schmeling.

Dad would eulogize over what a good fighter the German was and how he had shredded the label of invincibility attached to Louis. Later, as my knowledge of the sport grew from devouring second-hand copies of *The Ring*, I often questioned his loyalty to Schmeling. Hadn't Louis avenged his loss inside a single round of the rematch?

"Oh, but he never gave Max a chance" was his unswerving answer. But surely the object of boxing was to defeat your opponent as quickly and emphatically as possible, I persisted. Dad was unwavering in his conviction that Schmeling had been the victim of a mugging by the unsporting American.

When I was eventually able to view the evidence on film, I learned that Louis, far from the whirlwind aggressor my father had indicated, was the epitome of calm as he stalked his foe before moving in for the kill. It remains one of the most brilliant exhibitions of controlled aggression ever seen in the ring.

As a youngster, I never fully grasped the wider implications of a fight that is regarded as the most politically charged event in boxing history. As the grim prospect of a world war grew more likely by the day, the contestants for the world heavyweight championship at New York's Yankee Stadium on June 22, 1938, were seen as symbolizing the differences between their countries' ideologies.

Louis, the grandson of slaves, was handed the flag of "free" America to carry into battle against Nazi Germany, represented by Schmeling. It was up to Joe to discredit Hitler's convictions about the "master race." Max bore the responsibility of proving there was substance to the theory of the white man's superiority over the black man. That was the way it was perceived.

The fighters tried their best to put all this extra responsibility in the back of their minds as they got down to the business of boxing. To them it was a job, and they were determined to perform to the best of their ability.

Although the action in the ring lasted just two minutes and four seconds, the repercussions lasted for a very long time. Indeed, they never really went away.

Neither man is around to shed any new light on the debate. Louis passed away in 1981. Schmeling refused all requests for interviews in the last few years of his life. He was just seven months short of his centenary when he died on February 2, 2005.

My admiration for both fighters remains undiminished. I still have the autographed photograph Max sent me many years ago. I don't have one of Joe, although I'm sure I would have written to him had I obtained an address. Learning later of his troubled private life, I guess he might have had more on his mind than tackling what must have been a mountain of fan mail.

When I was writing my last book, a biography of Gentleman Jim Corbett, I contacted several former world heavyweight champions to ask if they would consider contributing a foreword. Schmeling was the only one who answered. Though in his midnineties, he took the trouble to thank me for my "friendly letter." I had reminded him that he once met Corbett socially. He said it was so long ago that he could not remember and apologized for not granting my request.

As for Louis, I recall how he once got me into trouble. As a skinny teenager, I joined the Arbour Hill amateur boxing club in Dublin, along with my brother Tom. Trainer Mick Coffey was giving us our first basic lesson—how to throw a left jab. He said the blow should come straight from the shoulder, the fist hopefully landing on target with the knuckles to the side, the thumb on top.

I boldly suggested that I had been studying a boxing how-to manual by Joe Louis, who instructed that the jab be thrown with the palm downward, the thumb to the side. Coffey, a highly respected amateur champion in his day, showed admirable restraint under severe provocation.

"Don't mind Joe Louis!" he said firmly, twisting my fist into firing position. "We'll do it my way here."

I never made it as a boxer, but that had more to do with a distaste of getting hit on the nose than confusion over the best way to throw a left jab.

PROLOGUE

THE VISIT

The well-built, neatly dressed man made sure of the Chicago address on the piece of paper before stepping out of the car. After ringing the doorbell, he passed his hat nervously from hand to hand as he waited.

He wanted his visit to be a surprise.

The woman who answered said Joe Louis was out playing golf, but she invited the caller to come inside and wait. She would send a message to the country club that there was a visitor.

After a short while, the door opened to reveal the large frame of the man they used to call the Brown Bomber, chubbier and with much less hair than the other man remembered.

For a few moments, Louis stood there, seemingly rooted to the spot, and gazed in astonishment at the last man on earth he expected to see.

There was no mistaking the smiling German with the dark hair brushed straight back from his high forehead and the black bushy eyebrows that stuck out like ridges over his eyes.

"Max, how good to see you again," he said, dropping his golf bag to the floor and rushing to wrap his arms around the ring opponent he once called "the only man I ever hated."

Max Schmeling settled happily into the embrace. This was how he had hoped the reunion would be—with whatever perceived enmities that had once existed being firmly buried in history.

He couldn't help but contrast it with the last time they were this close, when the American ripped through his guard with vicious punches, sending him crashing to defeat in the first round, and injuring him so badly that he spent six weeks in the hospital. Sixteen years had passed, but he still got occasional twinges of pain in his back to remind him of the brutal beating he took that night.

Whenever either man was back in the news, or there was an anniversary of their 1938 encounter, the events surrounding the historic event were recalled. Louis and Schmeling might have considered themselves no more than professional sportsmen doing their job, but the fight had assumed far greater significance. The world was on a direct course toward war, and the boxers found themselves reluctant pawns in the political game.

The fight was seen as symbolizing the looming conflict between the United States and Germany. Louis, who had suffered racial discrimination in his own country, carried the banner of "Free" America into battle with Nazi Germany, as represented by Schmeling. Adolf Hitler was convinced that victory for Schmeling would prove how superior, physically and mentally, the white man was to the black man. Americans put their faith in Louis to debunk the Aryan "master race" theory by thrashing Hitler's hero. To many, it was ultimately a showdown between good and evil.

Now, as they sipped coffee together in 1954, Schmeling hoped Louis would accept that so much of what had been written about the fight was not true. "The black man will always be afraid of me. He is inferior," he was reported to have said. The press had printed things like "Hitler sent Schmeling to America to beat Louis to pieces."

For years, Max had wanted to meet Joe, face to face, and tell him that the hateful words, the insults, that had been attributed to him were the product of Nazi propaganda.

Louis quickly put him at his ease. "Forget all that stuff," he said. "For a long time people tried the same with me. There were times when I believed what they wrote. But today I know better."

That evening, they went to a restaurant on the south side of Chicago. Max would recall that he was the only white person there, but most of the customers seemed to recognize him. The pair talked for hours, going over their fights, the people they had known, and discussing the directions their lives had taken. As they parted, they resolved that they would keep in touch.

It was the start of a remarkable friendship between two men whose onetime avowed aim was to beat the living daylights out of each other.

1

LEARNING THE ROPES

Jack Kracken made no special mark in boxing history other than that he was the first professional opponent of Joe Louis. Starting life in Norway as Emil Ecklund, he was regarded as a useful performer on the Chicago fight-club circuit and, some said, too stiff a test for the twenty-year-old debutant. He turned out to be the perfect fall guy. Less than two minutes into the fight on Independence Day in 1934, Kracken was sent crashing to the canvas for the full count. He never fought again. Louis's punch-for-pay career was up and running.

The result of the Chicago contest barely merited a mention in the local papers. It certainly wasn't picked up in Germany, where Max Schmeling was more concerned with the direction in which his own career was heading. With just one win in his last five fights, he feared his chances of regaining the world heavyweight title that had been stolen from him were slipping away. But, still only twenty-eight, he felt good. Four of those most recent results could be rationalized. Only Max Baer had beaten him convincingly. To reestablish himself, he needed an impressive win over one of the top contenders, or maybe one of the rising prospects. Even then, he feared outside forces could steer his ambitions off course.

The world outside Germany was growing increasingly concerned about reports of Adolf Hitler's suppression of democracy and, particularly, his determined anti-Semitic campaign. Within the past year, he had overthrown the old Weimar Republic, imposed his personal dictatorship, broken up the labor unions, abolished freedom of speech, stifled the independence of the courts, and driven Jews out of public and professional life. The first concentration camp had been set up at Dachau. Hitler's projected solution to the country's chronic unemployment problem was a vast rearmament program, in defiance of the Treaty of Versailles drawn up at the end of the First World War.

Although Schmeling considered the United States his second home, he was still a German. The Americans, ever wary of letting a foreigner take control of the world heavyweight championship, were now even more reluctant to accommodate someone they saw as a representative of Hitler. He would have to work doubly hard to prove his right to a title chance. As for his standing in Germany, he might find himself less of a hero with the Nazis if he continued to have an American Jew as his manager. Compared to these problems, fighting in the ring was easy.

Some support for Schmeling was guaranteed from an unexpected source: those Americans who would rather see a white man, *any* white man, as world heavyweight champion than a black man.

Joseph Louis Barrow knew all about racial discrimination almost from the time he was born in a sharecropper's shack about six miles from the town of Lafayette, Alabama. Conditions for most black Americans had progressed little in the half-century since President Abraham Lincoln declared an end to slavery. Segregation was entrenched in schools, in the workplace, in the armed forces, in places of entertainment, and everywhere else in daily life. Blacks could not eat in the same restaurants as whites and were pushed to the backseats of buses. Nowhere was prejudice more pronounced than in the Southern states. White politicians made big gains in elections and removed black postmasters and other minor officials from their jobs. Successive laws were passed limiting the opportunities and freedom of black citizens, and there was considerable support for one high-ranking Georgia official's contention that "a Negro's place is in the cornfield."

Munroe Barrow, a big, strong man, standing six feet tall and weighing around two hundred pounds, toiled from dawn till dusk working cotton in a field leased from a Lafayette landowner. He married Lillie Reese, a sturdy daughter of former slaves, who gave birth to eight children. Joseph, the future world heavyweight champion, was number seven. At his first weigh-in on May 13, 1914, he tipped the scales at eleven pounds.

Life for the Barrows was tough. Munroe had to share his crop with the landowner, as well as pay for the rent of a horse and plow, plus the cost of fertilizer and other essentials. As long as the breadwinner was able to work, his wife devoted most of her time to raising her family. Unfortunately, Munroe was prone to spells of mental instability, requiring intermittent stays at the Searcy Hospital for the Negro Insane in nearby Mount Vernon. This meant Lillie had to take over his sharecropper duties, trying to balance the work with looking after her children. By the time Joe was two, his father had been permanently institutionalized. Munroe died in 1938, unaware that his son had become heavyweight champion of the world and the most famous black man on the planet.

Nor did Joe know that Munroe Barrow was his father. The man he regarded as filling that role was Pat Brooks, a widower with nine children of his own. When Joe was six, Pat and Lillie, who mistakenly believed that her husband had died, remarried, and the two families shared a large house near Camp Hill, in the Buckalew Mountains. Despite the heavy burden of feeding the amalgamated brood, none of the kids went hungry. Chicken, potatoes, peas, and milk kept their bellies full. A devout Baptist, Lillie made sure the kids went to church every Sunday. She also insisted on them being obedient to their elders and that they should always tell the truth. "If she ever whipped us, I can remember her saying, 'I'm not whipping you for what you did. I'm whipping you for lying about it,'" said one of the girls, Eulalia.

Joe's schooling was irregular, and he used any excuse to avoid lessons. He did not talk properly until he was six and then with a slight speech impediment that compounded his shyness. Though a big, healthy boy, he was lazy and enjoyed nothing more than a sound sleep. It was a habit that was to remain with him throughout his life.

One day, Pat Brooks was visited by relatives from Detroit who filled his head with grandiose stories of the industry boom in Motor City and the good wages that could be earned. "They said the Ford factory didn't mind hiring Negroes," Joe recalled, "and for once we'd have hard solid money we wouldn't have to share with the landowner." If Brooks needed any further prompting to leave Alabama, it came after a scary encounter with the Ku Klux Klan. As he drove home with Lillie one night after spending the day sitting with the relatives of a dead friend, his old Model T Ford was forced to halt by a group of horsemen who suddenly appeared out of the shadows. They circled the vehicle menacingly and were about to drag the driver out, when one of the masked men recognized him.

"That's Pat Brooks," he said. "He's a good nigger." The Klansmen let him go on his way.

As soon as he could make arrangements, Brooks took his wife and some of the older boys to Detroit with the aim of finding a foothold for the rest of the family. Joe, twelve, and the younger children stayed behind with Lillie's brother, Peter Reese. Within a few months, word came that life was a whole lot better in Detroit and there were jobs for everyone old enough and able to do them. Pat had started work as a municipal street sweeper for fifty cents an hour while hoping to get hired at Ford.

Caught up in the excitement of moving to his new home in an area of Detroit known as Black Bottom, named after the rich, black soil of its original farmland, Joe remembered, "All of a sudden, I wasn't happy catching snakes, shooting marbles, fishing, and playing skin the tree." In the loft of a barn behind the house, the boys put together a makeshift boxing ring. Many of the neighborhood children were invited to take part in sparring sessions. Joe and a pal of his, Thurston McKinney, progressed from there to the Brewster Recreation Center, where boxing was encouraged.

Though initially bemused by the size and hustle and bustle of Detroit, Joe settled in well. Except at school, that is. He found it hard to keep up with his classes, and his parents agreed that it would be better if he went to an industrial school. He became fairly skilled at wood-working, and after school he had a job with an ice company. The youngsters who carried the ice from the horse-drawn wagon were paid according to their size and strength. Louis, a big kid, earned a dollar a day while his smaller friend, Freddie Guinyard, had to settle for fifty cents. Guinyard, who acted as Joe's personal secretary during his early career, said that whenever anything heavier than twenty-five pounds had to be carried, Joe was nominated.

Lillie, eager to have her children pick up some culture, innocently thought Joe might make a musician. She paid fifty cents a week for a violin and another fifty cents for lessons. Though it meant scrimping on her meager household budget, it was worth it to see Joe happily leaving the house and coming home with his violin case tucked under his arm. Too late, she discovered that the youngster had sold the violin and was using her weekly contribution to pay for a locker at the Brewster Center. The violin case carried nothing but his boxing gloves and training gear. Though she insisted that Joe's hands were worthy of something better than knocking other men's noses out of shape, she eventually conceded there was no point in arguing any further. "Very well"' she told him, "if you're going to be a fighter, be the best you can."

Joe thought he had made the wrong choice when he took a hammering in his first amateur fight. Badly overmatched against Johnny Miler, a tough, experienced light heavyweight, early in 1932, the seventeen-year-old novice was knocked down seven times and barely managed to survive the three-round distance. His ego as well as his body battered, he handed his seven-dollar merchandise voucher to Papa Brooks and got a lecture in return. Surely there were better ways of earning money, said his stepfather.

Still, there was no disgrace in the defeat. Miler would go on to represent the United States in that year's Olympic Games in Los Angeles, where he lost on a controversial decision against Ireland's Jim Murphy. Turning professional the following year, he acted as a sparring partner for Max Schmeling while the German was attempting to rebuild his career after losing the world heavyweight title to Jack Sharkey. By then, Joe Louis Barrow had put his unpromising debut behind him and advanced to become the Detroit Golden Gloves champion.

No one knows for sure when he dropped his surname and simply became known as Joe Louis, but it did cause some confusion in the early days and even at times throughout his life. Though pronounced as in "Lewis," his name often came out as "Joe Lou-ie" and he is still referred to as such by the uninitiated.

Despite an impressive run of knockout wins, Joe fell short when he tried for the national Golden Gloves title. He was outscored by the more experienced Clinton Bridges, a clubmate from the Brewster gym. In the American Athletic Union championships in Boston, Max Marek beat him on points. Marek would later capitalize on his success by displaying a sign outside his Chicago bar inviting passersby to "come in and shake the hand of the man who beat Joe Louis."

In 1933, Joe's perseverance paid off when he captured the AAU light-heavyweight championship. That summer, he lost for the fourth and last time in fifty-four amateur bouts when Stanley Evans took a points decision. "I had watched him train and I knew if he hit you, you were down," said Evans. "I had to outsmart him. I had to have more ring generalship."

After the fight, George Slayton, who had seconded Louis, invited a well-dressed middle-aged man into the dressing room. In recalling his first impression of John Roxborough, the man who was about to become his comanager and patron, Joe said,

> This man had real class. He was a very light-skinned black man about six feet tall, and he weighed about 190 pounds. He didn't seem flashy, but stylish and good-looking. He had a gray silk suit, the kind you don't buy off the rack. It made me look twice. His attitude was gentle, like a gentleman should be. Mr. Roxborough told me he liked the way I fought and he was interested in me. I couldn't understand why—hell, I'd just lost the fight. He told me to drop by his real estate office within the next couple of days.

When Louis next met Roxborough, he said he wanted to turn professional and earn some real money.

Max Schmeling's inspiration to become a boxer came about when his father took him to the movies to see the film of Jack Dempsey knocking out Georges Carpentier in their 1921 world heavyweight title fight. So enraptured was the teenager by what he saw that he took to sparring with a friend, using his father's socks as boxing gloves. He realized his natural power when he knocked out his companion in one of their friendly tussles, yet it frightened him. He saw the damage that could be caused by the human fist and was much relieved when his victim recovered consciousness.

Born Maximilian Adolph Otto Siegfried Schmeling in Klein-

Luckow, north of Berlin, on September 28, 1905, he was the oldest of three children born to Max Sr. and Amanda. His brother, Rudolf, was born in 1907 and his sister, Edith, in 1913. Max grew up in Hamburg and took an interest in all sports but especially in track and field and wrestling. His father, a navigator with a shipping firm, recognized the boy's strength and encouraged him to get involved in physical activity. Taking part in violent demonstrations was not quite what he had in mind.

Just a year after Germany's defeat in the First World War, the country was still suffering many deprivations, including a shortage of food. Max tagged along when he saw a local trader, who had been caught selling rats as canned meat, being lynched by an angry mob. The offender was tied to a wagon and paraded around the streets, to shouts and curses from onlookers, before being thrown into a river. He was later tried, found guilty, and sent to jail. When Schmeling excitedly told his father that he had joined the demonstration, he expected praise. Instead, he was punished. Such activities offended the older man's sense of order. Besides, he reminded the fourteen-year-old, there had been shooting in the inner city that day. The Hamburg Spartakists, a radical arm of the Social Democratic Party that developed into the German Communist Party, had riddled the city hall with bullets. Max, sheltering in a doorway, just escaped being hit.

During his apprenticeship at an advertising agency run by William Wilkens, the task he most enjoyed was washing his boss's Isotta car. One day, he dreamed, he would own such a magnificent vehicle. Wilkens encouraged the young man's passion for sports. Max played in goal for a youth soccer team and was so good that he thought about taking up the game professionally.

Boxing, which his well-traveled father had so often spoken about, was virtually nonexistent in Germany at the time. The sport had been illegal under the old Reich and was confined to just a tiny circle until some time after the end of the First World War. Even Otto Flint, the German heavyweight champion until 1920, had to fight mostly behind closed doors. It was only when returning prisoners of war, who had learned about boxing from their English guards, spread the word about the sport that it began to catch on again.

After his exciting experience watching the movie of the Dempsey–

Carpentier fight, Max drove his father to distraction enthusing about boxing and how he wanted to give it a try. Initially skeptical, Herr Schmeling soon saw that the young man would not be dissuaded. He said he would not raise any objections if Max wanted to take boxing lessons.

"A few days later I bought my first boxing gloves at a secondhand store," Max recalled over half a century later. "I still remember bringing home the worn and patched gloves and how I hung them over my bed like a sacred relic. Boxing's lure—dreams of epic battles—had captured me forever."

At seventeen, Schmeling left home to seek work, and this led him to Cologne, where the liberal lifestyle of the Catholic Rhineland was a welcome change from the restrictive Protestant north he had left behind. It was a special thrill to see his first Charlie Chaplin film and savor *The Cabinet of Dr. Caligari,* a masterpiece of the German cinema. Boxing, however, was his real passion.

He read about the history of the sport, learning of its development from bare-knuckle pugilism to gloved combat under the Marquess of Queensberry Rules, and diligently studied a book of instructions by Georges Carpentier. On joining the Mülheim amateur club, he practiced the basics of boxing such as footwork, body movement, defensive moves, and punching techniques. He made such good progress that, by 1924, he reached the light-heavyweight final of the German championships.

His opponent, Otto Nispel, was a rugged southpaw and much more experienced. After three rounds, the judges had the boxers level, so two tie-break rounds were fought. Nispel got the decision. Max's disappointment was tempered when he learned that his performance had impressed Arthur Bülow, the influential editor of *Boxsport.* Bülow told friends that if Schmeling could be taught some refinements, he could one day be a world champion.

Another who took notice of his ability was Hugo Abels, a Cologne roller-blind maker and part-time boxing manager. His suggestion that Schmeling was ready to turn professional was initially resisted, for Max believed that, at nineteen, he was too young. When told that his idol Jack Dempsey was the same age when he first fought for pay, he was persuaded that it was the right move. With Abels as his manager and

Bülow as his adviser, he became a full-time professional boxer.

Right from the start, Schmeling adopted a rigid, self-imposed discipline that ensured maximum physical fitness and mental preparedness. The delights of long evenings with friends were forsaken in favor of early nights, no drinking or smoking, a healthy diet, and total dedication to his chosen profession. It was a strict regimen, which would stand him in good stead throughout a career spanning twenty-four years.

On August 2, 1924, Schmeling had his first professional fight. His opponent on the Düsseldorf bill, Kurt Czapp, lasted into the sixth round before being rescued by the referee. The happy victor cut the reports from the local newspapers and sent them to his parents.

After three further wins, he suffered a setback when he was stopped in four rounds by Max Dieckmann. Caught early on by one of Dieckmann's heavy hooks, he began to bleed from his ear, and his cornermen were unable to stop the flow. A return match resulted in a draw, but on the third occasion that they met, in 1926, Schmeling showed how well he was learning his trade when he knocked out Dieckmann in the first round and became German light-heavyweight champion. By the end of that year, he had taken his record to nineteen wins, three draws, and three losses. Apart from Dieckmann, the only fighters to defeat him were the American Jack Taylor and Larry Gains, a Canadian who trained at the same Cologne gym as himself. Gains would later move to England, capture the British Empire heavyweight title, and beat Primo Carnera the year before the giant Italian won the world heavyweight title.

In a foreword to Gains's autobiography, Max wrote:

> We fought in the autumn of 1925, and, although I'd been suffering from flu shortly before the bout, it never occurred to me that I could lose. I had been winning my other fights so easily. But Larry knocked me out in the second round and, before doing so, demonstrated the value of a very English straight left. It was a priceless lesson from which I benefited in later years.

Schmeling's biggest thrill during that period was when Jack Dempsey visited Cologne on his honeymoon with film star Estelle Taylor. Max was one of three boxers chosen to spar with the world titleholder in an exhibition and was delighted to be told afterward by Dempsey that he was a champion of the future.

Looking to earn some money outside boxing, Schmeling talked Hugo Abels into backing him in an ice-cream venture. Seeing how hot and bothered city people were as they went about their daily business during the summer, he purchased a street cart offering cones for sale. Max left the business in the care of his partner, while he took up an offer from a circus owner to teach boxing to the two sons of Kate Sandwina, billed as "the strongest woman in the world." One of the boys, Ted, would go on to box professionally in England and America, where he fought Primo Carnera, losing on a knockout. When the four-week stint with the circus was over, Schmeling returned to Cologne only to discover that the ice-cream business, in which he had invested all of his savings, had melted away. Abels had sold the wagon to pay off their debts. "It would be a long time before I dared play the entrepreneur again," Max recalled.

The partnership split up, and Schmeling linked up with Max Machon, a Berliner with horseracing and boxing interests. Machon became his trainer and closest friend, with Bülow now acting as his manager. Schmeling moved with Machon to Berlin, a city he quickly learned to love for its "enormous energy" and "a hectic lust for life as if the whole world knew that it stood before an approaching catastrophe."

2

LIFE IS A CABARET

Lillie Barrow was understandably concerned when she heard about John Roxborough's background. The man who was about to manage her son's professional career fronted as a real-estate agent but made his real money from running the largest numbers racket in Detroit. The lottery game had been a popular pastime among poor urban blacks long before Roxborough got into it in the 1920s. Nearly everybody played it, intoxicated by the generous odds for a win. Lillie's misgivings were alleviated when she was told of Roxborough's contributions toward needy black causes, such as payments for rent, food, and coal, and helping promising young men to better their education.

Roxborough took on Julian Black, a business friend from Chicago, as a partner in managing Louis. Black had started his working life as an embalmer, moving on to running a speakeasy and involvement with the numbers game. As neither man knew an awful lot about boxing, they invited former lightweight Jack Blackburn to take charge as Joe's trainer. It was an inspired choice. Blackburn, who had fought some of the greats, including Joe Gans, Harry Greb, and Sam Langford, in over a hundred contests, knew the game inside out. The trouble was he carried a lot of baggage.

Back in 1909, just when Blackburn's career seemed to be going places, he got involved in an argument and shot three people dead, including his wife. Convicted of manslaughter, he was sentenced to ten to fifteen years in jail. Good behavior, along with teaching the warden and his children how to box, earned his release after four years and eight months.

After he retired from boxing in 1923, Blackburn became a trainer. He guided Sammy Mandell, a notoriously weak puncher, to the world lightweight title and also coached bantamweight champion Bud Taylor. His drinking problem and hot temper, however, got him into trouble again in 1935, a year after he took over as Louis's trainer. He was involved in an incident in which a man was shot dead. Blackburn was tried for murder, but, six days into the trial, the prosecution dropped the case.

It is for his expertise in guiding his star pupil that Blackburn would earn his place in the International Boxing Hall of Fame. Though he was tough with Louis, the pair hit it off from the start. He called the boxer "Chappie," and Joe addressed him as "Chappie" in return. Their close friendship endured right up to Blackburn's death from a heart attack in 1942.

Blackburn saw Louis as a somewhat unimaginative boxer at the start of their relationship. He overconcentrated on defense and threw punches singly rather than in combinations. The old-timer encouraged him to be more aggressive and showed him how to get maximum power into his punches, particularly his left jab. Realizing Joe would never be a dancing master, he taught him how to plant his feet firmly, shuffle forward, cut off the ring, and pressure opponents.

Critics of Louis would later depict him as something of a boxing robot, programmed to do exactly what his trainer wanted him to do. Such a suggestion does not bear up to scrutiny. No great fighter has his trainer, no matter how good he is, in the ring with him. In the heat of battle, unexpected things happen and the boxer alone must make crucial decisions to survive a crisis or capitalize on an opening. No one was better than Louis in figuring out how to deal with an awkward opponent or finding the right combination for a knockout.

Initially, Blackburn was skeptical about Louis's chances of making it. Not that he doubted the young man's natural talent, but he thought there were too many obstacles put in the way of black fighters.

"So you think you can get somewhere in the fight game?" he asked Joe. "Well, let me tell you something right off. It's next to impossible for a Negro heavyweight to get anywhere. He's got to be very good outside the ring and very bad inside the ring. Mr. Roxborough is convinced that you can be depended on to behave yourself, but you've got to be a killer;

otherwise I'm getting too old to waste any time on you."

"I ain't going to waste any of your time," Louis responded.

Berlin in the 1920s was an energetic city with a lively social scene and plenty of scope for intellectual stimulation. In contemporary writing, painting, architecture, music, and drama, there was accommodation for new trends and fine talents. People sat up till all hours of the night in the sidewalk cafés and plush bars or visited the countless artists' studios, talking endlessly about life.

"They were," wrote American foreign correspondent William L. Shirer, "a healthy, carefree, sun-worshipping lot, and they were filled with an enormous zest for living to the full and in complete freedom. The old oppressive Prussian spirit seemed to be dead and buried. Most Germans one met—politicians, writers, editors, artists, professors, students, businessmen, labor leaders—struck you as being democratic, liberal, even pacifist."

Schmeling, liberated from his strict upbringing, was delighted to be welcomed into the sporting and cultural circles. Though overwhelmed and slightly unsettled at first by the adulation, he embarked on a self-improvement course, reading books and conversing with intellectuals at the best parties. Still, he realized that he was seen as yet another exotic presence, a kind of mythical animal. Boxing was part of the excitement, the decadence, of Berlin. As a fighter, he was someone else to be talked about.

Max willingly posed for nude sculptures by Rudolf Belling and Renée Sintenis. At least he stripped off in private, unlike erotic dancer Anita Berber. Taking a prominent table in the Hotel Adlon's dining room, she slipped off her expensive fur coat and sat naked, sipping champagne with her two male escorts.

Schmeling wrote in his autobiography, published in 1977:

I think I served a double function in this era that had just discovered sports. The "natural" now reigned, and the fall of Wilhelminian conventions—the corset and the high collar— had brought with it a rather eccentric cult of the body: a glorification of the human body from the cabaret revue to nudism. No self-respecting intellectual journal refused to print nude photos. The Haller Revue brought dozens of undressed girls to the stage. *Querschnitt* published pictures of naked boxers reminiscent of classical and renaissance sculptures, and the 1925 UFA film Paths to Strength and Beauty offered the cultural history of the naked body from the beginning of mankind to the present. Some of this was truly comical, but behind it there was a longing for freedom.

At his favorite hangout, the Roxy Sportsbar, he met famous jockeys and athletes, sipped soft drinks with future tennis star Gottfried von Cramm, and shook hands with motoring aces like Sir Malcolm Campbell, holder of the world's land and water speed records. Screen heartthrob Conrad Veidt ("Women fight—for Conrad Veidt") and Oskar Homolka, the popular movie character actor, were among the regular clientele. Another notable entry on the tavern owner's guestbook would be Sonja Henie, the blonde Norwegian skater, whose three Olympic gold medals and ten world championship triumphs catapulted her into a successful Hollywood movie career. She later became one of Joe Louis's lovers.

With all the many distractions, Schmeling began to slacken his Spartan regimen of training hard and getting to bed by ten every night. He paid the price for his indolence when he came up against Gypsy Daniels at the Frankfurt Festhalle on February 25, 1928. Believing he had nothing to fear from a man he had already beaten two months earlier, he walked into a piledriver and was counted out in two minutes and forty-seven seconds of the first round. (Daniels wasn't really a gypsy but a dark-complexioned Welshman who was introduced to American fight fans by flamboyant manager Jimmy Johnston as the oldest of nineteen children and the son of a gypsy king. Johnston got him to wear a bandana and earrings, which were actually curtain pole rings.)

The news that Schmeling's twenty-fight winning streak had been snapped was greeted with incredulity in Germany. When the result was announced during a six-day bicycle race at the Berlin Sports Palace, the crowd broke into laughter, thinking it was a joke. Wild rumors were reported as facts. One suggested that Max had leaned over the ropes to speak with a friend when Daniels nailed him. Another explanation was that he was still feeling the psychological effects of an accident the previous year, in which his fourteen-year-old sister, Edith, was killed. Max was taking Edith and their mother for a ride in the countryside on his Harley-Davidson motorcycle with sidecar, when he lost control at some roadwork and crashed. While Max and his mother escaped injury, Edith, whose head hit the curb, died in the hospital without regaining consciousness. He was distraught for some time, partially blaming himself for the tragedy.

Max thought there was a more obvious reason for his defeat. As European and German light-heavyweight champion, he had been struggling to keep his weight down to the division limit of 175 pounds. It was time to take on the big boys. His challenge to Franz Diener, the German heavyweight champion, was accepted. It was a move not without risk. Not only was he facing a bigger, stronger man, but the fight was scheduled for fifteen rounds. Prior to this, all German title fights were limited to twelve.

This time he left nothing to chance. With Max Machon, he went over every available film of Diener's fights round by round. His trainer was especially concerned that Schmeling should use his left jab to keep off the champion until he got the chance to bring his favorite right into play. Diener, who had a number of tough American fights under his belt, would be his stiffest test to date.

Emphasizing the extent to which boxing in Germany had become a social as much as a sporting occasion, ringside seats at the Berlin Sports Palace were occupied by men in dress suits and starched shirts, while their womenfolk paraded in bare-shouldered, elegant evening dresses.

In the first round, Schmeling fractured his right thumb. Though this was a definite handicap, the excitement of the fight made him forget the pain. Besides, he had developed more variety to his boxing and no longer depended on a knockout to win. He boxed intelligently to counteract Diener's relentless aggression, and, though completely exhausted at the end, he was a comprehensive winner on points.

Now the holder of three titles, he couldn't defend any of them because of his hand injury. Skeptics suggested he was growing arrogant and was more concerned with social climbing than his boxing career. Somewhat depressed because he was unable to quickly prove the critics wrong, Max drew encouragement from the example of Gene Tunney, who had been mocked because he read the classics, corresponded with George Bernard Shaw, and posed for the Swiss sculptor Hermann Haller. Further encouragement came by way of a telegram from American promoter Tex Rickard, who offered him a fight on the undercard of Tunney's defense of the world heavyweight title against Tom Heeney. Unfortunately, Max was forced to decline, as the hand problem showed no sign of clearing up, but there was nothing to stop him from attending the big fight as a spectator.

The day before he boarded the liner *New York* with his hand heavily bandaged, he got word that he had been stripped of all his titles for failure to defend them. Arthur Bülow told him not to worry, that there were greener fields to conquer.

After watching Tunney easily defeat his New Zealand challenger on July 26, 1928, Schmeling was as shocked as the rest of the boxing world when Gene announced he was retiring to marry wealthy socialite Polly Lauder and go into business. The abdication meant that Max was very much in the mix for the vacant world heavyweight championship. The Americans, however, were anxious to keep the title in what they regarded as its natural home, and, besides, they never thought too highly of European heavyweights. It was clear that Schmeling would have to prove his worth by taking on, and beating, one or two of the other contenders. He would also need the help of someone who knew the American fight scene better than Bülow.

Enter Joe "Yussel" Jacobs.

There was no getting away from the fact that the biggest handicap facing Louis as he embarked on his professional career was the color of his skin. It didn't help that he had an all-black management and training team. Prejudice was as ingrained in boxing as in every other walk of American life. Ring history is full of cases where exceptionally talented black boxers were cheated of their rights.

John L. Sullivan, the first universally recognized world heavyweight champion, consistently ducked his leading challenger, Peter Jackson, bluntly stating, "I will never fight a nigger." The real reason, most experts agreed, was that he feared the gifted boxer from the West Indies. During Jack Dempsey's reign, one of the most deserving contenders was Harry Wills, a black man from New Orleans. Despite numerous efforts to get them together, it never happened, mainly because of political interference. Other great black fighters like Sam Langford, Joe Jeannette, and Sam McVey went through their long careers without ever getting a title shot. Ironically, the first black heavyweight to surmount the barrier, Jack Johnson, served to spoil it for everyone else.

Johnson, after chasing titleholder Tommy Burns halfway around the world, finally pinned him down in Sydney, Australia, in 1908. He took out his frustration on the hapless Canadian by torturing and jeering him through fourteen one-sided rounds until the police, fearing a riot, insisted that the fight be stopped. The new world champion showed his gold teeth in a wide grin, a natural action perceived as a boast of black supremacy. His flamboyant lifestyle further offended white society, especially when he married two white women in succession and had an affair with a third. Convicted of transporting a minor across a state border for immoral purposes, he was prosecuted under the Mann Act and sentenced to a year's imprisonment. After escaping to Europe for two years, he eventually surrendered his title to giant cowboy Jess Willard in Havana, Cuba, in 1915. Johnson, who loved driving at high speeds, was killed in a car crash in North Carolina in 1946.

Mindful of Johnson's excesses, Roxborough lectured his young fighter on how he must behave if he was to have any hope of success. He drew up a set of commandments for Louis:

Never have your picture taken alone with a white woman.
Never go into a nightclub alone.
Have no soft fights.
Have no fixed fights.
Never gloat over a fallen opponent.
Never speak negatively about an opponent before or after a fight.
Keep a solemn expression in front of the cameras.
Live and fight clean.

While many thought it unfair to burden the young man with such caveats, Louis's upbringing and personality made it easy for him to follow them. It was not in his nature to denigrate anyone he fought, black or white, and if his managers thought this was the way to do things, then he had no problem playing the game.

Characteristically, Joe would always refuse to judge Johnson, even though Jack was reluctant to give his successor credit as a great fighter. "When I got to be champ," Louis said, "half the letters I got had some word about Jack Johnson. A lot was from old colored people in the South. They thought he disgraced the Negro. I just figured he did what he wanted to do, and what he did had no effect on me."

For his early fights, Joe's comanagers let him keep the entire purses. They knew their rewards would come when he moved up the ladder. At Roxborough's suggestion, Louis sent most of his winnings back to his family. Whatever doubts Lillie Barrow harbored about her boy swapping his violin for boxing gloves were well and truly quashed by now. His take for his professional debut, the one-round knockout of Jack Kracken, was $60. By the end of 1934, his first year as a professional, he was making $3,000 for beating Lee Ramage. That Christmas, he spent freely on family and friends, while buying himself some snappy suits and his first car, a black Buick with whitewall tires. His reputation, too, was growing. Twelve straight wins, ten by knockout, even got him coverage in the *Detroit Times*, a William Hearst–owned paper that normally mentioned the black community only in crime stories.

The victory over Ramage, a tough, talented heavyweight considered the best on the West Coast, got Louis his first top-ten ranking by *The Ring* magazine. His managers thought he might be ready to make his debut in the hub of big-time boxing, New York City. They asked Blackburn what he thought.

"Yeah, he's ready for New York, but New York ain't ready for him," Blackburn replied.

When Roxborough and Black persisted in their plans, they were rebuffed by Jimmy Johnston, the matchmaker at Madison Square Garden. The only way a gifted black fighter would get a booking was to agree to lose, he told them. Blackburn, on being told of the ultimatum, said, "What did I tell you?"

New York would have to wait.

3

TAKING IT LYING DOWN

With the world heavyweight title up for grabs after Gene Tunney's retirement, Schmeling decided drastic action was necessary to ensure that he didn't miss out in the search to find a new champion. Showing an unexpected ruthless streak, he dumped Arthur Bülow to let Joe Jacobs take control of his affairs. It was a pragmatic decision. Jacobs had the connections in the United States to make things happen. Bülow didn't.

However, Bülow was not prepared to go quietly. He complained to the New York State Athletic Commission, accusing the fighter of breach of contract. The commission members heard both sides of the story and decided Max must keep Bülow as his manager. A furious Schmeling banged his fist on the table and stormed out of the meeting. He was followed by Jim Farley, an assistant commissioner, who managed to calm him down and took him back into the room. Schmeling later thanked Farley for smoothing things over with the commission, which had suspended boxers for less serious behavior. He would have reason to thank Farley again almost a quarter of a century later for helping him to become a highly successful businessman.

The commission backed down a little. The final judgment was that Schmeling could leave Bülow, but he would have to pay him his percentage until their contract ran out. Jacobs, when he heard, told Max he would manage him without taking any money until the boxer was clear of his debt to Bülow. "That impressed me a great deal," said Schmeling.

Jacobs, the New York–born son of Jewish immigrants from Hungary, was one of the most colorful characters in boxing history. Rarely pictured without a cigar stuck in his mouth, he was a small, astute businessman who never missed a trick when it came to getting publicity for his fighters. He got reporters to follow Max around as he visited schools, monasteries, and churches, had him photographed on top of skyscrapers, introduced him to politicians and cleverly played up his resemblance to Jack Dempsey. He also conspired with Schmeling to come up with a rather convoluted nickname, the Black Uhlan of the Rhine. To uninitiated Americans, it took some explaining. In the Franco-Prussian war of 1870–71, the Prussian Uhlans, a unit of cavalry lancers, won fame for their bravery and skill. The "Black" part of Schmeling's nickname came from his dark hair and bushy eyebrows.

In the one American fight arranged by Bülow, Schmeling made his U.S. debut at Madison Square Garden, in New York, on November 23, 1928. A perfectly timed right finished off Joe Monte in the eighth round. Jacobs, quickly proving his worth, already had three more bouts lined up for him. In the first of these, Max's sense of good sportsmanship cost him another quick victory. He had a habit of lifting his knockout victims off the canvas and helping them to their corners. Against Joe Sekyra, he was a bit too quick in going to his opponent's assistance before he was counted out. The crowd showed their appreciation of Max's gentlemanly act, but Sekyra recovered to last the distance. Schmeling wasted no time in his next outing, putting Italian-American Pietro Corri away in fifty-nine seconds.

Now it was time for the Americans to see just how good the European import was. Just ten days after his last fight, Schmeling stepped into the ring with Johnny Risko, considered by many experts as the natural successor to Tunney. The former baker's apprentice from Cleveland, Ohio, had an impressive record, including wins over future world heavyweight champion Jack Sharkey and former light-heavyweight king Jack Delaney. Known as the Rubber Man for the way he absorbed hard punches, he had never been stopped or even knocked off his feet. Schmeling spoiled that particular boast by bouncing Risko off the canvas in the opening round, and twice more in the seventh and eighth, before the American turned away and shook his head in the ninth round to signal that he had had enough.

It was a sensational win for Schmeling, who was fêted by the American public as a new hero. On the streets, people lined up to shake his hand. Requests for interviews poured in from broadcasters, newspapers, and magazines. Back in Germany, the result made big headlines, and his loyal fans eagerly awaited his homecoming. Just before he sailed for Europe, along with Jacobs and Machon, Max signed a two-year contract with Madison Square Garden. He promised he would be back soon to pursue his dream of capturing the world heavyweight title.

Just as he was settling into his well-earned vacation, Max was offered a part in a film with a boxing and love theme. Although the financial carrot was tempting, he hesitated at taking on a role for which he was not qualified. His misgivings about having to speak lines were dismissed by director Reinhold Schünzel, who assured him it was a silent movie. Some time into the shooting, the fledgling actor was hit with a double shock. Since talkies looked like they were becoming the rage, the rest of *Love in the Ring* would be done in sound. Not only would Max have to speak, he was required to sing a mawkish love song that did nothing for his he-man image.

Soon after the movie was completed, he found real-life romance. He had met Jarmila Vacek (Vackova), a Czech actress, on the voyage from New York and he visited her in Prague. They walked hand in hand over the Charles Bridge and through the city's old quarter. Sitting in a small bar overlooking the Waldstein Palace, Jarmila told of how she had tried to make it as a movie actress in America but found it impossible to make a breakthrough. Her best friend had wisely gone to Berlin to pursue a film career. Perhaps he had heard of her, queried Jarmila. Her name was Anny Ondra. If Max didn't know much about her then, he would certainly make up for it later.

The days in Prague were fun and carefree. In Berlin, Schmeling found it very different. Increasingly, the conflicts in parliament were spilling onto the streets. Public disturbances grew more frequent as Communists protested against perceived exploitation, while their far-right opponents, the National Socialists, denounced the Weimar Republic's attempts to bed down a progressive Western-style democracy. By the early thirties, the polarization had become increasingly extreme, and the scene was set for the emergence of Hitler's Third Reich.

While Schmeling was in Europe, Joe Jacobs, by now his official manager, had been working hard on pushing his man's case as a legitimate leading contender for the vacant world title. His diligence paid off when it was announced that Max would meet the Basque fighter Paolino Uzcudun as part of an elimination tournament. Jacobs pulled another masterstroke by enlisting the participation of the famous Hearst Corporation. Publishing giant William Randolph Hearst's wife was a leading charity organizer, and part of the proceeds of the fight would go to a milk fund for needy children. One of the Hearst newspaper group's top sportswriters was Damon Runyon, whose widely read column helped raise the German's profile throughout the United States.

On fight night, some 40,000 fans filed into Yankee Stadium, ensuring a gate of almost $400,000, a huge figure for a contest between two foreigners. Schmeling, win or lose, was guaranteed 17 percent of the total take. It was a long way from the time he had walked almost seventeen miles from Cologne to Bonn to cash a check for three marks, only to find the premises closed and have to walk all the way back to Cologne empty-handed.

Uzcudun proved a tough opponent and was still standing at the end of fifteen rounds, though well beaten on points. This was the first time that a sporting event in the United States had been simultaneously broadcast in Germany, and the flood of telegrams from listeners in both countries proved it was a winning innovation.

Jacobs cashed in on his man's popularity by arranging an exhibition tour in thirty leading U.S. cities. In between ring duties, Max took part in crowning Chicago's Blossom Queen, viewed the Grand Canyon and the Golden Gate Bridge, and was introduced at Hollywood parties to famous names like Clara Bow, Gloria Swanson, Walt Disney, Douglas Fairbanks, and Mary Pickford.

By the end of 1929, *The Ring* rated Schmeling second, next to Jack Sharkey, among the world's heavyweights. But if he thought that, by his elimination victory over Uzcudun, the way was now clear for him to meet Sharkey for the vacant title, he was in for disappointment. He was told that he would first have to fight Phil Scott. Despite being assured that he would have no trouble disposing of the vulnerable British champion, he refused to go through with the fight on principle. So he found himself suspended by the New York State Athletic Commission.

Instead, Sharkey took his place against Scott in a final eliminator. Because of the Englishman's habit of falling down when hit anywhere near the waistline, usually resulting in the perpetrator's disqualification, he had picked up some unflattering nicknames, like Phainting Phil, Horizontal Champion, and the Swooning Swan of Soho. As a precaution against a possible fiasco, the Florida authorities brought in a no-foul rule for the Miami contest. This prevented a boxer from being disqualified for landing a low blow that was deemed to be accidental. It proved to be disastrous for Scott. He was downed several times by reckless body punches from the American until, in the third round, he failed to rise from the canvas after what he claimed was the sixth foul committed by Sharkey. The referee completed the count and Sharkey was announced as the winner amid protest.

Shortly afterward, Jacobs traveled to Germany to give his brooding fighter the news for which he had been hoping. The New York Commission, after further consideration, had lifted his suspension, and he would meet Sharkey for the vacant world heavyweight title at Yankee Stadium on June 12, 1930.

After an exhibition tour to get back into shape, Max was due to leave for the States on April 1 when he came down with the flu and had to postpone his departure. He missed the chance to meet a special passenger on the *Bremen*, a sultry young German actress named Marlene Dietrich, who had been a sensation in Josef von Sternberg's *The Blue Angel* and was on her way to seduce America and the rest of the world. Max and Marlene, who became a U.S. citizen in 1937, would meet at various functions on Schmeling's subsequent visits to the United States.

Though still feeling feverish, Schmeling set sail on April 25 and on arrival immediately set up training camp at Endicott, near Sharkey's hometown of Boston. He found that his cocky opponent already considered the world championship *his* property.

"First I'll cut his face to ribbons," boasted Sharkey, "and then, around the seventh round, I'll knock him out. What does he have going for him other than his resemblance to Jack Dempsey?"

He berated Max as the luckiest boxer in history: "He pokes his nose into our country and gets a title shot just like that. If our leading boxers demanded that when we were coming up, we would have been slapped right down, and with good reason. This German comes over here and expects that, after two ridiculous elimination bouts, he has earned the right to face me."

Schmeling refused to be drawn into a verbal war, insisting that he never made predictions about his fights but expected the toughest contest of his career and would "do everything in my power to bring honor to my fatherland."

He was right to respect Sharkey, a formidable, if unpredictable, foe. Born Joseph Paul Cukoschay to Lithuanian immigrants in Binghamton, New York, he took his ring name from the rough, tough Irishman Tom Sharkey, who went twenty-five brutal rounds with Jim Jeffries in an 1899 world heavyweight title fight. Jack began boxing just after being discharged from the U.S. Navy in 1924, the same year that Schmeling made his debut. He progressed to impressive points wins over respected fighters like Harry Wills, Jim Maloney, and Young Stribling while numbering former light-heavyweight kings Mike McTigue, Jack Delaney, and Tommy Loughran among his knockout victims.

In between the big wins, however, Sharkey had his off-nights. He lost to Risko and Maloney and, in the biggest fight of his career so far, threw away likely victory over Jack Dempsey. He was ahead on points against the Manassa Mauler, who had lost his world title to Tunney the previous year, until, in the seventh round, he turned to the referee to complain that he had been hit below the belt. As he did so, Dempsey clocked him with a left hook to put him out for the count. That most elementary of boxing lessons, "Guard yourself at all times," had gone unheeded.

Sharkey again got it wrong against Schmeling, only this time it was he who delivered the foul blow. For the first time in history, the world heavyweight championship was decided on a disqualification, as the German lay on the canvas, his face contorted in pain and his left glove covering his groin, where Sharkey's left hook had landed in the fourth round. Up until then, the Boston Gob had been in control of the fight, his cool, calculating boxing frustrating Schmeling's pressure tactics.

The unexpected ending caused pandemonium. Referee Jim

Crowley, caught off guard, was about to start counting over the fallen German when Max's seconds came swarming into the ring. "It's a foul," yelled Jacobs, "Schmeling is the new champion."

The confused referee consulted with Harold Barnes, the judge best positioned to have seen what had happened. Barnes indicated that it was indeed a foul blow. Told by the other judge, Charles F. Mathison, that he was unsighted, Crowley twice more asked Barnes if he was sure about the illegal punch and was assured it was illegal. By now, Crowley was being assailed on one side by Jacobs, demanding Sharkey's disqualification, and on the other by Johnny Buckley, the American's handler, trying to convince him that the body blow was fair. The referee told master of ceremonies Joe Humphries to announce that he had ruled out Sharkey and that Schmeling was the new heavyweight champion of the world. Despite the disappointment of the 80,000 in attendance, there were more cheers than jeers.

Schmeling was in too much agony to celebrate his win, while the loser was utterly dejected. He stood motionless in his corner, head sunk to his chest, as his handlers ranted and raged at the perceived injustice. Bill Hennigan, one of the few reporters allowed into Sharkey's dressing room afterward, saw him take off his trunks, kiss them gently, and then throw them into a bag as he declared, "This was my last fight." His manager tried to console him, telling him he would still prove himself the best heavyweight in the world.

"I knew I had him beat," Sharkey told Hennigan. "I won all four rounds, easy. I was sure I was going to knock him out. I wanted to win the title by a knockout. He came in too high. I hit him with only two body shots in the whole fight. The first time was in the third round. That had him on the verge of a knockout. When he rushed at me in the fourth round, I started a left hook to the body. He came in high, just like he was doing all night. I thought I sunk the punch into his body. Maybe it was low, but if it was, it was unintentional. Hell, I'd be out of my skull to purposely foul when I had the title in my hands."

Sharkey called Schmeling "not much of a fighter who never hit me with one real punch." His resentment of the new champion was obvious.

Johnny Buckley was even angrier, claiming that Schmeling and Jacobs had concocted a scheme to deprive Sharkey of victory. "That was the only way they could win, and they knew it," he growled. "They planned to have Schmeling come in high when he moved into Jack, hoping that a body shot would land a little low so they could yell foul."

The *New York Times* man at ringside, James P. Dawson, was in no doubt that the verdict was fair. He wrote the next day: "I was advantageously seated to the left of judge Barnes and the action was directly above me. And I can say that the left hook which Sharkey directed for the body landed foul and merited disqualification because of its disabling effect." Dawson praised Barnes for having the courage to call it as he saw it. Most of the ringside journalists, as well as former heavyweight champions Tommy Burns and Tunney, thought the referee acted correctly.

It should have been Schmeling's proudest day. Instead, he felt anything but a world champion. He declared that he wouldn't accept the title, that it meant nothing to him winning it on a foul. His handlers tried to reason with him, saying he would have ample opportunities to prove himself a worthy champion. The New York Commission initially refused to recognize him as such and held up both boxers' purses until the controversy had been examined, before accepting that the result could not be changed. Within a month, the commission brought in a permanent no-foul rule. This demanded that all boxers wear an abdominal protector and made it impossible to win on a foul. Anyone floored by an illegal blow would be awarded that round, but if he failed to rise before the referee reached the count of ten, he would be declared the loser by a knockout.

Still feeling subdued on his return to Germany, Max kept a low profile as he took an apartment in Berlin's fashionable West End and met up with close friends, including Olga Tschechova, his costar in *Love in the Ring*. (After the Second World War, various rumors circulated about Olga. One suggested she was a spy for the KGB, another that she was a double agent for Poland as well as Germany, even that she was Hitler's mistress. She never denied her good contacts with leading Nazis, but insisted she never acted as an agent.)

One afternoon, as they sat sipping coffee in a café, Olga suggested they take in a movie, *The Girl from Rummelplatz*, which was showing nearby. It starred Max's next-door neighbor, Anny Ondra, whom he had never met, though he had noticed her blue chauffeur-driven

Cadillac parked outside. Captivated by Anny's screen persona, he rather undiplomatically asked his current escort if she could help arrange a meeting. Olga curtly said she wasn't a very good matchmaker and that he would have to make his own move. The next day, Max got a friend, Paul Damski, who had promoted some of his fights, to call on Anny with a bunch of flowers and ask if she would meet his friend. He got a polite, but firm, refusal.

Undaunted, Schmeling persuaded Damski to have another go. This time he had some luck. Anny later revealed that she had called up some friends to check out "this crazy man" who kept asking her out. She agreed to meet him at the Café Corso. He brought Max Machon along in case fear got the better of him and he would have nothing to say. The object of his affections quickly put him at his ease as she told him about her family, of how her father had been an officer in the Austro-Hungarian army, how she had gotten into acting and had been signed to a film contract by a director who saw her skating. She shared with Max happy memories of Prague, a city they both loved. On first meeting Anny, Max had asked her, "*Jak se vam dari*?" (How are you?) It was the only Czech phrase he knew, and he told her he had been taught it by her friend Jarmila Vacek.

After several more meetings with Anny in the company of Damski and Machon, Max thought he had finally gotten her on her own when she invited him to her apartment to listen to music. However, their privacy was interrupted every three minutes or so as Anny's maid appeared to put on a new record and crank up the gramophone. But he was truly smitten. During the weeks that followed, he left a bouquet every morning on the blue Cadillac parked in front of her door.

The first time Anny accompanied her boyfriend to a boxing tournament she was shocked to discover that, far from being a hero in his own country, he was the target of jeers and insults. The fact that he was Germany's first world boxing champion meant nothing. Cabaret performers and satirists lampooned him as someone who had become a winner by losing.

There was only one way to redeem his reputation in both Europe and America. He must take on, and defeat beyond doubt, one of the main contenders for his title. Just over a year after the Sharkey debacle, he faced Young Stribling, the New York Commission's mandatory challenger, at the Municipal Stadium in Cleveland, Ohio. Now the world would see what Schmeling was really made of.

Stribling, from Bainbridge, Georgia, was a terrific puncher. Indeed, he came close to registering more knockouts than any other fighter in history. His career total of 125 wins inside the distance was bettered only by Archie Moore's 141 short-route victories. Stribling, whose mother was a vaudeville acrobat, started boxing as a bantamweight at the age of sixteen. He first gained national attention when he held reigning world light-heavyweight champion Mike McTigue to a draw in a nontitle bout, then floored McTigue in a return match that he should have won but which was designated as a "no-decision" contest. He twice beat another light-heavyweight king, Tommy Loughran, but when he got a title shot, he was outscored by Paul Berlenbach. Moving up to heavyweight, he staggered Jack Sharkey with a right to the heart but failed to follow up his advantage and lost on points. In two controversial clashes with Primo Carnera, he was disqualified in the first match and won the return on a foul.

Against Schmeling, the Georgia Peach looked sweet for five rounds, but then the steely champion took over. Max gave the brave but outclassed American a systematic pounding until referee George Blake stopped the slaughter in the fifteenth and last round, as Stribling, after rising from a count, staggered against the ropes. Although there were only twenty seconds left in the contest, Blake thought there was a danger Stribling could suffer permanent damage if he didn't act quickly. The boxing world was shocked two years later when Stribling was killed in a motorcycle crash as he raced to a hospital to join his wife, who was about to give birth. He was just twenty-eight years old.

Schmeling, now hailed as a genuine world champion, took a year off before deciding on his next defense. He spent as much time as possible with Anny Ondra, trying hard to keep their romance away from the glare of publicity, although it was difficult. Anny was being swamped with movie offers. She had just finished working on a young Alfred Hitchcock's first sound film, *Blackmail*, and was then engaged on a German–French collaboration. Shortly afterward she and a few Czech friends started their own production company, which produced about eight films a year, most of them featuring Anny in the leading role.

Early in 1932, Schmeling was back in New York for the start of an exhibition tour and to discuss his next title challenger. Sharkey, the top contender, had fought twice since their still hotly debated meeting. He had looked unimpressive against beefed-up middleweight Mickey Walker, who held him to a draw, but showed a vast improvement in handing the massive Primo Carnera the first real beating of his career en route to a decisive points win. He was making lots of noise about his right to a rematch with the German.

When Max's exhibition schedule took him to Sharkey's home-town, he saw that the Boston Gob was about to milk the crowd's sympathy and support as he stepped up to take a bow. Schmeling nipped the reception in the bud by going up to Sharkey and giving him a warm embrace, then holding the ropes open as he gently ushered him out of the ring. A few days later, the contracts were signed for the pair to fight again on June 21 at the Long Island Bowl.

Shortly after setting up his training camp in Kingston, New York, Max got a message that the governor, Franklin Delano Roosevelt, wanted to pay him a visit. It was agreed that it would be a publicity coup for all concerned. The fight promoters were delighted because it would stir up interest in a bout that had so far failed to excite the public. For Roosevelt, it was a photo opportunity in his campaign for the presidency.

The polio-stricken governor delighted his host by speaking to him in German and telling him of the happy times he had spent in his country as a student. When it came to Max's sparring session, Roosevelt watched with great interest while his wife, Eleanor, covered her face with her hands. She said later that she couldn't bear to watch two men hitting each other.

"Of course I'm an American, Max," said Roosevelt when it was time to leave, "but I still wish you good luck with the fight."

With America still feeling the effects of the economic depression, the promoters were worried about ticket sales in the weeks leading up to the fight. On that night, however, a near-capacity crowd produced receipts of $500,000. Twenty-five percent of the net profits went to the Free Milk Fund for Babies.

The fight was a huge disappointment for a gathering that included notables from the worlds of politics, industry, show business, and the arts. Former world heavyweight champions Gene Tunney and James J. Corbett were among the boxers introduced to the 70,000 in attendance. Few highlights marked the tedious fifteen rounds, with Sharkey's cautious style negating the champion's more aggressive approach. Schmeling dictated most of the action and landed the better punches.

The only major talking point afterward was the split decision that went to Sharkey. Back then, fights that went the distance were decided on the votes of the referee and two judges, unlike today, when the referee has no scoring function, leaving it to three judges to render their verdict. Referee Ed "Gunboat" Smith, one of the "white hopes" of the Jack Johnson era, and judge George Kelly both marked their scorecards for Sharkey, while Charles F. Matheson favored the defending champion.

Schmeling showed exemplary sportsmanship by immediately going across the ring to shake the new champion's hand, even though he was feeling numb with disbelief. Sharkey, his left eye swollen tight from the attention of his rival's right hand, couldn't contain his delight. He joined his manager, Johnny Buckley, and his seconds as they danced and jumped around the ring, slapping each other on the back.

Although the verdict met with a mixed reception from the crowd, most of those asked for their opinions thought the German had gotten a raw deal. So did the majority of ringside reporters. A poll of the writers showed that twenty-two figured Schmeling had won, seven supported Sharkey, and one thought it should have been a draw. Radio commentators also thought the wrong man got the decision.

An outraged Joe Jacobs earned a special place in fight folklore when his complaint that an injustice had been done came out in the papers in mangled East Side New York dialect as "We wuz robbed. We shudda stood in bed." The pint-sized manager accosted referee Smith, screaming, "You oughta be arrested."

When several newspapers the next day were highly critical of the decision and pointed out that Smith might have leaned toward Sharkey, an old friend and a former navy man like himself, the Gunboat threatened to sue but was talked out of it by William Muldoon, chairman of the New York Commission.

Years later, in an interview with Peter Heller for his book *In This Corner*, Smith explained:

From the first round till the tenth or eleventh round, Jack Sharkey won every round. The other fellow did nothing but dance. He was the heaviest, shortest puncher I ever saw, Max Schmeling. He could hit like a bastard. He got the last four rounds, but how could I give him the decision when he only won four rounds? And that's where I got in bad. They hollered blue murder about that decision.

A flood of sympathetic messages lifted Schmeling's spirits somewhat before he departed for Germany. New York mayor Jimmy Walker called it "a bum decision." Gene Tunney said it was "a scandal" and questioned how a fighter who was on the defensive for the full fifteen rounds could have won. But nothing could change the harsh reality for Max that he was no longer heavyweight champion of the world.

4

MUSSOLINI'S MAN

Eighteen fights. Eighteen wins. Fourteen knockouts. Everything had gone to plan so far for Louis. Now it was time to take on a big-name opponent, someone who could show just how good was the twenty-one year old the papers were calling the Brown Bomber. The chosen one was Primo Carnera, the massive Italian who frightened off most of the other heavyweights with his appearance alone. He was a fistic Frankenstein.

Considering all the racial barriers they had to overcome, Louis's managers had done well to get him to this stage. For practical reasons, they had allowed one white man to infiltrate the black circle. Mike Jacobs (no relation to Joe Jacobs) was a wheeler-dealer promoter who could open important doors. He had inherited the mantle of the great Tex Rickard, king of fight promoters throughout the 1920s. Jacobs did a secret deal with the powerful Hearst press, getting it to back him as he set up the Twentieth Century Sporting Club to promote fights in opposition to Madison Square Garden. To herald his arrival as the new Mr. Boxing, he needed a heavyweight champion. He found Joe Louis.

Jacobs signed the Detroit prospect to a three-year exclusive deal, with an option thereafter, in return for giving Louis 37 percent of the gate receipts from his fights. Roxborough and Black were happy with the arrangement. At the same time, they had to fight off pressure from underworld figures like Owney Madden, an English-born racketeer and killer, to sell the young fighter's contract.

Jacobs somehow picked up the nickname of Uncle Mike, an image that was at odds with the way a lot of people perceived him. A young Sugar Ray Robinson, when he was desperately seeking a crack at the world welterweight title, growled, "Mike will manipulate anybody for a buck." *New York Mirror* columnist Dan Parker felt Jacobs should have been called Uncle Wolf, as the way he downed food mirrored his business practices. Parker regularly rapped Jacobs for his association with Frankie Carbo, an underworld character who controlled a string of boxers.

But Louis's evaluation of Jacobs, made twenty years after the promoter's death, was that "he was one of the finest men I ever knew."

Joe arrived in New York City four weeks before the fight with Carnera, set for June 25, 1935. The promoter's well-oiled publicity machine went into high gear. Newspapermen jostled for room at press conferences, though they were disappointed with Louis's lack of full response to their questions. Some considered his manner sullen, not realizing that he was overwhelmed by the surge of interest in him. He had never handled anything like this before.

Still, he enjoyed being taken to new places and meeting people he had only heard about. He shook hands with Jack Dempsey at his popular restaurant opposite Madison Square Garden, visited City Hall to meet Mayor Fiorello H. LaGuardia, and made an appearance on stage at the Harlem Opera House, skipping rope, punching the bag, and engaging in a skit with comedian Dusty Fletcher.

There were some objections from local residents about the sudden influx of blacks when the Louis entourage set up camp at Pompton Lakes, New Jersey. But Joe was happy there, playing golf on the local links and enjoying the buzz about the place. Despite being a professional fighter for less than a year, he was already well known, thanks in no small measure to Jacobs' publicity skills. The Hearst press, particularly, glossed up his image as a bible-reading former violin student who was very kind to his mother. As many as six thousand people attended the weekend sparring sessions, as vendors hawked souvenirs, hot dogs, and soda pop. The audiences were particularly intrigued by the sight of the 6 feet 1 Louis up against sparring partners who towered over him. This was no publicity gimmick. Blackburn wanted Joe to be ready for Carnera, who stood just under 6 foot 6 and weighed around 260 pounds.

Yet boxing history has shown that, in the heavyweight division, size doesn't really matter. If it did, the behemoths would crush all opposition like ants under an outsize boot. Instead, there are countless instances of smaller, faster boxers bringing down clumsy giants as emphatically as a lumberjack chopping down a large tree. Bob Fitzsimmons, the lightest man ever to hold the world heavyweight crown, once knocked out an opponent who outweighed him by sixty-two pounds, entitling him to boast that "the bigger they are, the harder they fall."

Carnera, however, was much better than the press of the day and boxing historians have credited him. Video evidence, now readily available, proves that he was surprisingly fast on his feet for a man of his immense bulk, had decent boxing skills, and when he landed with one of his big punches, it could have a devastating effect. And he did win the world heavyweight championship.

The main accusation clinging to the Italian's name is that his winning record was built on a succession of fixed fights, with opponents taking a dive for money or to avoid a beating. While there is evidence that some of his rivals were too eager to find the exit, it beggars belief that the fraud was as widespread as is commonly held. For starters, it seems scarcely feasible that Primo's handlers would have had the time and the organizational ability to travel throughout Europe and the United States prearranging the results of fights, many of them just days apart. The sheer logistics of such an enterprise would seem to rule that out. There is also the matter of professional boxers' natural pride. It could not have been easy to convince them that agreeing to lose would not harm their future careers and earning capacity. Even if they got offers they couldn't refuse, would the organizers of the fraud feel such a large cash outlay was justified? If the theorists are to be believed, Carnera's handlers must have been convinced he would eventually make it to the top and their investment would be recouped. If so, then why was it necessary to pay off so many heavyweights of modest talent who wouldn't have had an earthly chance of beating the Italian anyway?

If one is to accept the pretense that the tainted fights were designed to build up an impressive-looking knockout record, it would seem shortsighted on his managers' part to expect him to learn anything from opponents who weren't even trying. How, then, did he suddenly develop into such an able boxer when he had to face top heavyweights on a level playing field?

Much of the blame for the perceived scandal must be attached to Carnera's one-time manager, Léon Sée. The Frenchman, who had done much to further the sport in his native country and set up the French Boxing Federation, wrote a book in 1932 entitled *Le Mystère Carnera*. In setting out Primo's record, he included after each bout the words *combat arrangé* (fix) or *combat sincère* (genuine). By then, however, Sée was a bitter man. He had lost control of his protégé to the Mob before Primo won the world title. Owney Madden and Billy Duffy, who owned several speakeasies, were the principal members of a gun-packing syndicate that took over Carnera's American campaign. Sée was paid to step down, although he was allowed to retain a minor advisory role, but he was frustrated at his failure to properly cash in on his investment. His denigration of the big man he discovered and nurtured could be attributed to spite.

It took an unfortunate tragedy, when Ernie Schaaf died five days after being knocked out by Carnera, to eliminate much of the doubts about the Italian's punching power. The crowd had jeered the American for his apparent lack of effort and the way he collapsed under seemingly innocuous punches. Only when he was carried from the ring on a stretcher did they realize the truth. A distraught Carnera, the epitome of a gentle giant, was preparing to answer to a manslaughter charge when an autopsy revealed Schaaf had gone into the ring with brain damage suffered in a fight with Max Baer. The critics now claimed that the Italian was too big to fight so-called ordinary men and that a special dreadnought division should be introduced for boxers of his stature.

Yet there were fresh cries of "fix" when Carnera knocked out Jack Sharkey to become world champion in 1933. This was because many in the audience missed seeing the powerful right uppercut that finished the fight in the sixth round. It came quickly, as the defending champion was backed up against the ropes. Sharkey crumpled to the canvas to be counted out.

Sharkey's manager, Johnny Buckley, immediately called for the winner's gloves to be examined. He didn't believe the Italian could punch that hard. Billy Duffy raised no objections. No hidden horseshoe was found.

What evaporated along with the conspiracy theories was the bulk of Carnera's $12,000 purse. After his handlers made their deductions, together with training and other expenses, the new champion of the world was left with a few hundred dollars. The day after the fight, he was seen with Damon Runyon's wife, Patrice, with whom he was romantically linked, on a shopping spree with a duffle bag containing the banknotes.

Any lingering doubts about Carnera's pugilistic ability should have been buried when he comprehensively outpointed master boxer Tommy Loughran over fifteen rounds in defense of his title. Loughran, the former world light-heavyweight champion, was a vastly experienced fighter who had beaten International Hall of Fame inductees Harry Greb, Mike McTigue, and Mickey Walker, while showing he could handle top-notch heavyweights like Sharkey, Max Baer, Jimmy Braddock, and Young Stribling. In his last fight before facing Carnera, he had outsmarted Ray Impellitiere, an Italian-American who was even bigger than the Ambling Alp. Loughran said the reason he lost was that Primo restricted his movement by constantly stepping on his feet with his size 16 boots. The eighty-six-pound weight difference could also have had something to do with it, admittedly. In the final analysis, however, size alone could not have been enough to overcome someone of Loughran's renowned skill.

Though Max Baer exposed his limitations when the American took his title and made fun of him while administering a bad beating in June 1934, Carnera was still looked upon as a formidable force when he faced the Brown Bomber a year later. His reputation as a man-eating ogre meant nothing to Louis, laid back as ever, as he knuckled down to serious training. To him, the Italian's bulk only meant more target at which to aim his bombs. But many of the sportswriters who attended the Pompton Lakes camp were unsure of his chances. Shirley Povich wrote in the *Washington Post*:

My first impression of Louis was how young and strong he was and how he could punch. But here was Carnera, a mastodonic guy, with great height and reach and outweighing Joe by 50 or 60 pounds. There was a great curiosity as to how he would fare against him.

Normally, that sort of publicity would have guaranteed healthy ticket sales. But world events were transforming the ring at Yankee Stadium into a surrogate battlefield. By the summer of 1935, it was evident that Italy's Fascist dictator, Benito Mussolini, was getting ready to invade Ethiopia. In an era of widespread colonialism, Ethiopia was one of the few independent black countries left in the world. Though the gloomy forecasts meant little to the average black American, enlightened observers feared that Ethiopia's fall would destroy any remaining black nation's hopes of retaining self-rule. To them, Ethiopian Emperor Haile Selassie was a hero as he prepared to stand up to the bully.

The American press emphasized the symbolism of the boxing match in relation to what was happening in Africa. Louis was seen as representing the ill-equipped black patriots bravely resisting the jack-booted white imperialists. Cartoonists played up the David v. Goliath comparison, typically portraying the smaller, darker Louis under the shadow of the towering, intimidating Carnera. Willing or not, Louis was handed the banner of the Free World to carry against Fascism.

"They put a heavy weight on my twenty-year-old shoulders," Joe said in later years. "Now, not only did I have to beat the man, but I had to beat him for a cause."

For years, Carnera had proved a useful puppet for Mussolini, who pulled all the publicity strings to make sure that the fighter got large crowds wherever he went in Italy. Immediately after his victory over Sharkey, Primo had received a telegram from Il Duce: "My congratulations. Fascist Italy and its sports-loving people are proud that a Blackshirt has become boxing champion of the world."

Mussolini ordered an extra-large uniform for Carnera and he was shown wearing it, while giving the Fascist salute, in photographs distributed throughout the world. For his first title defense, against Paolino Uzcudun in Rome, Primo donated his purse to Fascist causes.

After the war, his defenders would say that the government exploited him, that if he had swum against the tide he would have suffered the inevitable consequences. Many Italians refused to accept the excuses. On the day Mussolini's body was hanged in Milan, Carnera was forced to face down an angry bunch of partisans in his home village of Sequals, in northeastern Italy. They wanted him to die as a hated symbol of the ousted regime. Brandishing a rifle as he emerged through his front door, he warned the group that he was prepared to go down fighting. The threat subsided.

When the Louis fight was announced, there were genuine fears about the political implications if it went ahead. American blacks had formed the Council of Friends of Ethiopians to make representations at the League of Nations on behalf of the besieged Africans. Fears were expressed that a Louis victory would be seen as an insult to the Italian flag and would prompt Mussolini into bringing forward his invasion plans. The Hearst organization, sponsors of the event, also showed anxiety about the bad publicity, but was swayed by the amount of requests for tickets from political and society figures. Still, there was concern in many quarters about possible street disturbances.

Police Commissioner Edward P. Mulrooney issued a calming, if patronizing, message: "There won't be a Harlem disturbance. The American Negro is by nature law-abiding, kindly, well-behaved. He is also happy and fun-loving. If Louis wins, there will likely be singing and shouting and dancing in the streets of Harlem." The worst that could happen, he believed, was "a few ashcans may be kicked over, as on New Year's Eve."

Still, Mulrooney prepared for the worst. He had some 1,300 uniformed policemen stationed all around Yankee Stadium, while 300 more men in plain clothes mingled with the crowd, ready to sound the alert if required. Four extra police wagons were parked nearby to haul off potential troublemakers, and Emergency Squad members stood by with tear-gas bombs and grenades.

Representatives of the black press were an unusual presence in the media section. Initially, the stadium authorities had sought to deny them ringside tickets, on the grounds that the area was reserved for the daily press. Black publications didn't have the money to appear more than weekly, principally because they couldn't attract advertising from the big stores. Louis made representations on their behalf to Mike Jacobs and, with the support of Hype Igoe, a sympathetic white writer for the *Journal American*, they got some black reporters installed close to the ring. Joe felt happy that he had played a small part in the campaign for democracy.

As the participants entered the ring, the dinner-jacketed announcer Harry Balogh, never known to use a few words when he could use a lot, took the microphone to address the 60,000 paying customers and 400 sportswriters, the biggest press delegation since Dempsey fought Carpentier in 1921. "Ladies and gentlemen," he began, "before proceeding with this most important heavyweight contest, I wish to take the liberty of calling upon you in the name of American sportsmanship, a spirit so fine it has made you, the American sporting public, world famous. I therefore ask that the thought in your mind and the feeling in your heart be that, regardless of race, creed, or color, let us all say, may the better man emerge victorious. Thank you."

It wasn't a fight. It was a slaughter. Before the first round was over, Louis had asserted his authority with solid shots that had his opponent already looking apprehensive. A vicious right drove Carnera's bottom teeth through his gum and started a flow of blood. In the fifth round, when the Ambling Alp tried to bull the smaller man around in a clinch, he was astonished to find himself lifted bodily off the floor. "Hey, I should be doing this to you," he told his tormentor as the referee broke them.

If nothing else, Carnera showed he packed a lot of courage into that massive frame. He absorbed a savage beating as Louis closed in for the kill in the sixth round. A right to the jaw dumped him head first in the middle of the ring. Upright at the count of four, he was rubber-legged, weary, and almost defenseless as he turned to face his relentless foe. A barrage of punches, culminating in a powerful right, put him back on the floor. Again, he was up at four. Utterly helpless, he succumbed to another attack and took his third and last count, which had reached three when he staggered to his feet. Referee Arthur Donovan, acting humanely, called a halt to the massacre.

"Louis, he's a good boy," said the gracious loser afterward. "He'll make a fine champion."

Joe still felt elated at his performance twelve years later when he said:

> This was my first night in New York and this was the night I remember best in all my fighting. If you was ever a raggedy kid and you come to something like that night you'd know. I don't thrill to things like other people. I only feel good. I felt the best that night.

The sportswriters covering the event were glowing in their praise of his performance. James P. Dawson told his *New York Times* readers that he had seen one of the greatest fighters of modern times in action: "He punches like Dempsey. He is a reminder of the one and only Sam Langford." Paul Gallico, of the *New York Daily News,* wrote: "Louis transformed a brawny, courageous man into a bubbling, goggle-eyed jelly."

While the scribes were unanimous in their appreciation of his remarkable fighting skills, they were less complimentary in assessing Louis the man. Indeed, they went further, projecting him as something savage or animalistic. Such caricatures pandered to the prejudice and fear that drove many white Americans' attitudes toward their fellow black citizens.

Davis Walsh's piece for the *International News Service* began, "Something sly and sinister and perhaps not quite human came out of the African jungle last night to strike down and utterly demolish the huge hulk that had been Primo Carnera, the giant."

Grantland Rice, one of the most widely read but blatantly racist sportswriters in the country, saw Louis as a venomous snake, likening him to both a bushmaster and a brown cobra. He also wrote of his "blinding speed . . . the speed of the jungle, the instinctive speed of the wild." Of the fight, he said, "Joe Louis was stalking Carnera, the mammoth, as the black panther of the jungle stalks its prey."

When they weren't implicitly denying Louis's humanity by comparing him to a jungle animal, the scribes rounded on his naturally impassive manner as a sign of heartlessness, a merciless engine of destruction.

"No killer with the ferocious scowl of Dempsey or the fiendish leer of Baer is this Joe Louis, but a killer nevertheless," wrote Shirley Povich in the *Washington Post.* "Like some machine, a methodical, mechanical destroyer, geared for destruction, did he attack the gargantuan specimen who opposed him with a sixty-four-pound weight advantage, and was cut down for the finish."

Povich's colleague on the *Post*, Bill McCormick, referred to "a cruel, destructive fighting machine trademarked Joe Louis." Syndicated columnist Heywood Broun remarked on Louis's "icy, dead-pan determination."

Paul Gallico saw "the fat-faced, café-au-lait colored, sloe-eyed" fighter as "something utterly vicious and pitiless. Not once is there a glimmer of sympathy or feeling on Louis's face." Reverting to the familiar jungle caricature, he went on:

> There will never be any complaint that Joe Louis is too nice a kid to be a fighter. He isn't. He is a splendid, vicious male animal, completely destructive. He was made for fighting and nothing else . . . Louis's handlers, Roxborough and Black, remind me more of animal trainers than fight managers. They gentle their animal around until feeding time and fighting time, and then they turn him loose.

Joe's skin color dominated almost every description of him. It gave the sportswriters great fun in dreaming up suitable nicknames. Some of the more outlandish suggestions included the Chocolate Chopper, the Dark Destroyer, the Dusky Downer, the Mocha Mauler, the Mahogany Maimer, the Panther with the Pin-Cushion Lips, the Saffron Sphinx, and the Shufflin' Shadow. They dug even deeper into the barrel to come up with the Tan Tarzan of Thump, Murder Man of the Maroon Mitts, and K.K.K. (Kruel Kolored Klouter) before finally settling for the Brown Bomber.

As for the unfortunate Carnera, the names he was called in the immediate aftermath of his fight piled on the pain he was suffering from his beating. Many Italians in the crowd had booed and jeered him as he stepped down from the ring, showing no sympathy for the punishment he had suffered. His left eye was grotesquely swollen and the blood from his gashed lip stained his chest. Even his manager, Billy Duffy, was heard to berate him for "a stupid performance." Neutral observers were more compassionate, praising his courage, especially the way he kept getting up after being floored. Louis's own brother, deLeon Barrow, speaking about the event many years later, said, "Carnera fought from bell to bell, and he didn't get no credit for it."

The repercussions in Italy, once the result became known, were immediate. A directive went out to all newspaper editors from the Ministry of Popular Culture, responsible for control of press and propaganda: "In no circumstances are you to publish any photograph of Primo Carnera knocked off his feet."

The former world champion didn't make it any easier for himself when, on his return home, he suggested that he had been doped by one of his seconds. At the end of the first round, as a sponge was passed over his open mouth, he said that he had smelled something "strong and acid." This had left him feeling weak as he left his corner for the next round, he claimed. Louis, when he heard about the allegation, remarked, "I guess he must mean the knockout drops I had in my gloves."

Fascist sporting circles in Italy, though skeptical, thought the matter deserved investigation. The Italian Boxing Commission sent a deputation to New York with orders to look into all the circumstances of the fight. They reported back that Carnera had been beaten fairly and that any suggestions of doping or threats by gangsters were nonsense. Achille Starace, secretary of Italy's Fascist Party, ordered the suspension of Carnera's passport and declared that he would not be allowed to fight German heavyweight Walter Neusel in Amsterdam that summer. Nor could he accept any more bouts in the United States in the immediate future. A directive was also issued to the Italian press prohibiting the publication of any more interviews that included references to the suspect sponge.

Disowned by the Fascists because of his "disgrace," Carnera was eventually allowed to return to America to resume his boxing career. Though he won his rescheduled match with Neusel in New York on a knockout, he suffered a brutal beating by Leroy Haynes, who stopped him in three rounds.

His brave handlers immediately threw him in with Haynes again. This time he lasted into the ninth round before being rescued by the referee. Taken to the hospital with a concussion, he was found to have a damaged kidney, which effectively ended his boxing career. Though he made a brief comeback after the war, it was only when he turned to professional wrestling, and he no longer had gangsters grabbing the bulk of his purses, that he was properly rewarded for stepping into the ring. He settled in America, appeared in quite a few movies, and bought a restaurant and liquor store. Diabetes and cirrhosis of the liver eventually brought him down, and in the 1960s he returned to his birthplace, Sequals, to die.

Louis had $60,000 to spend from the Carnera fight after his managers, for the first time in his career, took their share and 10 percent went to the Hearst Milk Fund. He bought presents for all of his family and some fancy clothes for himself. On trips to popular New York nightspots, he leaned on Duke Ellington's piano while the jazz maestro did his magic and enjoyed the company of "some sweet, beautiful girls."

There was one special girl, however, he wanted to be with more than anyone. Marva Trotter, a pretty nineteen-year-old stenographer, had first met Joe when she joined a crowd of onlookers at Trafton's Gym in Chicago while he was training to fight Lee Ramage in December 1934. They were introduced, and both later admitted it was love at first sight. From his purse for the Carnera fight, he bought Marva a car worth $7,200.

Joe replenished some of his spending spree with the $53,000 he got for an easy night's work against Harry "Kingfish" Levinsky, who got his nickname because he once worked as a fishmonger on Chicago's South Side. Usually billed as King Levinsky, he was, at twenty-four, just three years older than Louis, but was vastly more experienced and had a much-feared right hand. He had mixed it with some of the best in the business, including heavyweight champions Carnera, Sharkey, and Baer, and gave Dempsey such a going-over in an exhibition match that the old Manassa Mauler abandoned plans for a comeback.

Louis's growing reputation as a destructive force, however, scared Levinsky to death. He was so petrified in his dressing-room that promoter Mike Jacobs brought the fight forward by half an hour, hoping to catch him off guard. By then, the reluctant warrior had locked himself in the toilet and refused to come out. Finally, his handlers managed to half-guide and half-push him down the aisle toward the ring, only to see him freeze rigid when he caught sight of Louis sitting calmly on his stool like the executioner awaiting a condemned man. If that was what he was thinking, he was justified. In the two minutes twenty-one seconds the affair lasted, the King was knocked down four times, twice by jolting lefts, twice by hammerlike rights. The last time, as he sat on the bottom rope refusing to rise, referee Norman McGarrity counted to five, then stopped the fight. Levinsky later admitted that he had begged the referee to "get him off me."

5

BAER WITH A SORE HEAD

Louis had a double date on September 24, 1935. He married Marva Trotter at a friend's New York apartment, gave the bride a quick kiss, and then rushed to a waiting limousine to take him to Yankee Stadium to fight Max Baer.

"I wanted this to be a quick fight," he said years later. "I wanted to start being a married man as soon as possible, but I put all those thoughts out of my mind and concentrated on Baer."

Baer was the first common opponent for Louis and Schmeling. His sensational win over the German in 1934 set him up for his conquest of Carnera for the world heavyweight title the following year. In his first defense, he was dethroned by 10–1 underdog James J. Braddock, and in his next fight, he was stopped for the first time in his career by Louis.

Baer was one of those fighters who seem to have everything, except a dedication to his profession. While it is true that Max went all the way to the top, he could have enjoyed a much longer stay if he hadn't acted the playboy and clown. When he put his mind to it, he could look like a million-dollar performer, but his record was marred by defeats in fights he should have won.

A magnificent physical specimen at nearly 6 foot 3 and around 220 pounds, he was reputed to have to walk sideways through a doorway because of his wide shoulders. His body tapered to a slim waist that, whenever he was seen at a Broadway or Hollywood nightspot, usually had a woman's arm around it.

Nat Fleischer thought Baer had more potential than any of the heavyweight champions he had seen since Jack Johnson. He was immensely strong, could take a hard punch, and had a piledriver of a right hand. But Max's carefree, irresponsible personality ruined any chance he had of joining the all-time greats.

Variously known as Madcap Maxie and the Magnificent Screwball, he best summed himself up when he said, "I've got a million-dollar body and a ten-cent brain."

It wasn't just his fistic activity that kept Baer's name in the headlines. He allegedly signed over so many parts of himself to various managers that the total came to an incongruous 110 percent. Most of his time between fights was spent in courts and lawyers' offices. Then there were lots of spicy tales of his love affairs to keep the gossip columnists happy. He traveled around in his own chauffeur-driven limousine and had a staff of "social secretaries."

Born in Omaha, Nebraska, Baer was said to be of mixed German, Scottish, and Jewish blood. His family moved to California when he was eight, and by his teens he was working for his father, a successful butcher and cattle breeder. Carrying heavy slabs of meat developed his upper-body strength.

It was in a row with a train driver that he showed he had a naturally powerful punch. He had stolen the railwayman's flagon of wine as a joke, but, when forced to defend himself, he laid out the irate driver with a right to the jaw. Max bought a punching bag and set up a small gymnasium on his father's ranch.

He started punching for pay in 1929 and was earning national recognition when, in his twenty-seventh fight, he knocked out Frankie Campbell in five rounds. When Campbell failed to regain consciousness, Baer was distraught and had to be talked out of quitting the ring. He lost four of his next six fights but bounced back with impressive wins over Johnny Risko, King Levinsky, Tom Heeney, and Ernie Schaaf.

By June 1933, the heavyweight scene was stagnating. It was exactly a year since Jack Sharkey had taken the world title from Schmeling, and he hadn't fought since. Now public clamor forced him to come out of hibernation to defend against Carnera.

Three weeks before the championship fight, an even more attractive match between two of the top contenders took place. Max v. Max,

Baer against Schmeling, was a natural. The winner would be a ready-made next challenger for whoever emerged victorious between Sharkey and Carnera.

Schmeling had made just a single ring appearance since the Sharkey fight. In what was regarded as his most impressive performance since he first arrived in America, he battered the former world welterweight and middleweight champion Mickey Walker to defeat in a New York thriller. Although it seemed an uneven match, a 5 foot 7 middleweight against a top-ranking heavyweight, Walker had proved his ability to jump the two weight divisions by beating several leading heavyweights and holding Sharkey to a draw over fifteen rounds. Although floored by Schmeling in the first round, the Toy Bulldog fought back so well that he established a points lead before succumbing to the German's greater strength. He took a frightful beating before his manager, Jack "Doc" Kearns, got the referee to call a halt in the eighth round.

"Walker was a study in pain in the last round," Paul Gallico observed. "Can you imagine how he must have been hurt? His mouth was cut. Both eyes were shut. One of them was cut. His lips were mashed. He had nothing but a smear on his face and into that smear Schmeling kept driving his fists."

So, going into 1933, Schmeling was riding high. How could he be aware of the great fall that awaited him before the year was halfway through?

Maybe he was distracted to some extent by what was happening in Germany. In January, President Paul von Hindenburg appointed Hitler, whom he disparagingly referred to in private as "the Bohemian corporal," to the office of Reich chancellor. Berlin friends told Schmeling of the torchlight parade through the Brandenburg Gate, and he witnessed for himself the mass celebrations and hysteria.

In his autobiography, Max acknowledged:

[the] sense that something new had begun, a bustling energy had come over the country, new confidence, new hope. The most visible sign of this was to be seen in a both emotional and silly new form of expression that had suddenly swept through the entire country: there were marches practically everywhere.

He admitted to being disturbed to see, marching behind a band of musicians, a threatening-looking division of *Sturmabteilung*, Hitler's brown-shirted storm troopers, known as the SA. With their banners and uniforms, they turned an entertaining event into a propaganda exercise, with the aim of instilling in the public a mixture of fear and excitement, he noted.

One day in April, Schmeling was dining in a popular sporting restaurant when an SA officer entered, saluted the room with an outstretched right arm, and approached Max's table.

"Herr Schmeling," he announced, "the Führer requests that you join him for dinner at the Reich Chancellery."

Max replied that he had already eaten, but would be happy to accept the invitation. At the Reichstag building, he was led into an anteroom and asked to wait a moment.

"I had barely walked over to the window when the door opened and Hitler appeared, surrounded by [Hermann] Göring, [Joseph] Goebbels, and most of the other cabinet ministers," he recalled.

> Without hesitating, Hitler came directly over to me and said, "Good day, Herr Schmeling, how good of you to come. I wanted to invite you to join me for dinner." He was shorter than I had imagined, but, more than anything else, there was none of the rigid, overdone intensity of his public appearances. When we had driven into the city from Saarow-Pieskow in the last few years, we would see his election posters in the villages and towns that we drove through, and Anny would always laugh at his resemblance to Charlie Chaplin. But in this moment there was nothing comical or absurd in his bearing; he moved about in a relaxed way, he was charming and seemed quietly confident in these surroundings. I answered, "Herr Reichskanzler, thank you very much, but I have just eaten." Hitler accepted that in a friendly manner and said only, "Well, let's at least just chat a bit."

Schmeling remembered that the mood in the room was relaxed and friendly. Göring slapped him heartily on the shoulder. Goebbels made a joke about the Sports Palace. Franz von Papen, who had been instrumental in getting the reluctant von Hindenburg to appoint Hitler, asked a trivial question about America. After about twenty minutes, the get-together ended, with Hitler wishing Schmeling luck in his upcoming fight with Baer. As he was being driven home, Max concluded that the purpose of the meeting was to get him to spread the word, in interviews with the American press, that the doom merchants had got it all wrong and that everything in Germany was just fine.

Initially at least, Schmeling embraced the new optimism sweeping Germany. He saw signs of how life had improved for the people. Hitler had begun to fulfill many of his election promises. Unemployment had been significantly reduced. Violence and shootings, it appeared, had all but stopped. But not everyone was seduced. At the once fashionable Berlin cafés, many of the familiar faces were no longer to be found. They had seen the dark clouds gathering and had emigrated. The movies and theater, especially, suffered a hemorrhage of talent, losing the likes of Fritz Lang, Ernst Deutsch, Ludwig Bergner, Albert Bassermann, and Fritz Kortner. Soon the world-famous tenor Richard Tauber and film director Billy Wilder, both Austrian-born, would join the exodus. Marxist dramatist and poet Bertolt Brecht eventually made his way to California. He would return after the war to found and direct the Berliner Ensemble.

Back again in New York, Schmeling reflected that most of his American friends were Jews, Joe Jacobs foremost among them. When he told them of his reception at the Reich Chancellery, they kidded him about what Hitler must have thought about him fighting Baer, who sported the Star of David on his boxing shorts. Wouldn't the Nazis consider it a race crime? They laughed at the idea.

Goebbels wasn't amused the following year when he learned that a Hollywood movie called *The Prizefighter and the Lady* had been released in Germany. Baer played the lead opposite Myrna Loy, with Carnera in an important supporting role. The script called for Max and Primo to meet in the ring, and it was during the filming that Baer discovered the Italian was open to a right cross. The knowledge proved useful when he later faced Carnera for real. The movie's subtitled version had already been showing for ten days when the propaganda minister slapped a ban on it. His objection was that "it was not in the spirit of the New Germany because the chief actor was the Jewish boxer Max Baer."

If Goebbels had listened to leading American trainer Ray Arcel, he wouldn't have gotten so worked up about the movie. Arcel firmly debunked the myth of Baer's Jewishness. "I should know," he said, "I saw him in the shower."

Another fighter-turned-aspiring-movie-star almost spoiled Schmeling's preparations for the Baer contest. Jack Dempsey, one of the backers for the fight, had followed his actress wife Estelle Taylor into making movies. Someone thought it would be a good idea to get Dempsey and Schmeling to spar together as a publicity gimmick. It came close to backfiring.

Dempsey, in order to look the part of a matinee idol, had just had his nose straightened. He jokingly asked Schmeling to be careful not to undo the surgeon's handiwork. The trouble with Dempsey was that whenever he had the gloves on, his old instinct to slug it out quickly surfaced. He stormed from his corner and floored Schmeling with a barrage of punches. Promise or no promise, Max elected to hit back, and a hard right landed on the Manassa Mauler's most precious feature, causing him to throw up his hands in surrender. Laughing, Dempsey told reporters that Max was in great shape and had an outstanding right hand.

While Schmeling maintained his normal fanatical dedication to conditioning, reports from his opponent's camp suggested that Baer was failing to reach the same high level of fitness. Indeed, the American looked so poor in sparring that a poll of the twenty-four newsmen assigned to cover the fight had twenty-two picking the German to win. Schmeling was also a hot favorite with the fans. Dempsey was skeptical about the odds.

"No man who can punch like Max Baer should be a 6–1 underdog," he said. "Not even if he's in there with a gorilla."

It turned out Dempsey knew what he was talking about. Baer took control of the fight from the start, and, in the tenth round, exploded one of his trademark booming right hands on Schmeling's left cheek for the first of two heavy knockdowns. Referee Arthur Donovan stopped the fight at one minute fifty-one seconds into the round.

Over forty years later, Schmeling was still unable to explain his shock defeat. Maybe it was the fierce heat that day in New York, he suggested. He just knew he fought as if his legs were paralyzed. His arms, too, felt like lead. The newspaper writers had noted that he seemed way off form and was barely recognizable from the Schmeling of earlier fights. Max Machon told him in his dressing room, "That wasn't a defeat, it was a disaster."

There was some consolation for the loser when it was shown the fight had been a resounding financial success. The standing-room-only crowd was clocked at 56,300, and the top ticket price was $26.25, remarkable returns for those dark Depression days. Schmeling pocketed his agreed upon 37.5 percent of the $239,195 gross gate, leaving the winner with a meager 12.5 percent.

While Schmeling slipped back in the world ratings over the next year by winning just one of his three fights, Baer struck gold when he knocked Carnera off the heavyweight throne. In between giving the Ambling Alp a systematic hiding, he found time to joke with ringsiders and wink at the women who had come to see him. On one of the eleven occasions Carnera hit the floor, he pulled the challenger down with him in a tangle of arms and legs. Baer teased the Italian by shouting, "Last one up is a sissy," before jumping to his feet. Referee Arthur Donovan had seen enough by the eleventh round and stopped the massacre.

Showing the erratic form that characterized his career, Madcap Max lost the title in his first defense in a stunning upset to James J. Braddock. He didn't take the challenger seriously and spent time entertaining on stage and radio when he should have been training hard. Braddock, labeled the Cinderella Man after his rags-to-riches success, was a 10–1 underdog. He made nonsense of the odds, using stiff jabs and jolting rights to decisively outscore Baer over fifteen rounds.

The philosophical loser, interviewed on radio afterward, said, "Who likes to lose? But I will say it's good for a family man like James Braddock to win. He's got a lot of children to look after. I don't have any, not that I know of."

After a three-month break, Baer took a foolish gamble by taking on the all-conquering Louis at Yankee Stadium on September 24, 1935. Victory would have reestablished Baer as top contender for Braddock's title, but he never stood a chance. Apart from a right near the end of the first round that momentarily stunned his opponent, Baer hardly landed a solid punch. In contrast, Louis missed just two out of more than two hundred and fifty blows in the eleven minutes fifty seconds the affair lasted, according to one reporter's calculation.

"Louis's left hooks were deadly," wrote Nat Fleischer in *The Ring*. "His left jabs were cobra-like stings, and he poured into his adversary's body deadly right crosses that rocked the Californian almost from the start. Halfway through the first session, Louis knew he was Baer's master, even if he hadn't known so before, and from then on it was only a question of how soon Louis would end Baer's misery."

In the third round, Baer, bleeding profusely from his nose and mouth, was floored for the first time in his career. He rose, only to be knocked down again. The bell saved him from being counted out. It was a doubtful relief. A succession of stinging jabs followed by a terrific right had Max clinging on desperately in the fourth round. Once separated, Louis measured his distance for a long right that was quicker to the target than Baer's tentative jab. Baer was already sinking to the canvas when Joe's follow-up left glanced off his head. He took the full count on one knee, making no attempt to rise. The crowd booed his apparent act of surrender.

When asked afterward why he hadn't made more of an effort to continue the fight, he mixed pragmatism with humor: "When I get executed, people are going to have to pay more than twenty-five dollars a seat to watch it."

Baer fought on for another six years but never again got within reach of a title shot. Having shrewdly invested much of his ring earnings, he supplemented his income with movie and stage appearances, as well as public relations work. He died of a heart attack in a Hollywood hotel room in 1959 while in town filming a television commercial. A bellboy, noticing the guest was unwell, asked him if he should call the house doctor. Max, a joker to the end, quipped, "No, you'd better get a person doctor."

Louis's emphatic victory over Baer sparked off celebrations in black neighborhoods all across the nation, none more enthusiastic than in Harlem. The *New York Sun* reported: "Milling thousands of Negro men, women, and children turned the district into bedlam as they surged through the streets, howling gleefully, blowing horns, dancing madly, pounding on pots and pans."

For the still downtrodden section of the population, it was a rare chance for a celebration, however fleeting. Generally, American blacks had little to cheer about. The same year that Louis came into the spotlight with his victories over Carnera and Baer saw eighteen blacks lynched. The vigilante executions occurred while thirteen of the victims, accused of murder, rape, organizing sharecroppers, and "communistic activities," were supposedly in the care of law enforcement agencies.

Undoubtedly, Louis was also earning the respect of a growing number of white people, who expressed admiration for his talent and sportsmanship. Many spoke patronizingly of his deferential nature.

Boxing experts acknowledged he was good for the sport. His exciting knockouts had brought back the million-dollar gates of the Dempsey era. There was no frantic search for a "white hope" to halt this black man's rise to the top, unlike the relentless campaign to dethrone the despised Jack Johnson a couple of decades earlier. The writers were almost unanimous in proclaiming Louis a certain world heavyweight champion, just as soon as Braddock could be lured into putting his title at stake.

"Louis, a boxer still two years removed from his peak, is being pronounced as a greater fighter than John Lawrence Sullivan, James J. Corbett, Robert Fitzsimmons, James J. Jeffries, and Jack Dempsey," wrote Harry Salsinger in the *Detroit News*:

> Nothing like this has ever happened before. No heavyweight champion in history was ever considered as anything more than a good prospect after 18 months of professional boxing. Louis should continue flattening the heavyweights of the world and by the time he retires he undoubtedly will be nominated the greatest fighter of all time by acclamation.

Joe, typically, wasn't as caught up in the hysteria as everyone else seemed to be. Over the years, however, whenever he was asked about his most satisfying performance, he would always refer to the Baer fight.

"I felt better that night. I felt like I could fight for two or three days. I threw more strikes at that man than anyone else."

6

NAZI SALUTE – WITH A CIGAR

Schmeling, feeling down after his heavy defeat by Baer and wondering if he still had a future in boxing, had the consolation of knowing he had a woman who loved him. On July 6, 1933, a month after the Baer fight, he exchanged marriage vows with Anny Ondra before a registrar in Charlottenburg, on the outskirts of Berlin. A large crowd waved the couple off to their honeymoon in the resort of Heiligendamm on the Baltic Sea.

Max acknowledged how lucky he had been to find Anny. Not only was she a very popular movie star but she was also a very successful businesswoman. Her stunning looks and charming personality meant she could have had her pick of eligible men.

Born to Czech parents in Tarnow, Poland, on May 15, 1902 (not 1903 as listed by some sources), Anny Sophie Ondráková grew up in Czechoslovakia. The golden-haired, brown-eyed daughter of a colonel in the Austro-Hungarian Army was a dancer before she broke into the movies. Although she played many straight roles, she was best in cute comedy parts, once being described as "Buster Keaton in skirts." Spotted by Alfred Hitchcock, she got a small part in his silent film *The Manxman.* When the English director made his first talkie, *Blackmail,* in 1929, he signed Anny to play the heroine. Disappointed to learn she only spoke German and Czech, he got around the problem by dubbing her voice. A movie career in England or America was clearly not a viable prospect, and she continued to make German movies. Altogether, she appeared in more than eighty films, the last in 1957.

Though her marriage to Schmeling was childless (Anny once suffered a miscarriage), it lasted for fifty-four years, right up to her death in 1987. Several English-language film sources state that she was previously married to Karel Lamac, who directed many of her early films and became her business partner, but this is denied in a recent Schmeling biography published in Germany. Briana Cechova, of the Department of Film History, Czech National Film Archive, is also adamant that Lamac was a lifelong bachelor.

In the early months of her marriage, Anny was required to show her strength of character. Not only was she deeply hurt by nasty letters she received suggesting Max was finished as a fighter but she also tried to ignore newspaper stories alleging he was having an affair with another actress. Schmeling firmly quashed the rumors.

"I love my wife more every day," he told reporters in December 1933. "I don't see what interest anyone could have in spreading such a story. They must be crazy."

While Anny settled into married life, her business interests began to suffer in the prevailing political climate in Germany. She had never given much thought to the fact that four of the six business partners were Jews, while she and the remaining partner were Czechs. Work for the company had almost dried up, and only a handful of scripts were waiting to be considered. Anny, who had received several tempting offers from Hollywood, considered moving the business to America. But, after consultations with her partners and legal representatives, she reluctantly accepted that the best course was to liquidate Ondra-Lamac Productions.

If that wasn't bad enough, there was another blow in store for the Schmelings. Max, anxious to get his boxing career back on track, accepted an offer to face a young American, Steve Hamas, in Philadelphia. Hamas, a former college football hero, was nicknamed Hurricane because of his aggressive style. His best win was a second-round knockout of Tommy Loughran. He outpointed Loughran in a return, but lost two subsequent matches with the former world light-heavyweight champion on points. Despite his good record, he was not looked upon as much of a threat to Schmeling. In a stunning upset, Hamas won a clear points decision.

An opportunity to make up lost ground came along when Max was paired with Paolino Uzcudun in Barcelona. It was a risk, as the Spaniard was a much bigger man and would have the overwhelming support of the 30,000 spectators in attendance. Also, he was thirsting for revenge over the man who had beaten him in New York five years earlier.

In his last ring outing, Uzcudun had gone fifteen rounds in a world heavyweight title challenge to Carnera, a contest that earned its place in ring history for the record combined weight of its championship contestants. The champion weighed 259½, and the Basque tipped the scales at 229½.

Schmeling described the rematch with Uzcudun:

> Paolino, normally an attacking fighter, never got a chance to come off the defensive. With the first exchange of punches I felt like my old self and knew that Paolino couldn't hurt me. Again and again he ran into my left, but he took these punches along with my hardest rights. He didn't go down once. Breathing heavily and with a swollen face, he wearily returned to his corner after the final gong. To the amazement of even Paolino's most dedicated fans, the decision was a draw.

Even the Spanish press thought the verdict was farcical. The Catalonian paper *Diagraphico* observed that, from the first round on, Uzcudun had been nothing more than a punchbag. *La Vanguardia* commented: "There can be no more decisions like this one, which hurts the prestige of Paolino, Spain, and the sport of boxing."

Schmeling, though disappointed at the result, was pleased at his improved performance. He felt he had shown good ability and punching power, while recapturing the reflexes that had been missing against Baer and Hamas.

On his return home, Max aimed to spend a few days relaxing with his wife in Munich, where she was filming. The plan was changed when the couple received an invitation from the Führer to have coffee at the home of Franz Xavier Schwarz, the Reich treasurer. Hitler, in his first meeting with Anny, turned on the charm, saying how pleased he was to make the acquaintance of such a "gracious lady" and hoping she had brought a shawl, as they were sitting outside in Schwarz's large garden on the Tegernsee.

As the guests sipped their coffee and accepted offerings of cake with large dollops of cream, Hitler only once brought the conversation around to the Uzcudun fight, and never mentioned the loss to Baer.

In his reminiscences, Schmeling wrote:

> I noticed a young woman who appeared to be in her mid-20s, pretty in a simple way, with a charming laugh that often seemed to have no reason. She remained in the background and, despite all modesty, seemed to speak to Hitler in an open and extremely intimate way. When I asked [Heinrich] Hoffman [Hitler's personal photographer] at the coffee table who she was, he brusquely waved me off. Only later, away from the group, did he tell me: "That's Eva Braun; she works for me." He said this with a certain pride. Somewhat surprised, I asked him what the big secret was all about, at which point he flashed a smile that said volumes and turned away.

As the group was driven to dinner at the home of Adolf Müller, proprietor of the Nazi Party newspaper *Völkischer Beobachter,* Hitler sat in the front alongside his chauffeur while the Schmelings occupied the backseat. Max couldn't help thinking it incongruous that as the convoy of six to eight black Mercedes roared through the idyllic countryside stirring up clouds of dust, Hitler rhapsodized about the landscape, the mountains, and the quaint Bavarian villages.

On his return to Berlin, Schmeling was shocked to find an official notice awaiting him, stating that he had been sentenced to six months in prison and ordered to pay a ten thousand–mark fine for a currency violation. Because of his celebrity status, the jail term was reduced to probation. Still, Max was annoyed that what he considered a trivial matter had got into the newspapers. He had bought some shares and gold bars from an American acquaintance after the Hamas fight and put them in a safe deposit box. Without realizing it, he had contravened currency regulations. In his absence, the Justice Ministry had issued a press release about the findings of the case.

Remembering how Hitler had offered his help if ever it was

needed, Schmeling decided the time was now. The Führer answered his call by inviting him to the Reich Chancellery, and after listening to the details, angrily denounced "the bureaucrats in the Finance Ministry." He put through a call to the minister, Roland Freisler, whose efforts to offer an explanation were cut short. "There will be no discussion. Take care of the matter immediately," Hitler barked before slamming down the phone. Two weeks later, Schmeling got official notice that the verdict had been overturned and the case dismissed.

While his financial investment bore fruit within six months with a twenty-one-point rise in the price of his shares, Max's boxing stock wasn't anywhere near as healthy. Another talented German heavyweight, Walter Neusel, had come along to compete for the fans' affections. Many saw him as likely to take over from the fading Schmeling as a serious world championship contender.

Neusel was managed by Paul Damski, who had guided him through an impressive run of victories over Larry Gains, Reggie Meen, George Cook, and Max's nemesis, Gypsy Daniels, before taking his tall, hard-hitting prospect to America.

Billed as the German Tiger because of his aggressive style, Neusel made an immediate impact, knocking out Stanley Poreda in ten (Joe Louis did it in one) and defeating Tommy Loughran and the giant Ray Impellitiere. He held the highly rated Natie Brown to a draw and showed he could box as well as punch in an impressive points win over King Levinsky.

Inevitably, demand grew for a showdown between the top two German heavyweights. Walter Rothenburg, still active as a promoter in Germany despite his Jewish background, put the fight together for Hamburg on August 26, 1934. The venue was a dirt track next to Hagenbeck Zoo. Within a few weeks, Rothenburg had built a fine arena that could hold 95,000 spectators.

It didn't escape the Nazi leaders' attention that here was an event being staged by a Jewish promoter between boxers who both had Jewish managers. No doubt fearful that intervention could create a public backlash, they chose to turn a blind eye. Later, both Schmeling and Neusel would come under strong pressure to dump their mentors "in the interests of Germanhood." To their credit, they refused.

In any case, Damski didn't travel to the fight from Paris, where he was domiciled since coming to the uncomfortably close attention of the Gestapo. Nor did Joe Jacobs make the trip from America. However, his presence at Schmeling's next fight would cause quite a stir.

Meanwhile, for the first time, a boxing match in Germany attracted international interest. One reporter sent to cover the event, Sparrow Robertson of the *New York Herald*, told Schmeling that opinion was divided in the States as to who would win. Among former heavyweight champions, Jack Dempsey and Max Baer both predicted a Schmeling victory, whereas Gene Tunney thought Neusel's aggressiveness and youth would be the deciding factors.

From the opening bell, Neusel went on the attack in an attempt to overwhelm his more experienced rival. He found his efforts nullified by Schmeling's clever defensive boxing and precise counterpunching. By the seventh round, Neusel was slowing down and losing confidence. A hard right shook him badly. He made a brave effort in the next round to get back into the fight but took a lot of punishment. The ninth round had hardly begun when the referee, seeing Neusel in some distress, with blood coming from cuts over both eyes and his face badly swollen, stopped the fight.

The impressive win put Schmeling well and truly back in the world heavyweight picture. He looked again toward America, where Max Baer was enjoying his reign as king of the heavyweights after his thrashing of Carnera. But the one everybody was talking about was an exciting young black fighter who was bowling them over like ninepins. Joe Louis was someone they would all have to reckon with sooner or later.

While awaiting news from Joe Jacobs about a resumption of his American campaign, Schmeling got an offer he couldn't refuse—the chance to avenge his defeat by Steve Hamas. Walter Rothenburg scooped the Madison Square Garden Corporation, who wanted the fight for New York, by staging it in Hamburg. Hamas, despite conceding home advantage, felt that what he had done before, he could do again. For Schmeling, it was a make-or-break fight. A second loss to the American would effectively finish his world title hopes. A decisive win would put him back among the top contenders.

Max invited his manager to Berlin so they could have a few days together before traveling on to Hamburg. Booked into the Hotel

Bristol, Jacobs was shocked to find on arrival that his reservation had been canceled. Word had gotten through to the management that he was Jewish. A furious Schmeling confronted the head clerk and told him that if the story got into the U.S. papers, the hotel would never again have an American guest. The register was produced for Jacobs to sign in.

If that attempted Nazi snub didn't work, the next one did. Jacobs discovered that he was barred from Schmeling's corner for the fight, but he would be allowed to watch from a ringside seat. He didn't object. The opportunity would come before the night was out to register his protest.

Schmeling got a tremendous reception as he made his way to the ring in the newly built Hanseatic Halle. He looked grim and determined, with not the slightest trace of nervousness. Hamas, on the other hand, appeared extremely ill at ease.

From the start, Max was in command. He constantly beat his opponent to the punch, and by the fifth round, the American was looking the worse for wear. In the next round, a powerful right to the body sent Hamas back against the ropes. A following right to the jaw floored him for a count of eight. Twice more the visitor hit the deck before the bell ended the round.

A pitiful sight as he bled from the nose, mouth, and a cut above his eye, Hamas should never have been sent out for the ninth round. A merciless Schmeling pounded the game American with both fists until the referee made his belated intervention. So badly beaten was Hamas that rumors spread he had died from his injuries. Though the stories were untrue, he would never again step into a boxing ring.

As Schmeling was declared the winner, the audience cheered lustily and broke into a spirited rendition of *Deutschland über Alles*. The jubilant victor, after accepting a laurel wreath bearing a swastika ribbon, joined the multitude in raising his rigid right arm in a Heil Hitler salute. So did Jacobs—only he kept his lit cigar gripped firmly between his fingers. He turned his head toward Max and gave him a wink.

It didn't take long for the storm to erupt. The Nazi newspaper *Fraenkische Tageszeitung*, in a front-page editorial, denounced Jacobs's action as "a despicable insult by a Jew toward our Führer." It further attacked both Schmeling and Walter Neusel for retaining their Jewish managers and called for the immediate reform of such "shameful conditions in the German sport world."

A few days later, Schmeling was summoned to the office of the newly appointed Reich minister of sports, Hans von Tschammer und Osten. Spread out on the desk in front of him were numerous newspaper clippings showing the offending Jacobs salute.

The minister's opening remarks were conciliatory: "You should really box more often in Germany, Herr Schmeling. That would be a more appropriate surrounding for you."

Schmeling told him fights and locations were decided by who made the best offer.

Von Tschammer, after a pause to gather his thoughts, said, "Our youth need role models to emulate, to inspire them."

"Role models can be found everywhere," Schmeling replied. "What I accomplish in America can inspire German youth, too."

The minister, showing signs of annoyance, said, "It's athletes like yourself that are needed in our new Germany."

Max held his ground. "When I box in America, I represent Germany."

Raising his voice, von Tschammer said, "You shouldn't be so shortsighted, Herr Schmeling. Think of your age. You will want to be a trainer here some day. Over there, no one is going to care about you when you're washed up. Force yourself to listen. It's dumb to burn all your bridges behind you."

Schmeling, remaining calm, said he hoped to be able to live off his savings and investments when he grew old.

Von Tschammer abruptly ended the meeting but reiterated his feelings in a letter to Schmeling a few days later.

Max felt so strongly about the sports chief's attempts to pressure him into turning his back on America that he decided to take his objections to the top. His request for a meeting with Hitler got an immediate response.

Invited to tea the next day at the Reich Chancellery, Max and his wife were greeted with excessive courtesy by the Führer.

"Would the gracious lady prefer coffee or tea?"

To Anny's request for tea, Hitler nodded agreeably and said, "Tea, how nice, Frau Schmeling. I, too, only drink tea, but it can't be too strong."

After Max interrupted to say he was a passionate coffee drinker, Hitler again turned his attention to Anny, debating the merits of the various pastries from which to choose. He was delighted to hear her refer to one cake, generally called *Napfkuchen*, as *Gugelhupf.*

"How long it is since I heard that word," he said with a laugh. "Imagine that. *Gugelhupf.*"

They talked about her upbringing in Czechoslovakia.

"Ah, yes, Prague, beautiful old German Prague," Hitler said, deep in thought. (Four years later, his army would enter and take control of the city that the Germans had first occupied in the thirteenth century.)

Max, irritated by what amounted to being ignored while Hitler flirted with his wife, waited for a break in the conversation to declare his reason for being there.

Referring to the letter he had received from the minister of sports, he made clear that he didn't wish to split with Joe Jacobs, who had been his manager since 1928. He owed all his success in America to Jacobs, whom he always found to be "competent, respectable, and correct."

Hitler listened carefully but said nothing as he slurped his tea loudly.

"Besides," Schmeling reminded his host, "loyalty is a German virtue."

That was too much for Hitler. He made an angry gesture and sat staring at the floor for a few moments. Then, after briefly turning on the charm again with Anny, he beckoned to an attendant to show his guests out.

Schmeling saw that his appeal had got nowhere. Hitler had listened to what he had to say but refused point blank to discuss it. Max heard no more from the Sports Ministry, but von Tschammer would later get his revenge.

Whenever he was in Berlin, Schmeling still met up with his friends at the Roxy Bar, on Joachimstaler Strasse, and they would lament how many of the old circle had disappeared. Alfred Flechtheim, art collector and publisher of the avant-garde journal *Querschnitt*, had sold his gallery and gone to live in London. Heinrich Mann, author and older brother of Thomas Mann, had left Amsterdam for southern France. Carl von Ossietzky, leftist-pacifist who published the activist journal *Weltbühne*, had been sent to a concentration camp (the Nobel Prize winner would be released as a result of international protest, but died from the effects of his mistreatment). Kurt Tucholsky, author, journalist, and satirist, whose works were burned and banned by the Nazis in 1933, committed suicide in Sweden.

The Roxy was where the world met, Schmeling wrote in his autobiography, but now the whole world was only half the world:

We could still speak freely and openly—Ditgens [the owner] knew how to cultivate and hold together a circle of friends among whom caution wasn't necessary. Not that there were particularly inflammatory conversations at the Roxy; many of us, and in some ways I was among them, were impressed by the new optimism in Germany as well as by the success of the new regime.

But in our sphere we came to know this regime's other face soon enough. Each of us had at least one person we were close to who had been forced to leave the country; others had been forced out of a profession or simply made to live in fear. And we all knew—or at least knew of—persons who had already been arrested.

After the war, many, perhaps hoping to fool themselves, claimed to have had no knowledge of what went on. In truth we all knew. It was no secret that there were concentration camps in Germany; it was openly discussed in the Roxy Bar.

At this time, on March 19 and 21, 1935, the first air-raid drills were held in the Berlin area. There was something both surprising and almost absurd in the sights of the cosmopolitan city blacked out while grown people ran to their posts with fire apparatus in hand. We went out in the street, and many of us laughed. But at the same time, we felt that something strange was happening.

7

WIVES AND LOVERS

"You booked me into sixteen fights," Schmeling often said to Paul Damski, "but the best match you ever made was the seventeenth, the one with Anny."

Like most famous fighters, he could have had his pick among female admirers, but he was happy being a one-woman man. It was not that he was short of offers. Once, while in London to sign contracts for a fight with Tommy Farr that eventually fell through, a bellboy at the Savoy Hotel handed him a message: "I have just read that you're in London and that we're staying at the same hotel. I would be frightfully pleased to see you again after all these years. This evening I'm giving a cocktail party in my suite. Will you come? Yours, Marlene Dietrich."

The sultry movie star had always been a fan of her fellow German. She had flown from her home in Los Angeles to New York to see him fight Sharkey, and they nodded to each other as Max stood in the ring awaiting the announcements. She also accurately predicted he would knock out Louis.

Flattered by her invitation to the party but concerned that he might be the only guest, Max asked in his reply if he could bring some friends along. Dietrich never got back to him.

Louis, in his private life, was the direct opposite of Schmeling. All a pretty woman, black or white, had to do was flutter her false eyelashes at him and he was ready for a new relationship. Throughout his four marriages, two of them to the same woman, he was regularly unfaithful. He would try to make it up to his wives by giving them expensive presents of clothes, jewelry or, if he was feeling particularly guilty, a car.

After his retirement, he said, "I could never resist a pretty girl with a sparkle in her eyes. And there were lots of those girls coming on strong, you'd better believe it."

His hundreds of lovers included many who were anonymous, while others were household names. Among those who snuggled into his brawny embrace were Norwegian skater-turned-movie-star Sonja Henie, Hollywood "sweater girl," Lana Turner, and torch singer Lena Horne.

Indefatigable sex siren Mae West was said to have been another. Just before Louis married Marva Trotter in 1935, he visited the Buick showroom in Detroit. A fancy black limousine with whitewall tires caught his eye. He thought the built-in mahogany bar was a neat extra, even though he didn't drink. While he was discussing terms, the salesman excused himself to talk to an attractive white woman with blond hair who had entered the premises. After a few minutes, he returned to Louis and told him, "The car is yours. The lady has bought it for you."

In *Joe Louis: My Life*, he recalled:

> My mind immediately flashed to Jack Johnson and my managers' warning about "having your picture taken with a white woman," and I tried to get out of it. But what the hell can you do when the lady is insistent and charming as hell? I took the car and promised her two ringside tickets for the Max Baer fight.

For the next five years, Joe got a new Buick every Christmas as a present. His benefactor insisted on complete discretion, and neither ever talked about their meetings. All he ever said was: "She was a very important white woman, and I was a very important black man. She taught me the meaning of discretion."

Maurice Leonard, author of *Mae West: Empress of Sex*, had little doubt that she was the person who kept Louis supplied with top-of-the-line rides. Certainly, it would have been in keeping with West's renowned fondness for pugilistic types. One would-be lover, summoned to her mirrored bedroom but dismissed as not living up to expectations, caustically remarked, "You could be a combination of

Einstein and Cary Grant, but you would mean nothing if a well-built fighter with a crooked nose, cauliflower ears, and the IQ of an ape appeared."

The daughter of ex-professional "Battling" Jack West was often taken to fights by her father during her adolescence. She loved boxing—and boxers. Among her conquests were world champions "Gorilla" Jones and "Speedy" Dado. She lived for a while with Johnny Indrisano, who taught her to box after appearing with her in a movie. West successfully sued the scandal magazine *Confidential* for alleging that she had had a lengthy affair with world featherweight champion "Chalky" Wright, employed as her chauffeur. Asked by a friend why he didn't wear a uniform, Wright said the job was a front and he was *the man.*

If Louis was one of West's lovers, her romantic partners certainly spanned a lengthy period of world heavyweight championship history. "Gentleman" Jim Corbett, champion from 1892 to 1897, was in his fifties when he supposedly accepted Mae's invitation to "come up and see me." Max Baer (1934–35) boasted of a one-night stand with West, while Louis was champion from 1937 to 1949.

Although Joe didn't discriminate in matters of race or creed when it came to bedding a succession of waitresses, actresses, models, cigarette girls, singers, secretaries, showgirls, and whoever else was ready to jump into the sack with him, his long-term relationships were typically with partners who were elegant, self-assured, and fair-skinned. It was important that these affairs with white women were kept as secret as possible.

In 1936, while in Hollywood filming *Spirit of Youth*, in which he played a dishwasher who soars to become world heavyweight champion, he rarely spent a night alone. On his subsequent trips to the movie capital, it was the same story.

"A big movie star would see me, the heavyweight champion of the world, and wonder how I am in bed," Joe said. "I'd see a big beautiful movie star and wonder how she was in bed. We would find out very easily. These were just one-night stands. But we both knew to keep it cool. Neither of us could afford to be found out in America in those days."

Sonja Henie, with whom he had a longer relationship, was "a pug-nosed blond with bright blue eyes and one of the best sports I've ever known. We had a nice thing going, but she was a smart woman and kept everything undercover."

Lana Turner, once accurately described as "not a great actress, but one of the best cheap broads in the movies," was equally discreet about her romance with Louis. "A beautiful girl she was," Joe remarked, "and real likeable." (Turner was at the center of one of Hollywood's greatest scandals when, in 1958, her fifteen-year-old daughter, Cheryl, stabbed to death Lana's gangster boyfriend, Johnny Stompanato, while attempting to protect her mother.)

In today's age of almost daily exposés in the sensation-hungry media, it seems remarkable that there was a time when celebrities could keep their love lives out of the headlines. Potential scandals were often covered up in deference to the parties involved. Mixed-race entanglements, especially, could be very harmful to both sides if the news got out. While they might be considered daring, and therefore chic, in some circles and simply tolerated in others, it was still a highly inflammatory issue, particularly in the American South. Swedish sociologist Gunnar Myrdal, who toured southern states studying race relations for his book *An American Dilemma,* ranked the various taboos considered important to southern whites. Top of the list was "the bar against intermarriage and sexual intercourse involving white women."

Louis got away with it mainly because his meetings with white women usually took place in the black enclave of whatever city he was in. That way, both parties were protected from inquisitive white reporters. Even those who did know what was going on usually kept quiet.

Shirley Povich, long-time sports columnist with the *Washington Post,* explained:

> We respected an athlete's private life. We overlooked their peccadilloes, though we knew about them. Joe was a womanizer, a lot of us knew that or had heard the rumors, but we didn't write anything about it, just like we didn't write certain things about Babe Ruth and other sports figures. Those were the mores of the time. I personally didn't feel any hypocrisy. There was no conflict there. The feeling was that it was none of the public's business.

All the while Louis was away for fights, or playing golf, or doing the rounds of the nightclubs, his wife was expected to stay at home and patiently accept his double standards. He once told Marva, "All you have to do is just be beautiful, gracious, a good mother, and a good wife. Just be my doll-baby."

Eventually, tired of too many lonely nights, Marva got a divorce.

Destiny was moving Louis and Schmeling closer to a ring showdown. They both closed out 1935 with victories over the same opponent, Paolino Uzcudun.

For Max, it was gratifying to get the Basque to agree to a rematch in Berlin. There, Schmeling felt assured of a fairer deal than he had got in Barcelona. His faith was justified when he secured his win, but he wasn't entirely satisfied with how it was achieved. Uzcudun spent almost the entire twelve rounds of a tedious encounter covered up like a clam, intent only on lasting the distance, which he did.

Louis did much better when he met Paolino, pulverizing him inside four rounds. A tremendous right drove two of the Spaniard's teeth through his bottom lip and bounced him off the canvas. Just about upright by the count of nine, Uzcudun was in such a sorry state that referee Arthur Donovan immediately stopped the fight.

Famed trainer Whitey Bimstein, who worked in the loser's corner, said he had never seen anybody hit a man as hard as Louis hit Paolino. It was the first time in his career that Uzcudun had been beaten inside the distance. After twenty minutes resting in his dressing room, he stood up and fell over in a faint.

Among the crowd at Madison Square Garden was Schmeling. Though impressed by the American's power, he was encouraged by what he saw as a serious flaw in his style. Pressed as to what that was, he would only say, "I saw something." He would elaborate in good time.

A week earlier Mike Jacobs had announced that Schmeling and Louis would meet in June of the following year at Yankee Stadium.

The Olympic Games were due to be held in Berlin in the summer of 1936. However, there were fears that the United States would boycott the event in protest at the Nazis' racist policies. The nonappearance of one of the world's most powerful nations would not only devalue the

Games, but would mean a serious loss of face for the Third Reich.

Knowing how popular Schmeling was in America, Arno Breithaupt, the deputy sports minister, asked if he would act as an intermediary. The hope was that he could exert a positive influence on the right people.

Max agreed to deliver a letter to the president of the American Olympic Committee, Avery Brundage, while he was in New York for the Louis–Uzcudun fight. At their meeting, Brundage was courteous but expressed his concern about the situation in Germany and produced newspaper clippings showing photographs of the arrests of Communists and harassment of Jews. One of the reports told of Jews being prohibited from using public swimming pools.

"What about this, Max?" Brundage asked. "A good number of black and Jewish athletes will be on the American team. Who is going to guarantee us that they won't be abused?"

Schmeling assured him that the German athletes would guarantee the integrity of the Games and would not allow any discrimination. Afterward, he wondered if he had been too presumptuous. After all, how could he be sure that what he said would be honored by Hitler? Still, his intervention undoubtedly helped swing the vote by the American Olympic Committee, by a small majority, in favor of taking part.

Once American participation was assured, the Reich pulled out all the stops to show how wrong the world was in painting such a black picture of life in Germany. More naive visitors to Berlin would be almost led to believe that anti-Semitism was a myth. All anti-Jewish posters and literature were removed. Newspapers were forbidden to print anti-Semitic material for the duration of the Games. Even the population of the city was instructed not to express racist feelings.

Behind the phoney goodwill, Hitler was intent on using the Olympics as a showcase for the doctrine of Aryan superiority. Sweeping success by German sportsmen and women in the various events would also vindicate his enormous investment in sport as a means to developing a superfit nation.

Nazi ideology upheld physical strength, more than intellectual ability, as a supreme virtue. To this end, a tough training program required all able-bodied males between the ages of sixteen and fifty-five to be involved in some sort of fitness activity. In the industrial sector, this meant that calisthenics formed part of the working day for most employees. Whole factories would come to a halt for periods of up to half an hour to conduct stretching, strength-building, and aerobic exercises.

The young were taught to endure pain and exhaustion as something normal. In one of Hitler's speeches, he expounded on his ideal of German youth as "quick like greyhounds, tough like leather, and hard as Krupp steel."

On another occasion, he observed that education must not stuff the student with mere knowledge, which was the ruin of many young men. "A violently active, dominating, brutal youth—that is what I am after. Youth must be indifferent to pain. There must be no weakness and tenderness in it. I want to see once more in its eyes the gleam of pride and independence of the beast of prey."

Sports were seen as a way to erase all vestiges of humanity and tenderness, ultimately to prepare participants for the possibility of war. Boxing was a compulsory activity in schools and youth camps, leading inevitably to many children suffering beatings by bullies. Even less demanding sports took their toll. Often games were played to the point of exhaustion. Rates of physical injury and nervous strain soared. The intensive sports regimen led to another common problem. Some 37 percent of eighteen-year-olds called up for military service in 1936 were found to be suffering from flat feet caused by fallen arches.

Sports were often given priority over intelligence in school entrance exams. This meant that nonathletic types could struggle to get the education they merited. High school diplomas were issued only to those who had attained the recommended physical fitness standards. Youths leaving school to start apprenticeships were obliged to continue the school fitness program while they were learning their jobs.

Adults, too, suffered the consequences of overindulgence in mandatory physical activity. In the late 1930s, all German adults were required to perform a test that included a long jump of 2.8 meters (9.2 feet), a 1 kilometer (0.6 mile) run in under six minutes, and tossing a medicine ball a distance of 6.15 meters (20 feet). Older participants regularly suffered from pulled backs and torn ligaments and tendons as well as physical exhaustion. Failing the test could mean additional training and even problems with their employment.

"German sport has only one task," said Propaganda Minister Goebbels in a speech, "to strengthen the character of the German people, imbuing it with the fighting spirit and steadfast camaraderie necessary in the struggle for its existence."

In a parade through the Olympic village two days before the Games began, the Nazis proudly showed off their greatest sporting hero—Max Schmeling. Maybe he didn't quite look the part of the idealized blond, blue-eyed Aryan, but for the Nazi propaganda machine the Black Uhlan of the Rhine had shown how a true German warrior could conquer the world. Two months before, he had exposed the myth of Joe Louis's invincibility, sensationally ending the American's winning streak in one of the greatest upsets in ring history.

8

FALLING STAR

One summer day in 1936, Eddie Frayne, sports editor of *American*, called columnist Jimmy Cannon into his office. He gave him a choice. Did he want to go west with the Yankees or stay in New York to cover the Louis–Schmeling fight? Cannon knew there was a kid with the Yankees who was making his first road trip, so he decided he would rather travel with Joe DiMaggio.

"Schmeling's all washed up," he told Frayne. "It won't be much of a fight."

In a Detroit hotel room with Tony Lazzeri, he listened to the radio broadcast of the fight. Above the roar of the crowd, he heard commentator Clem McCarthy's hoarse, excited voice: "He's down."

"I told you," Cannon said to Lazzeri.

But it was Louis who was down. Only when it became clear that the Brown Bomber was heading for a sensational defeat did Cannon regret missing one of the biggest sports stories of the decade.

In the eight years since Gene Tunney's retirement, five men had held the world heavyweight championship. Though Schmeling, Sharkey, Carnera, Baer, and Braddock possessed talent, none was regarded as an outstanding champion. They were mere stopgap titleholders until someone exceptional came along. Louis seemed certain to fit that criterion. Winner of his first twenty-three fights, all but four by knockouts, he was already being proclaimed by many experts as one of the greatest heavyweights in history.

As part of his buildup toward a title fight, Joe had gained valuable experience and boosted his confidence by taking on, and easily beating, two of the former champions, Carnera and Baer. Next on the agenda was Schmeling. There was nothing to suggest the German would prove more troublesome than the others. Coming up to his thirty-first birthday, Schmeling was considered over the hill. Now in his twelfth year as a professional, he had struggled in several of his last few fights and seemed destined to become the latest victim of the rampaging Louis.

Max, however, wasn't prepared to roll over and die as easily as had so many of Louis's victims. On the contrary, he entered into preparations with meticulous planning on how to win. He spent countless hours with his trainer, Max Machon, studying films of Louis's fights with Ramage, Carnera, Baer, Levinsky, and Uzcudun, probing for any signs of weakness. They even showed the films backward, frame by frame, following a punch from its point of impact back to the instant it was thrown.

Styles make fights, it has often been said, and Schmeling thought he had the perfect style to counteract what Louis could offer. He noticed that Joe, after delivering a jab, tended to drop his left hand, thus leaving himself open to a right-hand counterpunch. It so happened that a short, straight right was the best weapon in Schmeling's arsenal. Most of his knockout wins had been gained via his powerful, deadly accurate right hand.

To ensure the success of his strategy, he knew there would be no gain without pain. Louis had a brilliant left jab that was almost impossible to avoid. In order to stay within range to fire his own missiles, Max would have to absorb countless jabs to the face, the weapon Louis employed to soften up opponents for the kill. He would have to rely on fitness, courage, resilience, and a determination to stick to the game plan. He believed he would finish the fight bloody and bruised—but victorious.

Seven weeks before the fight, Schmeling set up training camp at a Jewish country club in the Catskills, seventy miles upstate from New York. At the same time, John Roxborough and Julian Black installed Louis at Lakewood, New Jersey. Joe preferred Pompton Lakes, but he approved his managers' choice as it could accommodate more paying customers eager to see him working out. Besides, it had a beautiful golf course, and nothing pleased Louis more than spending his free time on the greens. Unless it was with women.

Joe celebrated his twenty-second birthday on May 13 with a party. One of his most welcome presents was a gold and silver medal delivered by Nat Fleischer in recognition of his selection as *The Ring*'s "Fighter of the Year." Among several famous boxers in attendance was world heavyweight champion Jimmy Braddock, who wondered why they hadn't yet met in the ring.

"Are you trying to duck me?" he asked Louis. "I'm the champion and you should be chasing me, but since you won't do that, I'm coming after you. Do we fight or do we fight?"

Louis laughed and said, "Sure I'll fight you, Jim. As soon as I smack down this Smellin', I'm your man." (Louis always pronounced the German's surname as Smellin', not in a derogatory sense, but that was simply how it came out in his Alabama drawl.)

In those days, long before political correctness became fashionable, many writers exaggerated his unsophisticated speech patterns to the extent that he came across as nothing more than a primitive moron. The *Washington Post*'s Mary Knight, after a visit to Lakewood, told of Louis's admission that he never swam: "Ah don't never fool wid no water. Ah's skairt o' water. Ain't nuthin' else in di' world Ah's got a fear of cep water. But Ah sho' is a-feared o' dat stuff."

Cartoonists enjoyed depicting Louis as an Uncle Remus stereotype, complete with outsize lips and a wide grin. In a *New York Evening Journal* cartoon, a reporter asks him to talk about defeat. The Louis character replies, "Sho'. I pops 'em on de chin and dey drags 'em out by de feet."

(Schmeling, who spoke good English, also gave the newspapers the chance to poke fun at his heavy German accent. His revelation that he had discovered a flaw in Louis's style appeared in print as "I zink I zee zomzinks.")

Behind the blatantly racist treatment of Louis by the press, however, there was a growing acceptance of his popularity with the general public. Most writers agreed that his modesty, good behavior, and sportsmanship in the ring had earned him the tolerance of the white population. People felt good that here was someone who had epitomized the realization of the American Dream by showing how a poor black boy could become rich through his natural talent and earnest endeavor.

Promoter Mike Jacobs, far from trying to hide Louis's graduation to affluence, took pride in revealing the exact percentages he received from gate receipts, radio and movie fees, and other contractual agreements. The ritual after every fight was that Louis would visit Jacobs's office and pose for cameramen accepting a five-figure check. For the period, his earnings were phenomenal. For beating Carnera he earned $60,000; for King Levinsky, $53,000; for knocking out Charlie Retzlaff in a single round, $23,000. Of course, Joe had to meet his own expenses and split his purse with his managers and trainer as well as pay income tax. But the press preferred to dwell on his gross purses. It made better reading. A popular game was working out how much Joe earned per minute. For demolishing Levinsky in the first round, for instance, they figured he made about $25,000 for every 60 seconds. The countless hours he spent training for the fights were conveniently ignored.

Jacobs and Louis's managers were at pains to emphasize that Joe was saving for his future, that as soon as he had enough stashed away, he would retire. By late 1935, Roxborough had predicted, Louis would have over $100,000 in life assurance annuities. It was good for his image, but the truth was that he spent money as fast as he earned it.

Louis was raking in the dollars because he was drawing big crowds. Though a fine technical boxer, he was most admired for his explosive hitting power. Fight fans love a puncher, and Joe was the most exciting heavyweight since Dempsey. On top of that, his exemplary behavior in and out of the ring had won him universal admiration. In short, he was sensational.

Before the Schmeling fight, Damon Runyon wrote:

It is our guess that more has been written about Louis in the past two years than about any living man over a similar period of time, with the exception of Charles Lindbergh. The Louis record in this respect is utterly astounding in view of the fact he isn't a champion.

Though the American press continued to dwell on Louis's popularity and his role as a flag-bearer for the black race, other symbolic implications of the Louis–Schmeling fight got little attention. Schmeling would usually be identified as a German or a Nazi, just as his opponent would be referred to as a Negro. Writers gave Max silly tags like the Terrific Teuton, the Nazi Nudger, and the Heil Hitler Hero but refrained from casting him as an out-and-out villain. Schmeling had fought in the United States and made friends there before most Americans had even heard of the Nazis. One reporter wrote: "Almost every sportswriter in this country likes Max, who is good-natured, gentlemanly, sportsmanlike, polite, thoughtful, and almost every good thing imaginable."

Schmeling's calm conviction of his ability to upset the American destroyer also impressed the scribes. Other Louis opponents like Levinsky and Baer had been petrified going into the ring. Schmeling, constantly probed for signs of apprehension, always answered questions as to whether he was afraid with a decisive "no."

"Why should I be afraid?" he asked. "This boxing is my business, my trade, my profession. I have been hit before and I did not like it, I admit. But I was not scared then and I will not be scared when Louis hits me."

The Nazis, who thought his almost inevitable defeat would reflect badly on the dogma of Aryan superiority, did not share Schmeling's confidence. The party's official *Reich Sport Journal* observed that there was "not much enthusiasm" for the fight and criticized those Germans who had organized a special trip to attend. Julius Streicher, the Nazi in charge of racial purity, had recently expelled a black wrestler from a Nuremberg tournament on the grounds that mixed-race encounters were contrary to official policy. Anyway, professional combat was not encouraged by the Third Reich, who saw sports more as a means of attaining peak physical fitness than a stepping stone in the pursuit of wealth and fame.

Asked by an American reporter if Hitler had wished him luck on his departure from Germany, Schmeling replied, "Why should he come down to the boat to see me off? He's a politician."

The sole Nazi correspondent sent to cover the fight, Arno Hellmis, told readers of *Völkischer Beobachter* that America was hoping for a Schmeling victory. He wrote:

The racial factor is placed strongly in the foreground, and it is hoped that the representative of the white race will succeed in halting the unusual rise of the Negro. In fact, there is no doubt that Max Schmeling, when he enters the ring on Thursday evening, will have the sympathy of all white spectators on his side, and the knowledge of this will be important moral support for him.

A month before the fight, an uproar broke out in the British House of Commons when Foreign Secretary Anthony Eden announced the end of sanctions against Fascist Italy as the best way to avoid a major European war. Angry cries of "Shame" and "Resign" greeted Prime Minister Stanley Baldwin's defense of the action. The principal power in Europe was Germany, not Italy, he argued, and it was time for Britain to reconcile itself with the new Germany.

Baldwin backed Hitler's claim that the Nazis had saved Germany from the threat of Communism. He went on:

It is no wonder, considering the desperate troubles Germany had gone through, that her people now worshipped ideals of force and violence. Yet Chancellor Hitler has told us he wishes for peace and if a man tells me that I wish to try it out . . . the part Germany can play for good or evil in Europe is immense, and if we believe the opportunity is presented, let us do what we can to use it for good.

On June 18, the appointed day of the fight, a heavy downpour drenched New York. Fearing its effects on the gate at open-air Yankee Stadium, the promoters postponed the event until the following day. The weigh-in, however, went ahead as planned.

Louis took the 9:10 A.M. train from Lakewood, laughing and joking most of the way with his fifteen companions and playing the blues on his harmonica for the crowds gathered at every station to wish him well. By the time they reached New York, he was asleep.

Schmeling, accompanied by Machon and cornerman Otto Petri, was driven from Napanoch by a New York policeman, Sergeant Jim Hopkins, who had to be careful, as the mountain roads were treacherous after the rain. Their car followed another containing Joe Jacobs, who had predicted a ninth-round knockout victory for his man.

The weigh-in was due to take place at noon at the New York Hippodrome. Louis arrived on time, to rapturous applause, but Schmeling was half an hour late. As the fighters met for the first time, they greeted each other with the utmost courtesy.

"Hello, Joe, how do you do?" Schmeling inquired.

"Fine, Max," Louis replied. "And you?"

"Very good, Joe. Thank you."

After both men weighed in and shook hands for the cameramen, Schmeling, at 192 the lighter man by five pounds, said, "Good luck this evening, Joe."

The announcement of the twenty-four-hour postponement didn't unduly concern either fighter. Both decided to stay in New York rather than go back to their training camps.

As Louis left for the Hotel Theresa in Harlem, he said to Jack Blackburn, "That German sure was a pretty cool bird."

"Chappie," the trainer observed, "it looks like you got a fight on your hands this time."

Schmeling settled in at the Plaza, where, from his high window, he could gaze at New York's skyscrapered skyline. He tried to get some sleep but was disturbed from time to time by Machon looking into his room to repeat what he had already said a thousand times: "Leave your calling card right after the first bell. The kid has to know who he's dealing with."

At 7:45 P.M. on June 19, Joe Jacobs told Schmeling a car was waiting to take them to the arena. As he was leaving the hotel, the desk clerk called, "Good luck, Max." The route to the stadium was badly congested, but a motorcycle escort with blaring sirens cleared the way for the group.

Sitting in his dressing room awaiting the call to the ring, Schmeling was visited by Tom O'Rourke, a former promoter and one of America's most respected boxing experts. The eighty-three-year-old, sitting on the rubdown table next to the fighter, said, "I know you can win, Max, but you've got to be careful and use your head." Suddenly, without warning, O'Rourke slipped soundlessly to the floor. Machon and Petri tried to convince Schmeling that the visitor had just fainted, but Max knew he was dead. Some unscrupulous American writers would seize upon the incident to demonstrate what a cold, heartless man was Schmeling. He watched a man die without showing a flicker of emotion, they said.

The threatening weather, together with an attempted boycott of the fight organized by Jewish store owners, meant a disappointing turn-out of 45,000 paying customers. That was nearly half as many as had attended the Louis–Baer fight at the same venue the previous September.

Schmeling, the underdog in the betting by 8–1, was first to enter the ring. Just after Louis stepped between the ropes, the contestants glanced briefly at each other. Louis's face, noted Max, was "as expressionless as a mask." Referee Arthur Donovan called them to the center of the ring for their last-minute instructions and bade them, in the time-honored manner, "Now go back to your corners and come out fighting."

The fight began quietly, each man watching warily for the other's first move. Schmeling, remembering Machon's advice to "give him your calling card quickly," kept his right hand at his chest, cocked and ready for the first opportunity. It was Louis, however, who landed the first telling blow, a hard left hook to the head. "I realized the power behind the punches that had finished so many world-class boxers," Max observed later.

Only once in the opening three minutes did Schmeling connect with his pet punch. The short right to the face surprised Louis, but the American was soon back on the offensive and clearly won the round. "Well, you're still alive," joked Machon as Max sat on his stool. "Yes, but Louis can punch," replied Schmeling.

Although Louis took a stinging right that made him blink in the second round, he had surged into a good points lead by the end of the third as his solid jab regularly found its target. Already there was puffiness around the German's left eye and anxiety in his corner. "Come on, Maxie, what's happening?" yelled Joe Jacobs. Machon glared at the agitated manager before advising Schmeling, "You caught him with a good one early on. He really felt it. Keep patient—you'll get your chance to unload that right again."

That opportunity came in the fourth round. After attempting two rights that grazed his opponent's jaw, Schmeling found the range for the punch he had honed and perfected over his previous fifty-nine fights. His powerful right swept past Louis's drooping left arm and exploded against the side of his head. The Brown Bomber, cool and collected seconds earlier, staggered backward, his eyes blinking, his mind foggy, and his legs unsteady.

Immediately, Schmeling followed up his advantage, smashing further blows to the head until a powerful right landed cleanly on Louis's jaw and sent him tumbling to the canvas for the first time in his professional career. With the crowd in an uproar, and Louis's mother, who had never before attended one of her son's fights, deeply regretting her change of heart, Joe climbed to his feet at the count of two. He would have been better off taking a longer count to give his head time to clear, but instinct, or pride, drove him back into action quickly. Somehow, Louis managed to stay upright for the rest of the round in the face of heavy fire from the German, who continued, in his anxiety, to punch after the bell.

"Okay, Chappie," said Blackburn as he sponged down Louis's face and massaged the back of his neck, "listen to me. You're still in there, but you gotta keep your guard up. You took that right hand 'cause you were wide open after your left hook." Before pushing Joe out for round five, he repeated, "Whatever you do, Chappie, keep that guard up."

"That fourth round was the beginning of the end for the 'Super-Man,' " Nat Fleischer reported in *The Ring*.

> The idol who had replaced Jack Dempsey as the magnet, slowly but surely from that fourth round, was nearing the end of his reign. He seemed not only to be wobbly, but in a daze. He acted in the next three rounds just as he did when he was severely criticized by the scribes during the first fortnight of his training. It was a lackadaisical Joe Louis who was tossing punches at his foe. He was in a complete fog. The power behind those punches of his that had floored Baer, Levinsky, Carnera, Retzlaff, and Paolino seemed gone. They were tame blows compared to the dynamite right hands that were landing flush on his chin with regularity, round after round.

Schmeling, sensing that victory was within his grasp, continued to pour in right-handers at every opportunity, constantly jarring the American right down to his heels. Louis's jabs were still landing, but their sting had gone and Max simply ignored them. Two terrific rights near the end of the fifth round hurt Louis badly and brought the crowd to its feet. The excited roars echoed all across the ballpark. So great was the earsplitting din that neither fighter heard the bell, nor did referee Donovan. The punches continued to fly as frantic cornermen clambered into the ring. Just before the boxers were separated, Schmeling staggered his rival with a powerful right to the jaw. Louis lurched toward his corner and fell onto his stool, almost in a state of collapse.

Five times during the sixth round, Schmeling's deadly right thudded against his opponent's head with sickening force. Yet he remained cautious, watching for his openings and at times backing to the ropes in a bid to draw Louis's fire, so he would have the opportunity to counter with a finishing blow. This hesitancy almost cost Max dearly in the seventh, when Louis opened up with a barrage of lefts and rights that clearly shook him. But the German resumed the offensive in the next round, staggering Louis with successive rights. The referee warned Louis for a low blow.

The left side of Louis's face was swollen as he started the ninth, while Schmeling's left eye was almost closed. Yet the German was the fresher of the two and more accurate with his punches. Another series of rights to the head hurt the Brown Bomber, and he looked shaken as he returned to his corner.

The weary American was late getting off his stool for the tenth round. His pain and dejection were apparent to all. Schmeling was all over him, mercilessly pounding him with his precise, powerful blows. Louis hit out erratically, and a left hook landed below the belt. It didn't seem to bother the recipient, who sent Louis staggering into the ropes with another barrage of punches. Max piled on more punishment throughout the eleventh, and it was clear that Louis would not survive the distance.

The end came after two minutes and twenty-nine seconds of round twelve. After being hurt by a low blow, for which the referee again warned Louis, Schmeling shook his foe with a heavy right and followed up with a similar punch that sent Louis stumbling against the ropes. As the crowd roared, sensing the finish, Max punched and punched with his right hand to Louis's head, face, and jaw.

The final blow, a tremendous right that slammed into the left side of the American's battered, swollen face, sank him to his knees against the ropes, his limp arms hanging over the middle strand for support. He then fell onto his back and rolled over as if trying to get up. "When the referee counted," he recalled later, "it came to me faint, like somebody whispering." At five, his shoulders were off the floor, but he was still stretched out, face down, as Donovan spread his arms to indicate he had completed the count. A delighted Schmeling leaped into the air, arms above his head, before racing across the ring to help his victim's seconds drag his limp form to the corner.

Suddenly the ring was filled with people, most of them eager to slap the winner on the back and offer congratulations. Joe Jacobs, his suspender buttons flying off as he jumped into the ring, cut a comic figure as he manfully tried to hold up his pants while yelling at reporters, "What did I tell you? Didn't I keep saying that we'd beat him? What do you say now? We beat him."

Across the ring, few took notice as the crestfallen loser, his head covered in a towel, was led down the steps. The *New York Herald Tribune* reported the following day:

> The Brown Bomber staggered to his dressing room. They laid him carefully on the rubdown table, massaged him, gave him smelling salts and, after fifteen minutes, got him into the shower. But he was still groggy. His eyes were closed and he groaned on trying to make a fist. Dr. Walker and Dr. Nardiello examined him and found that he had sprained both thumbs. Louis, still in a trance, mumbled a few words, "I just couldn't get at him. There was no way. Schmeling danced in front of me and then he was gone. Oh God, my face!"

Hearing a reporter ask John Roxborough about low blows, Joe sat up. "Did I hit him low?" he asked. "Yes, twice," his manager replied, after hesitation. "Roxy, you go tell him I'm sorry," Louis said. He was plainly upset at the implication that he had tried to foul his way out of trouble. "I don't want to foul nobody. Tell him I didn't know what I was doing."

It was Julian Black who elbowed his way through the crowd packing the winner's dressing room. He shook Schmeling warmly by the hand and said, "You were great, Max." When a reporter brought up the question of low blows, Schmeling said, "Oh, you can't blame the guy for those. He didn't know what he was doing. Anyone could see that." Later, in an article published in the *Saturday Evening Post*, he accused Louis of deliberately fouling him.

The car ride from Yankee Stadium took the German party from the Bronx, through Harlem, to Manhattan. In Harlem, they saw many signs of the hysteria and despair over the result of the fight. Cars heading downtown were spat upon and hit with boards. Schmeling's car picked up speed and took shortcuts to the Plaza. The next morning, the newspapers reported that hundreds had been hurt in rioting. Outside Yankee Stadium, buses were stoned, windows were broken, and a man was shot. The *New York Times* told of thirty blacks kicking a fifty-year-old white man unconscious.

Outside his hotel, reporters besieged Schmeling, asking what he meant when he said before the fight that he had "seen something." He explained that he noticed how Louis dropped his left hand after jabbing. Surely Blackburn should have been aware of that, said one questioner, especially when he was facing a renowned counter-puncher?

"Films of later fights showed me that Louis never quite broke that one bad habit," Schmeling wrote in his autobiography. "But the fact that he remained heavyweight champion longer than anyone else proved his incomparable skills."

9

GERMANY REJOICES

Just a short time ago, they hadn't wanted to know him. Now, suddenly, Schmeling was the Nazi party's darling. "Congratulations," cabled Goebbels immediately after hearing the result. "I know you won it for Germany. We are proud of you. Heil Hitler." The Führer followed with his own message: "Most cordial felicitations on your splendid victory." To Max's wife, Hitler sent flowers.

A week after the fight, Schmeling was invited to fly home on the *Hindenburg* zeppelin. An officer gave up his berth so the hero could travel in style. After sixty-one hours in the air, the craft landed at Frankfurt Airport to tumultuous cheers from the waiting crowd for the VIP passenger. From there, he journeyed on to Berlin, where Hitler invited him, along with his wife, mother, and several friends, to lunch at the Reich Chancellery.

The Führer's short, but overly formal, speech of congratulations embarrassed Schmeling, but he soon relaxed as Hitler invited his special guests to sit around a large table. Although well informed from what he had read of the fight in the papers, Hitler wanted firsthand details. Did Max know, for instance, that even before the fourth round he would "beat the Negro?"

Schmeling had brought along some American press clippings, which Hitler and Goebbels read with obvious relish. During the conversation, Hitler said it was a shame he couldn't have seen the fight. Max told him he had brought back a film of the contest. It was being held at airport customs. (Mike Jacobs had given Schmeling full rights to overseas distribution of the films for a modest fee, because he didn't think the bout would last long enough to make them profitable.) Hitler sent an aide to pick up the canisters, and they watched the unedited reels later in the day. Schmeling was amused at Hitler's running commentary and the way he slapped his thigh in delight every time Max landed a hard punch.

"Schmeling," he said at one point, "have you read what I wrote in *Mein Kampf* about the educational value of boxing? Boxing is a manly sport. That's why I tell everyone, Schirach [head of the Hitler Youth] and von Tschammer [Reich minister of sports], that boxing should be introduced into the public school curriculum."

Hitler ordered that the film, instead of being shown as a newsreel in movie theaters, should be made into a full-length documentary by adding footage of Schmeling and Louis in training and of Max's homecoming welcome. Released under the title *Max Schmeling's Victory: A German Victory*, it played to full houses throughout Germany for several weeks.

American papers took up the story of Schmeling's meeting with Hitler. In the minds of some writers, this identified him as a Nazi supporter. Westbrook Pegler of the Scripps-Howard newspaper group was scathing about the Third Reich's overnight conversion to the boxer's cause:

> At no time during the months when Schmeling was preparing to fight Louis did the Nazi government accept any responsibility in the matter. Schmeling did not then enjoy the status of official patriot and representative of Nazi manhood. He was absolutely on his own, because there seemed an excellent chance that having already been knocked out by a Jew [Max Baer] he would now be stretched in the resin at the feet of a cotton-field Negro . . . But before the night was over Schmeling had become a great German patriot, and his unexpected conquest of the colored boy had been taken over as a triumph for Adolf Hitler and his government.

The American press, so completely off the mark in its predictions of an easy win for Louis, searched frantically for excuses. Joe wasn't fully fit, he was overconfident, took his experienced opponent too lightly, and had been softened by easy living. What they all agreed on was that the myth of the indestructible Brown Bomber had been shot down in flames. A typical headline ran: SCHMELING VICTORY PROVES TO RING WORLD EVERY MAN IS HUMAN AND CAN BE LICKED.

Much of the soul-searching resulted in the widespread conviction that Louis's ability had been blown up out of all proportions. The *New York Sun*'s Grantland Rice wrote, "The Louis defense against Schmeling's right was not even up to the average amateur standard. The near superman of many fights suddenly turned into a duffer with nothing to offer but fighting instinct and a stout heart."

Southern newspapers took delight in kicking the man while he was down. O. B. Keeler, in the *Atlanta Journal*, sneered, "You can have the Brown Bomber." Louis, "the Pet Pickaninny," was "just another good boxer who had been built up." Ben Wahrman, a correspondent for the *Richmond Times-Dispatch*, suggested changing his nickname to "the Brown Bummer."

Nat Fleischer presented a more compassionate and reasoned view. While praising Schmeling for his triumph against the odds, *The Ring* editor refused to write off Louis as a has-been. "Louis was a great fighter before the fight and he'll be great again. Make no mistake about that."

Among the fighters whose ghosted words appeared in print, Jim Braddock, in a feature for *The Ring*, expressed his conviction that Louis's bubble had burst and his superman myth exploded. Though he had picked Joe to win, the reigning world heavyweight titleholder said he had seen how fit and confident the German was and had expressed the view that he could do some damage with his powerful right. Braddock admitted he had resented all the publicity garnered by Louis. "It was mighty discouraging to think that I was the world champion, yet Louis got the bulk of the headlines in boxing."

In the same magazine, Jack Dempsey, who had predicted a Louis win inside five rounds, suggested that it would be very difficult for the beaten man to regain his former status. New opponents wouldn't have the same fear of him as they had before, and good right-hand punchers especially would like their chances of emulating Schmeling's feat.

In the final analysis of what went wrong for Louis, there was practically unanimous agreement that he had gone into the fight unprepared, physically and mentally. The training camp at Lakewood had had more of a carnival atmosphere. All sorts of people, including top entertainers, dropped in at random. Joe, flattered by the attention, spent too much time in their company when he should have been concentrating on the job at hand. Other times he could be found lying around in the hot sun or enjoying his new hobby, golf.

Jack Blackburn continually stressed that golf wasn't compatible with boxing, because different muscles were brought into play, and a golf swing was a lot different from a boxing swing. Blackburn had been a fighter forty years before Louis was born, so he knew what he was talking about. But his advice fell on deaf ears.

Joe said years later:

> Good God, I really was in love with the game. When I entered training camp, I had the idea that I was going to do a lot of hard work for nothing. I thought I could name the round that I would knock Schmeling out. Instead of training as I should have, I'd cut my training short and jump in the car and head for the golf course . . . Instead of boxing six rounds, I'd box three. Punch the bag one round instead of two.

There was another major distraction—women.

Female admirers were swarming around like flies, Louis recalled. "I remember one time Chappie actually took a stick and threatened them. I found them anyway."

While John Roxborough had previously banned women from the training camps, he could no longer deny Joe his say in how everyday things were run. The fact was that Louis, who had entered boxing as a teenager largely influenced by his family, his religion, and the poverty of his upbringing, then guided by his managers into becoming a model athlete, had grown up. By the time of the Schmeling fight, he had become a confident young man swayed by fame and fortune. He had his own opinions and wasn't afraid to express them, even in the face of well-meaning advice offered by friends and family. This compulsion to reject sound advice when it didn't fit with his personal preferences was a character flaw that would haunt him for the rest of his life.

Roxborough thought he had found a way of keeping the swarm of lusty female admirers at bay while making sure that Joe wasn't feeling too deprived, by inviting Marva to visit her husband every day. It wasn't such a great idea.

Louis related in his memoirs:

> This was the first and only time Marva was this close to me at camp time. I mean, we were real young then—Marva was twenty years old on May 7 and I was twenty-two on May 13. She stayed at the Stanley Hotel, about two blocks from the stucco house called the Alpert Mansion where I was staying. What can I say? I was young, she was younger, and we'd just been married must be nine months.

Regular sex before a fight has always been regarded as a taboo. Not only does it dissipate vital energy, goes the perceived wisdom, it tends to induce an overrelaxed state. Fighters need to be mean, aggressive, hating everyone around them, so that when they get into the ring they're eager to take out their frustration on the guy opposite them. (Not that regular romps by such clouting Casanovas as Harry Greb, Jack Johnson, and Muhammad Ali seemed to do them much harm!)

Marva was eventually persuaded, in her husband's best interests, to stay away, but that only gave him the freedom to accommodate the rest of the hungry pack. If Roxborough and Blackburn banned girls from the camp, Joe would go out and find them. "I'd even sneak off to Atlantic City when I got the chance to see some girl whose name I don't even remember," he said years later.

Describing his routine for the Schmeling fight, he admitted the difficulty of keeping his weight steady:

> I was on the road at seven in the morning for six miles. I always ran off four pounds. Then I'd drink fruit juices, eat prunes and toast, and go to bed for about three hours of sleep. Usually during this nap I'd get back the weight I lost. But this time it didn't work—those camp-following girls took too much out of me. When I came to the camp, I weighed 216 pounds, and then I went down to 204 two days before the fight.

When he wasn't bedding girls, Louis was most often to be found on the golf course. His handlers thought a deep-sea fishing trip might be a welcome diversion, and hired a boat. Joe approved at first but changed his mind when he got down to the dock. He preferred to play a few rounds of golf. No amount of warnings from Roxborough, Black, and Blackburn could persuade him to take his training more seriously.

When the fight was over, and the big-time loser had time to reflect on his foolishness, everyone agreed on the one stark fact: Schmeling was in top shape, physically and mentally; Louis wasn't.

To his credit, Louis made no real excuses for his poor display beyond acknowledging his overconfidence and lack of proper preparation. To the scandalmongers suggesting he had been drugged, he replied, "Sure I was doped, by his right-hand punches."

Others claimed that a punch from Schmeling that landed after the bell at the end of the fifth round, when Louis's guard was down, had done irretrievable damage. Joe commented laconically, "We were both fighting at the bell. I heard it and dropped my hands. He didn't, I guess. Anyway, he'd caught me before in the second and fourth rounds."

To add to Louis's misery, he learned that his stepfather, Pat Brooks, had suffered a paralyzing stroke two days before the fight. The news had been kept from him because everyone knew it would upset him. When he visited his former home, along with Marva, he was shocked to see how feeble the old man was. Brooks was the only father he had known, and when he died, Joe wept for quite a while. Though he felt sorry that Brooks had never seen him fight as a professional, he was glad no one told his stepfather the result of the Schmeling bout.

To put his mind at rest, Joe soon decided to get back to the training camp at Pompton Lakes. He felt his body was getting better and his confidence had returned. Bring on the next fight! He hoped, above all, that would be a return with Schmeling. Every time he boxed with a sparring partner, he imagined he was in the ring with the German. "I wanted that rematch so bad I could taste it," he said. "I had been humiliated, and I had to prove to everybody that I was the best heavyweight around."

While Louis prepared for his redemption fight, the eyes of sports fans around the world turned to Berlin, venue for the 1936 Olympic Games. The Nazis were proudly proclaiming it the biggest Olympics in history.

An enormous stadium accommodating 110,000 spectators and an indoor pool seating another 18,000 had been specially built. Nearly three and a half million tickets were sold for competition between 3,936 athletes.

The occasion was also a golden opportunity to show the skeptics how progressive and tolerant Germany really was under the Third Reich. Signs proclaiming *Juden unerwünscht* (Jews not welcome) were quietly removed from stores, hotels, beer gardens, and places of entertainment. The persecution of Jews and other minorities was temporarily halted while the country was put on its best behavior.

In his memoirs, Schmeling noted that the anti-Semitic hate sheet *Der Stürmer* disappeared from the newsstands, while foreign newspapers and books by Hermann Hesse and Thomas Mann, ordinarily banned by the Nazis, were suddenly available again.

"No previous games had seen such a spectacular organization nor such a lavish display of entertainment," wrote William L. Shirer in *The Rise and Fall of the Third Reich.*

> Goering, Ribbentrop, and Goebbels gave dazzling displays for the foreign visitors—the propaganda minister's "Italian Night" on the Pfaueninsel near Wannsee gathered more than a thousand guests at dinner in a scene that resembled the Arabian Nights. The visitors, especially those from England and America, were greatly impressed by what they saw: apparently a happy, healthy, friendly people united under Hitler—a far different picture, they said, than they had got from reading the newspaper dispatches from Berlin.

Avery Brundage, the American Olympics Committee president, was quick to grasp Hitler's extended hand of friendship. He told his hosts at a welcoming ceremony for the U.S. athletes, "No nation since ancient Greece has captured the true Olympic spirit as has Germany." Brundage had been at the forefront in opposing a proposed boycott of the Games, spearheaded by Jewish, Christian, and secular athletic organizations. In a shameful act of appeasement toward Hitler, he removed two Jewish members of the U.S. track-and-field relay team, Marty Glickman and Sam Stoller, from the competition.

At the opening ceremony, Hitler released 20,000 carrier pigeons from the Sportpalast, while the 800-foot *Hindenburg* circled over the stadium towing a huge Olympic flag. In the midst of the pomp and ceremony, athletes from forty-nine nations paraded before the crowds. A series of runners had carried the Olympic torch, lit in Greece, to Berlin.

The enormous German investment in athletic training for the Games was justified by their winning thirty-three gold medals, far more than any other nation. Nazi pride was shaken, however, by the outstanding performances of black American competitors, who carried away fourteen medals. The star of the show was undoubtedly Jesse Owens, the first American in the history of track and field to take four gold medals at a single Olympics.

Infuriated by the success of what the German press labeled the "black auxiliary tribes" of America, Hitler left the stadium each day before they stepped up to the rostrum to receive their prizes. His excuse was that he was forbidden by agreed Olympic protocol to meet the winners.

What had happened was that on the first day, when two German athletes won their nation's first-ever gold medals in track and field, Hitler invited both victors to his box and congratulated them enthusiastically. He treated the three Finnish winners of the 10,000 meters similarly. Later in the day, two black Americans, Cornelius Johnson and Dave Albritton, won gold and silver in the high jump. Five minutes before they stepped up to the medals rostrum, Hitler and his contingent departed quickly. The Americans refused to see it as anything other than a deliberate snub.

That night, the IOC president sent word to Hitler that, as guest of honor, the Führer must shake the hand of every winner or none at all. Hitler chose the latter course.

Word circulated that Hitler arranged to meet all the German medalists privately to offer his congratulations. A former Nazi Youth leader, Baldur von Schirach, raged, "These Americans should be ashamed of themselves for letting their medals be won by a *Neger*. I would never shake the hand of one."

While the American press kept the controversy on the boil, Owens told reporters that he didn't think Hitler had snubbed him. After one of his wins, he said, he passed the Nazi stand as he made his way to the radio booth for an interview. Hitler saw him, waved his hand, and Owens waved back. On another occasion when the subject was raised, Owens caustically commented, "I wasn't invited to shake hands with Hitler, but I wasn't invited to the White House to shake hands with the President either."

Perhaps some saw him as naive in his interpretation of Hitler's actions, but Owens was more likely using the opportunity to highlight the racial discrimination in his own country. An Olympic hero he might have been, but just after his return home from Berlin, he found himself barred from taking a seat at the front of a bus. Within days of the end of the Games, Owens's athletic career began to disintegrate. He was suspended for refusing to join a money-making European tour organized by the American Athletic Union. After he decided to cash in on his fame and take advantage of some the flood of offers he received, the AAU banned him for life. Denounced as a "professional," he would never again thrill the crowds with record-breaking feats.

Though Owens found work in various jobs ranging from public speaker to custodian, at other times he was reduced to racing against greyhounds, horses, and trains to earn a buck. On July 4, 1938, he took part in the most bizarre contest of all—a race against his friend Joe Louis. Billed as "the Fastest Man in the World v. the Heavyweight Champion of the World," it drew 7,000 spectators to a Chicago ballpark.

The concept, of course, was ridiculous. Louis, not even a fast mover in the ring, would hardly raise a puff of dust before Owens crossed the finishing line. Just as in a boxing match, Jesse wouldn't survive Joe's first punch. So who won the race? Louis, of course!

Owens, fooling nobody, tripped and fell to let Louis get to the line first. As the crowd cheered, the contestants smiled at each other and embraced. "You ran real well, champ," Jesse said.

"Yeah," Joe replied.

10

RETURN ROUTE

Louis could have spent months moping about, playing golf, and doing a bit of fishing while brooding over his defeat. Instead, like a person who gets quickly back behind the wheel to recover from a car crash, he opted to return to the ring as soon as it could be arranged. On August 18, sixty days after the Schmeling fight, he returned to the scene of the execution, Yankee Stadium, to face Jack Sharkey.

The Boston Gob was a good choice of opponent. Sharkey was a former world heavyweight champion and still a rated contender. Victory over such a big-name opponent would do much to repair Louis's image with the public. In truth, Joe had little to beat. Sharkey was way past his prime and had slowed down considerably. Best remembered for his two controversial title bouts with Schmeling, he appeared to have lost his way following his knockout defeat by Carnera. In the ensuing three years, he had won only two of his six contests.

Still, the last thing a fighter loses is his punch, they say, and Sharkey packed plenty of power in his right hand. He was encouraged, naturally, by Schmeling's success with his right counters. Speaking to reporters on the eve of the fight, he predicted he would win easily. Louis, he claimed, "can't fight a lick and built his reputation knocking over a bunch of has-been stiffs."

Joe was cagey when asked how he thought it would go. "I ain't predicting," he said. "I'm going to do my best, and I hope to win."

Jack Blackburn had no doubts that Louis would be back to his devastating best. Sticking to the forecast he made the first day the fight was signed, he said, "Joe will knock out Sharkey inside three rounds."

The wise old trainer was spot-on. After one minute and two seconds of round three, referee Arthur Donovan completed the count over an outclassed Sharkey. The ex-champ had failed to land a significant blow and had been floored four times. At the age of thirty-three, he wisely hung up his gloves for good.

Talented but temperamental, Sharkey had often been criticized during his career for losing fights he should have won. Like so many unpredictable performers, he discovered he was best liked when he was down. Years after his retirement, he said, "I wasn't very popular anywhere. You know, the first time anybody went for me was the night I fought Joe Louis. I got belted to the canvas in the first round, and the referee, standing over me, said in a low voice, 'Try to get up, Jack. Everyone's with you tonight.' There I was on all fours. My head was full of bees. I felt as if I had an awful toothache. But I heard the referee and I had to laugh. I said to myself, 'So everybody's for me, eh?' Well, that's the way they've always been. They love me when I'm getting my brains knocked out."

Ring historians who enjoy rating the greatest heavyweights of all time usually have Louis and Jack Dempsey near the top. The question they nearly always come up with is: who would have won had these two clashed when both were at the top of their game? The man considered the best judge of that was Sharkey. He was the only one to have fought both Louis and Dempsey. He was beating Dempsey in their 1927 bout when he turned to complain to the referee after taking a painful low blow in the seventh round. Dempsey, never one to miss an opportunity, socked him on the jaw and knocked him cold.

"I fought Louis when he was on the way up and Dempsey when he was on the way down," Sharkey said in 1954. "At their primes, I think Dempsey would have won. But, of course, just one of those TNT rights from Louis could have changed the whole picture."

After his KO of Sharkey, Louis was visited in his dressing room by legendary dancer Bill "Bojangles" Robinson, who, as he beat out a rhythm on his Panama hat with his fingers, said jubilantly, "You done it, boy." Louis rubbed his neck reflectively and said, "Yeah, but I still got a long way to go."

He couldn't get Schmeling out of his mind. Beating Sharkey and other top contenders, even taking the world title from Jim Braddock, would count for nothing if he couldn't get the chance to avenge his sole defeat. He feared, as did many Americans, that Schmeling, if he beat Braddock, would take the title back to Germany and keep it there.

A window of opportunity opened when Braddock pulled out of his scheduled title defense against Schmeling. Backed by reports from several doctors, he told the New York State Athletic Commission that he was suffering from arthritis in both elbows and his left hand. There was no way he could meet Schmeling in that condition, he insisted. The commissioners accepted his plea and postponed the fight until the following year. Louis had offered to take Braddock's place, even putting up $300,000 as an extra inducement. Schmeling refused flatly, saying he wanted a world title bout and nothing else.

While Max stayed idle for eighteen months, fuming over Braddock's repeated excuses for not fulfilling the terms of their contract, Louis kept busy. He flattened Al Ettore with a terrific left hook in the fifth round. Any doubts about his ability to take a hard shot were answered when Jorge Brescia, a bulky Argentine, landed a solid right to his chin in the third round. Joe responded by meeting Brescia in a toe-to-toe exchange, then dispatching him with a left hook to the jaw.

He rounded out the year in a mismatch against Eddie Simms in Cleveland. The bout was to benefit a Christmas fund for the city's poor. Joe showed no charity toward his hapless opponent, taking just twenty-six seconds to send him to Cloud Cuckooland. Simms, his eyes glazed, used the ropes to drag himself aloft after a heavy knockdown. Turning to the referee, Arthur Donovan, he mumbled, "Come on, let's take a walk on the roof." Donovan immediately stopped the fight and led the bemused loser back to the safety of his corner.

American support for Schmeling was dwindling as stories, pumped out by the Nazi propaganda machine, had him referring to Louis as "an amateur" and implying that he was stupid, a trait derived from the circumstance of his race. German athletes taking part in the recent Olympics had told Max they were inspired by his victory over Louis. Schmeling was quoted as saying that the ultimate reason for the country's success in sports was Hitler's inspiration. It was even rumored that the world championship belt he would get if he regained the title would be handed over to Goebbels to be hung on the wall of his trophy room. Louis, when told of the reports, vowed he would make the Black Uhlan pay for his arrogance and insults.

Later, Schmeling denied making the remarks attributed to him. His anxiety to distance himself from the Nazi's propaganda output was as much to protect his career interests as a kick at those who used his name for political gain. It was essential to stay as friendly as possible with the Americans if he was to regain the big prize, the world heavy-weight title. Go too far with his denigration of Louis, as put out by Goebbels's ministry, and he would be frozen out of the picture.

An example of how the Nazis tried to secure Schmeling's loyalty was their decision to make him an honorary commander of the SA. Shortly after the Olympics, a high-ranking SA officer called at his home to tell him of his appointment and present him with the Dagger of Honor. Schmeling, caught off guard, asked for twenty-four hours to think about it. He called an old friend, Heinrich Hoffman, Hitler's personal photographer, in Berlin. At first, Hoffman couldn't understand the problem. Racing drivers Rudolf Caracciola, Manfred von Brauchitsch, and Bernd Rosemeyer all wore the pin of the Dagger of Honor with pride, as did many other German sports stars. It was only when Schmeling explained that being an SA commander would create problems for him in America that Hoffman saw his point of view. When the SA officer returned the next day and learned of Schmeling's refusal, he took the case holding the Dagger of Honor under his arm, made his way to the door, gave the Nazi salute, and uttered his only words "Heil Hitler."

While realizing his decision would cast further doubts on his patriotism, Schmeling had to be careful not to put himself completely out in the cold. There were times when his status allowing him access to the Nazi regime came in handy. Such an occasion was when his sculptor friend Josef Thorak got into trouble for violating the race laws. The situation was complicated. Thorak had married into a Jewish family, but the couple, fearing a forthcoming ban on mixed marriages, had decided the best course was to divorce while continuing to live together. The Nuremberg Laws of 1935 then created a new situation. Couples like the Thoraks were deemed to be committing the punishable crime of *Rassenschande* (race mixing) between unmarried persons. Josef moved out of the house, while the Gestapo, who had been tipped off by an informer, kept guard to make sure he didn't sneak home at night.

Frau Thorak, fearing she would be ordered to leave, along with her three school-age children, turned to Schmeling for help. He promised to do what he could. After driving to Berlin, he was received by Goebbels at his ministry near the Brandenburg Gate.

"What's wrong, Herr Schmeling?" the propaganda minister wanted to know. Told of the situation and how exemplary a mother was Frau Thorak, Goebbels said, "But she is a Jew, isn't she?" Schmeling explained that she had never tried to influence her children against the regime and had even encouraged them to listen to Hitler's speeches on the radio. "But she's still a Jew," Goebbels insisted.

Eventually yielding to his visitor's persistence, the minister asked, "What do you want me to do, Herr Schmeling?" Shocked at the suggestion that he meet Frau Thorak personally, Goebbels conceded to let his assistant hear her case. The outcome was that Frau Thorak could stay in her home, on the understanding that she would have no contact with her former husband. In an unexpected sequel, Josef Thorak later became an official sculptor to the Third Reich and was chosen by Albert Speer to design the statues that graced the Nazi Party parade grounds at Nuremberg.

In the summer of 1937, Schmeling accepted an invitation to attend a European title fight in Rotterdam and used the opportunity to visit some old Jewish friends, exiles from Germany. On his return to Berlin, he learned that news of his visit had gotten out and that the Propaganda Ministry wasn't at all pleased. Schmeling angrily defended himself against the criticism. He explained that he always conducted himself abroad as would any good German, and he wouldn't be told how he should treat old friends.

Some time later, he ran into Goebbels by chance. "What are you thinking, Herr Schmeling?" the minister barked. "You just go ahead and do whatever you please. You don't concern yourself with laws. You come to the Führer, you come to me, and still you continue to socialize with Jews."

While Schmeling awaited definitive news of his delayed title challenge, Louis kept fighting—and winning. Steve Ketchell was dumped inside two rounds. Natie Brown, who had taken Joe the distance two years earlier, was knocked out in the fourth of their return. It was a record Louis maintained throughout his career—he always beat an opponent more easily the second time they met.

Bob Pastor found a way to survive, if not win, by backpedaling furiously for the entire ten rounds. Ironically, Pastor was considered a poor football player at New York University because he was slow, but he was quite a nifty mover in the ring. He made Louis look cumbersome and lacking in the savvy to solve a clever, fast-moving style. Pastor still complained, in an interview forty-five years later, that he should have gotten the decision. Referee Arthur Donovan, an unashamed Louis admirer, scored it eight rounds to two in Joe's favor. The two judges weren't as generous, but they made Louis a clear winner. The crowd showed its sympathy for the underdog, who finished the fight unmarked, and booed the winner for his pedestrian performance.

"He just won a race," Louis told reporters. "I couldn't hit him because he wouldn't stay put. Jack [Blackburn] told me to pin Pastor in a corner, but I couldn't do it. Nobody got hurt but the people who paid money."

Promoter Mike Jacobs shocked the boxing world, and left Schmeling fuming, by announcing that he had reached agreement with Louis and Braddock to meet for the world heavyweight title in Chicago on June 22, 1937.

Joe Gould, Braddock's manager, said he was withdrawing from his agreement with Madison Square Garden for the Braddock–Schmeling fight because of public opposition. For several months the Non-Sectarian Anti-Nazi League had pressured the New York State Athletic Commission to ban the bout or risk a boycott. The league had enough clout in political and press circles to have a significant influence on public opinion. Some of the most prominent men in the country were members. New York lawyer Samuel Untermeyer, who had campaigned for the United States to drop out of the previous year's Olympics, was president. Mayor Fiorello LaGuardia of New York and James W. Gerard, ambassador to Germany before the First World War, were vice presidents. J. David Stern, publisher of the *Philadelphia Record*, was treasurer. The league's stated aim was to "ruin this fight from a financial point of view."

The growing protest campaign included the American Federation of Labor and various Catholic and Protestant groups. The Jewish War Veterans of the United States, boasting 250,000 members, denounced the fight.

Gould claimed that he had conducted a poll of leading sportswriters to plumb the depth of anti-Nazi feelings. The writers had agreed a boycott would hurt attendance figures. It was clear that a fight between Braddock and Schmeling was too risky. The findings suited Gould's campaign to have Louis as Braddock's challenger rather than Schmeling. Louis was a bigger box-office draw, and everyone would make more money.

Before the contracts could be signed, however, there was still some hard negotiating to be done. Gould knew that Braddock, approaching thirty-two, was too slow and too stale (he hadn't fought since taking the title from Max Baer two years earlier) to last many rounds with the young, destructive Brown Bomber. Therefore, the champion would have to be well compensated for handing the title over on a platter.

"All we want is fifty percent of Louis," Gould informed an incredulous John Roxborough. "We'll let you keep half."

"No fifty percent, no fifty cents, nothing," snapped Louis's manager. He was aware that Gould had links with underworld figures like Pete Stone, known as Pete the Goat, and Owney Madden. Even when Gould dropped his demand to 25 percent, then 20, Roxborough held firm. Braddock's manager decided to put the squeeze on Mike Jacobs instead.

Jacobs understood that if he wanted to wrest control of heavyweight boxing away from Jimmy Johnston, the powerful matchmaker for Madison Square Garden, he would have to play ball with Gould and Braddock. He said he would guarantee them $500,000, or half the gate and radio revenues, whichever was the greater figure for the fight. On top of that, he made an extraordinary offer. He was prepared to concede 10 percent of all his net profits from heavyweight title promotions for the next ten years. The deal was done.

Contrary to popular belief, it was not Louis who had to surrender

10 percent of his purses to Braddock for the decade after he became champion. The agreement was that the deductions came from the promoter's gate receipts. As it happened, Jacobs eventually got fed up with the seemingly never-ending debt and stopped paying the money. He was taken to court and managed to persuade his tormentors to accept a financial settlement.

The Madison Square Garden bosses, angered on hearing that Braddock was committed to defending his title against Louis, weren't prepared to give up without a fight. They obtained an order demanding that Braddock show up in court to explain his failure to live up to his obligations under the prior contract with Schmeling. When the process server finally caught up with the elusive champion, Braddock went to court to present his case. To his relief, he found that Federal Court judge Guy L. Fake had denied the temporary injunction sought by the Garden. The Louis fight could go ahead. Judge Fake ruled that the contract binding Braddock to meet Schmeling before Louis "places an unreasonable restraint upon his [Braddock's] liberty." There was an appeal, but the Supreme Court upheld Judge Fake's decision.

Braddock took some flak for snubbing Schmeling, the legitimate number-one contender, in favor of taking on Louis, who had been decisively beaten by the German. But few begrudged him trying to ensure his family's security after struggling so hard for so many years. Braddock's was the classic underdog-makes-good story.

Born on June 7, 1905, in the notorious New York district known as Hell's Kitchen, he grew up in New Jersey. He dropped out of school when he was thirteen and, after winning several state amateur boxing titles, turned professional in 1926. Within three years he was good enough to challenge Tommy Loughran for the world light-heavyweight title but found himself outsmarted over fifteen rounds. A series of unimpressive performances, not helped by a hand injury that never properly healed, saw him slide down the rankings. Between 1930 and 1933, he lost sixteen of his thirty fights. To help put food on the table for his wife and three children, he took work on the docks. When that wasn't available, he joined a government work program paying $17 a week.

Braddock had almost given up on making it as a boxer when

Gould, who had stuck with him through the Depression period, got a call from Jimmy Johnston. An opponent was needed for Corn Griffin on the undercard to the Carnera–Baer title fight. Would Braddock be interested? Gould said he thought Jim had retired, but he would ask him. Braddock, told his purse would be $250, eagerly grabbed the chance. Although he knew Griffin was a leading heavyweight contender who had impressed observers as a sparring partner for Carnera, he told his manager, "If I'm licked, at least I'll go down fighting."

Griffin swarmed all over Braddock in the first round and dropped him for a count. It looked all over for Jim as he made his way shakily to his corner at the bell. Things changed dramatically in the second round, when Braddock found, from somewhere, a mighty right that sent the odds-on favorite down and out. The delighted winner told his even more ecstatic manager, "I did that on stew and hamburgers. Get me some steaks and see what I do."

The sensational result shot Braddock up the heavyweight ratings. He followed up with a convincing points-win over future world light-heavyweight champion John Henry Lewis, who had beaten him handily two years before. Matched with Art Lasky for the right to meet champion Baer, he gave one of the best performances of his career to outsmart his much bigger opponent for a decisive points victory.

Finding that Schmeling was demanding first crack at Baer, Gould offered to settle the issue by matching Braddock with the German in a final eliminator. Schmeling refused, so matchmaker Johnston announced that Baer would defend his title against Braddock on June 13, 1935.

Despite his recent good wins, Braddock was given little chance of dethroning Baer. The champion treated him with contempt in the buildup and spent more time in nightclubs than the gym. Braddock made the 10–1 favorite pay for his lack of preparation by soundly trouncing him over fifteen rounds. The superbly fit challenger piled up the points with an accurate left jab while using smart footwork to keep away from Baer's wild swings. It was one of the biggest upsets in boxing history. Damon Runyon nicknamed Braddock the Cinderella Man in recognition of his remarkable rags-to-riches story.

Now that he was world champion, Braddock was in no hurry to accommodate the pack of hungry contenders. Nobody could really blame him for cashing in on his popularity through endorsements, testimonials, and personal appearances, but it meant that the title was kept in mothballs for two years.

Schmeling, especially, felt badly treated. He had turned down several lucrative matches while waiting for Braddock to fulfill his contractual obligation. Both fighters had signed up in August 1936 for the fight to take place in September. That date was scrapped when Braddock claimed his hand and elbow problems required extended rest. Schmeling, skeptical about the American's excuses, put out a statement that he had no interest in fighting a champion who wasn't completely healthy.

The situation reached farcical heights the following year with the event that has gone down in boxing history as the Phantom Fight. At first, everything seemed in order when both sides met in the spring of 1937 to sign new contracts. The rescheduled date for the contest was June 3 of that year.

Schmeling went into serious training at Speculator, in upstate New York, despite persistent rumors that Braddock had no intention of fighting him. Whatever happened, he was determined to keep to his side of the bargain. He would be fit and ready to challenge Braddock for the championship on the designated date. If the champion pulled out, then he should be stripped of his title. Schmeling, as the official number-one contender, would then be matched with the winner of an elimination tournament for the vacant world championship. That was the only fair conclusion.

Fairness, however, has never had much to do with big-time boxing. Gene Tunney, a visitor to the German's training camp, whispered an ominous warning: "Be ready for anything, Max. You don't know what's possible in this country."

Schmeling stuck to his guns. He had a contract with Braddock for the fight on June 3. He would be there on that date, even if the champion was not. It was around midday when he strode into the offices of the New York State Athletic Commission. Fulfilling to the letter the procedures laid down by the organization, he stripped for a physical by Dr. William Walker, who declared him in excellent shape. When he stepped onto the scales, his weight was announced at 196. The challenger's hard work at his training camp had paid off.

But where was the champion? No one expected Braddock to show up for the weigh-in, of course. He was away training at Grand Beach, Michigan, for the Louis fight on June 22 and had only academic interest in what was happening in New York.

Schmeling, with the attitude of a man who is about to come into an inheritance, awaited the commission's next move. Having done everything that was expected of him, he was entitled to expect justice.

Major General John J. Phelan, the commission chairman, called Schmeling into his office to read out a prepared statement:

> This body, after due and lengthy consideration of the matter, finds James J. Braddock and his manager, Joe Gould, in violation of the commission's orders and hereby imposes a civil fine of $1,000 apiece on Braddock and his manager. In addition, this board suspends Braddock from fighting in this State, or in any State affiliated with the New York Commission, for an indefinite period. Also, any fighter meeting Braddock will be suspended automatically. Gould is also suspended. The forfeit money of $5,000 put up by Madison Square Garden for Braddock shall be divided in equal parts by the Garden and by Max Schmeling, who is ready, willing and able to fight tonight.

Schmeling didn't know whether to laugh or cry. The $1,000 fine amounted to no more than a slap on the wrist for Braddock and his manager. Nor would the New York ban have any bearing on Braddock's intention to fight Louis in Chicago later that month, as the Illinois State Athletic Commission wasted no time putting out a statement asserting that they would not recognize the suspension of Braddock imposed by its New York counterpart.

Back at his hotel to meet the press an hour after the meeting, Schmeling let his frustrations erupt in expressions of outrage. "The ruling is a joke," he kept repeating over and over. Furthermore, he complained, his act of faith had cost him around $25,000 in traveling and training expenses.

In the midst of his tirade against the New York Commission, he was handed a telegram. It was a demand for tax due from his training sessions, when people had paid to see him work out. "What's this, another joke?" he exclaimed. Joe Jacobs assured him the wire was genuine. He would have to pay the grand total of $18.75.

The last straw was a reporter's query whether he would attend the Braddock–Louis fight. Max virtually shrieked "No" before storming out of the room.

Later in the day, he was still angry but calm when he turned up for a scheduled coast-to-coast radio broadcast. This was his chance to express his grievances to the American nation, and he was sure he would get a sympathetic hearing. But the National Broadcasting Company refused him permission to use his prepared script, as it was considered too caustic toward the New York Commission. Schmeling, in turn, rejected a proposed substitute script, and so the broadcast was canceled.

He would have to be patient. Louis was an overwhelming favorite to beat Braddock, and if he was the proud and honorable man he made himself out to be, he must make an early defense of his title against the most deserving contender. Max should have had no worries on that score. Louis had said that if he beat Braddock, he wouldn't consider himself a true world champion until he whipped the only man who had beaten him.

11

A CHAMPION'S PROMISE

Old-time fighters used to training in cold dingy gyms or sparse out-door camps reacted scornfully to reports of Louis's plush setup as he went into training for the Braddock fight. He relaxed, ate, and slept in an opulent ten-room Spanish-style stucco summerhouse in Chiwaukee, Wisconsin, owned by Fred Fisher, a Chicago bed manufacturer. It had lots of expensive antique furniture, a pool, and two bathrooms to every bedroom. From his window, Joe had a magnificent view across Lake Michigan.

But there was none of the fooling around that had been routine at previous camps. This was serious business. In just over a month, Louis would be fighting for the heavyweight championship of the world. Nothing could be left to chance. He had to be in the best shape of his life. Jack Blackburn was so dedicated to the task that he vowed to stay off booze completely until the fight was over.

Louis willingly knuckled down to the rigorous schedule. He was up at five o'clock every morning for a ten-mile run while Blackburn and bodyguard Carl Nelson followed in a car, measuring the miles on the odometer. Then it was back to bed, where he would sleep until awakened for a ten o'clock breakfast consisting of prunes, orange juice, and liver or lamb chops. He could then relax for a few hours until the afternoon sparring sessions. Helping out was Harry Lenny, a veteran white trainer, who advised Joe on ways to combat Braddock's right-hand punches. Blackburn raised no objections. "If it helps Chappie become champ, it's good," he said.

Once the afternoon workouts were finished, chef Bill Bottoms prepared a large dinner for Joe that included lots of chicken, fish, and vegetables, with ice cream for dessert. For his twenty-third birthday, on May 13, Bottoms baked him a giant cake. A less disciplined Louis would have dived in for a hefty chunk, but he restricted himself to a modest slice. He needed to lose ten pounds by the day of the fight. Joe's evenings were spent playing cards or Ping-Pong with members of his entourage, scanning the newspapers and listening to his favorite jazz recordings, or just taking a stroll by the lakeside before turning in at nine o'clock.

Blackburn's aim was to bring Louis along slowly to his best condition. He didn't want him to peak too soon. Joe was also told to hold back in sparring so as not to risk damaging his hands. Reporters unaware of the trainer's strategy wrote that the title challenger looked terrible.

"I don't know what has happened to Louis," Jack Miley informed readers of the *New York Daily News*. "Nobody does, including himself. But, judged by his training camp workouts, the boy just isn't there. He is slow and lazy. He has lost his sock. He acts as if he doesn't care. He seems to be just going through the motions of preparing himself for his shot at the title."

Other writers took up the theme of Joe's laid-back demeanor. Bill Corum, of the *New York Journal*, observed, "There isn't an ounce of killer in him. He's a big, superbly built Negro youth who was born to listen to jazz music, eat a lot of fried chicken, play ball with the gang on the corner, and never do a lick of heavy work he could escape." *Life* magazine ran a series of photographs with captions noting that "the challenger rarely smiles . . . Here Louis grins because a workout is over . . . He hates workouts and getting up out of bed." R. G. Lynch, of the *Milwaukee Journal*, said that uninformed visitors to the training camp "would never have thought that anybody had ever called this smooth-faced, placid, slightly sullen Negro youth a jungle killer."

Mike Jacobs was reading all this and rubbing his hands with glee. Knowing that Braddock had no chance, he was afraid that if the public saw the fight for what it was, a mismatch, few would pay to watch it. It was in his interest to build up Braddock and tear Louis down. Jersey

Jones, the promoter's publicist, did little to counter the growing conclusion that Louis was fat and lazy, that success had gone to his head and soft living had taken its toll.

In assessing both men's fighting qualities, the writers tended to exaggerate Louis's weaknesses while discovering admirable qualities in Braddock. Again and again, they questioned Joe's ability to take a punch, pointed to his vulnerability to a right-hand punch, and doubted his intelligence as a fighter. The latter could be largely put down to ingrained prejudices. Had Louis been the white man, they would hardly have failed to explain that he had lost just once in his career. Braddock had been beaten 29 times.

Frank Graham, of the *New York Sun,* came out with the utmost absurdity when he suggested that Louis "doesn't even know how to jab." It wasn't a view shared by the people who really understood boxing and had studied Joe's style in depth. They were convinced that no heavyweight in history had bettered his jab. After the fight, Braddock would liken the punch to "getting a light bulb rammed into your face."

Right up to the day of the fight, Braddock and his manager did their best to unsettle the challenger. Gould kept repeating that Louis wouldn't be able to complain about sneak punches, as he did after losing to Schmeling, because Braddock would give it to him clean, and it would be all over in a few minutes.

Just as Louis was packing his bag for the noon weigh-in, a messenger delivered a slim square package. Blackburn snatched it from the fighter's hands and ripped it open. Inside was a record of the popular song, "They Can't Take That Away From Me." The label was signed "James J. Braddock."

Louis got his chance to hit back when they met at the scales. "I hear you had a birthday, Jimmy," he said. "You were thirty-two. I had a birthday, too. I was twenty-three."

Close to 48,000 people crammed into Chicago's Comiskey Park on the night of June 22. Most of the 20,000 blacks in attendance had scraped up $3.75 for distant seats overlooking the outfield, where the ring was set up. "They must have saved real hard to get that money together," Louis said later. "Half of them must have been on welfare, but

Lord knows what they sacrificed to see me. I had a responsibility to them."

At ringside, where seats cost $27.50, better-off blacks rubbed shoulders with rich white businessmen, society couples, gangsters, Hollywood stars, and famous ex-champions. Most black Americans who heard the fight, though, were at home, huddled in groups around their radios, waiting to cheer their man to victory or weep if he lost.

In the ring, Louis slipped out of his red-trimmed blue dressing gown to reveal purple trunks with the initials *JL* embroidered on them. Braddock, as always, wore shorts bearing a shamrock emblem, even though he had to go back a couple of generations to find his Irish roots. The champion weighed 197, just a quarter of a pound less than Louis, the 2–1 favorite.

Braddock came out fast at the opening bell, winging a couple of rights that were easily avoided by the challenger. Louis, calmly watching for an opening, whipped in a couple of hard body shots and staggered Braddock with a powerful right. They clinched, and as they parted, Braddock landed a short right uppercut that sent Joe to the canvas. The crowd was in an uproar. Were they about to witness a replay of what had happened when Louis was felled by Schmeling's lethal right-handers?

This time, however, Louis was unhurt. He jumped quickly to his feet before referee Tommy Thomas could start to count. Furious at himself for being caught so early in the fight, he attacked Braddock with both fists flying, shaking the champion with a left hook and right cross and drawing first blood. At the end of the round, Blackburn admonished Joe for not taking advantage of a longer count. Pride wouldn't let Louis play that game. In the other corner, Braddock was telling Joe Gould that Louis's punches were very hard.

After battering the champion with a sustained attack in the second round, Louis eased off for the next two rounds, content to bide his time. He later maintained that he could have finished off Braddock any time after the first round. But Blackburn told him to play it safe, jabbing and countering until the champion slowed and tired. "I'll tell you when to shoot," said the ringwise old trainer.

Braddock came out for the fifth round with his eyes puffed and blood trickling from a cut above his left eye. For a brief spell, he matched Louis for jabs landed and even managed to bloody his nose. The better boxing and the harder punches were coming from Louis, however. It was just a matter of time.

A powerful right split Braddock's lip in the sixth, and a right uppercut in the next round staggered the brave champion as he tried to mount an attack. Braddock leaned to his right in a bid to avoid the big right-handers, but was straightened up by a left hook. There was just no escape from the relentless Brown Bomber. Gould told his fighter at the end of the round that he was going to throw in the towel. "If you do," Braddock spluttered through his bloodied lips, "I'll never speak to you again as long as I live."

Louis provided a graphic description of the finish in his autobiography:

> When the bell rang for the eighth round, he came out wide open. His legs were gone. He couldn't keep his arms up. Joe Gould kept yelling from the corner, "Keep your hands up! Keep your hands up!" But I knocked him out with a punch we called the D.O.A. (dead on his ass) in the gym when I was an amateur. It was a left to the body and a right to the chin. The punch took him off his feet. He whirled in the air and fell flat on his face. I knew he couldn't get up.

It was fully ten minutes before the now ex-champion could leave the ring under his own power. He later admitted that when he was knocked down, "I could've stayed down for three weeks."

Louis never looked at Braddock as the referee counted him out. He stood passively in a neutral corner, gazing out over the crowd and listening to the excited roars. Poker-faced as always, he accepted the referee's hand as his left glove was raised to signal the new heavyweight champion of the world. As his handlers had taught him, he would never gloat over a fallen white opponent.

It was back in the dressing room that the pressure of the occasion and the realization of his new status hit him. Suddenly feeling faint, he lay down on the rubbing table and closed his eyes. Some of the reporters who elbowed their way into the packed room told of having to "wake up" the new champion, who had fallen asleep. All Joe wanted was to go home to Marva and talk to his mother on the phone. Through all the fog, he vaguely heard Blackburn say he wanted to keep Joe's right glove as a souvenir. He had earned it.

When he eventually reached his mother on a long-distance call to Detroit, the first thing she asked him was if he was hurt. Assured that he was fine, she said she had first prayed to God that he wouldn't get hurt, then prayed that he wouldn't hurt Braddock. On being told that Joe and Marva were coming to spend a few days with her, she said, "Good, now I can go to bed."

Black people all over America wildly celebrated their hero's victory. Harlem Holds Maddest Revel ran the banner headline in the *New York Sun*, which told of jubilant blacks leaning out of hotel windows and yelling, "How do you like that, white man?" British journalist Alistair Cooke reported from Baltimore's Darktown that the scenes "looked like Christmas Eve in darkest Africa," with "cops barking and women screaming and men going down grabbing their toes and snarling oaths." In Chicago, Louis's wife said it was "bedlam, sheer bedlam." South Side blacks took over trains and taxis and rode around for free. Others disconnected trolley cars and burned bonfires in the streets. The *Chicago Defender* gave over most of its front page to the fight, allowing just a two-column space to report the U.S. Senate vote favoring an antilynching bill. The makers of Sweet Georgia Brown Hair Dressing announced they would give away a nine-by-twelve-inch photograph of Louis with every sale of their product.

Generally, the press, while crediting Louis for outclassing Braddock, focused more on the fallen champion. They praised the courage of a man who had absorbed such terrific punishment that his face required twenty-three stitches and had refused to quit. Braddock, they said, was an old man who had never been a great fighter, yet he would never accept the inevitability of his defeat. When it came, he accepted it with courage and dignity.

In contrast, the victor was seen as dominant, cruel, impersonal. The old savage, animalistic imagery resurfaced in much of the writing. Louis "rose from the floor like a jungle man" to achieve his win, according to Jack Cuddy of the United Press.

On Louis the fighter, the consensus was that he had learned from the Schmeling defeat and was a much-improved all-rounder. Dan

Parker, of the *New York Mirror*, admitted:

> How wrong almost everyone has been about Louis. They called
> him dumb. They said he was a sucker for a right. They
> questioned his courage—all after a lucky combination of cir-
> cumstances, that perhaps could never happen again, enabled
> Max Schmeling to score a knockout over him a year ago. I think
> it was lucky for Mr. Schmeling he wasn't in there Tuesday night
> instead of Braddock.

The most prophetic comment came from Shirley Povich in the
Washington Post: "Methinks Louis is in for a long reign as champion—
the longest perhaps in the history of the heavyweight division."

But the press would not fully accept him as a true champion until
he could meet and beat Schmeling. On that score, Louis was in full
agreement. He would not rest until he erased the only blot on his
record. "Bring him on" was his stock answer to questions about the
German.

Scorning the Chicago result, Schmeling was in London trying to
arrange a fight with Tommy Farr, heavyweight champion of Great
Britain and the British Empire. Schmeling insisted that, as Braddock
had ducked out of his contract to fight him, a meeting between Farr
and himself should be recognized as a world title contest. "I have no
intention of putting myself in the position of challenger," he said.
"Louis has to come to me if he wants a fight."

When Mike Jacobs approached Schmeling about a possible
rematch with Louis, he was surprised to hear the German demanding
30 percent of the gate. That was out of the question, the promoter
retorted. Max would have to accept the normal challenger's 20 percent,
or there was no point in discussing it further. Schmeling refused to
back down.

Although the American press was not wholly dismissive of his
claims of injustice, Schmeling felt humiliated and suspected a conspiracy to keep the title from going to Germany. He hoped a convincing victory over Farr would put him in a better bargaining position with Jacobs.

Again, he found himself outmaneuvered. Jacobs offered Farr a

$60,000 guarantee, plus 25 percent of the radio and film rights, to fight Louis in New York. That was nearly double what the Welshman could expect for facing Schmeling.

The British Boxing Board of Control backed Schmeling, announcing it would not recognize a fight between Louis and Farr as being for the world title. It would only be a final eliminator, with the winner to meet Schmeling for the vacant championship. The board's decision would have no bearing on Louis continuing to be recognized as champion in America, and it failed to deter Farr, who signed up to fight Louis at Yankee Stadium on August 26.

Schmeling still didn't give up.

Not much was known about Farr, who had never fought in America, but his record showed worthy points wins over Max Baer and former world light-heavyweight champions Tommy Loughran and Bob Olin. Each of those fights took place in London. Reports from Britain noted he was a clever boxer, courageous, with a hard chin, but prone to getting cut easily. Not considered much of a puncher, he had caused a minor shock by knocking out another top-rated German, Walter Neusel, in three rounds.

Farr had a hard upbringing and had already boxed for pay when, at age fourteen, he started work in the Welsh mines. He had barely settled into his job when he was caught up in a tunnel explosion that sent jagged lumps of coal flying into his face and body. He bore the scars of the accident for the rest of his life. It was in the pits that Farr learned how to fight, in brutal, bare-knuckle bouts staged in waist-high holes dug out of the ground. The holes were just a few feet wide, so the contestants would have little room to maneuver or even to fall down if knocked unconscious. The adult miners, betting on the outcome, would cheer loudly as the boys went at it hammer and tongs. "After the pits," Farr would recall, "fighting in the ring was child's play."

Maybe he was trying to emphasize what a tough nut he was, but Farr insisted on sparring without a headguard or gumshield. Mike Jacobs nearly had a heart attack when he heard. If the Welshman got cut, it would cause a postponement and that wasn't in anyone's interest. Eventually Farr listened to the promoter's pleas and wore the protective gear.

Louis's managers brought in Mannie Seamon, who had trained legendary world lightweight champion Benny Leonard, as assistant to Blackburn. Seamon was given responsibility for hiring the right kind of sparring partners. Marty Gallagher, a rough, mauling type of fighter, was instructed to crowd the champion, getting him used to the kind of fight he could expect from Farr. Gallagher bobbed and weaved his way in close, where he attempted to rough up Louis, while Joe sought to keep his distance and box. In case the challenger adopted a cautionary approach, another sparring mate, Pat Silvers, was told to box on the retreat and force Joe to lead.

On the day before he wound up his training program, Louis had a surprise visitor. He saw Schmeling at the back of the large crowd watching him sparring and noticed him whispering to his trainer, Max Machon. Joe's wife was also there that day, and when the session was over, he told her he was going to talk to Schmeling. She said she would go with him.

Marva, confronted with the man who had cost her so many tears and so many sleepless nights, was polite but straightforward. She left Schmeling in no doubt that there was still unfinished business between him and her husband. Max was friendly and respectful. Afterward, when they were alone, Marva said she had liked Schmeling's quiet manner. "He was more gentle than I expected," she said.

"Yeah," Joe agreed. "If we wasn't fighting, I might almost like him."

Rain caused the postponement of the fight for four days, and it was August 30 when Louis and Farr finally climbed between the ropes at Yankee Stadium in front of 32,000 spectators. Louis, a 5–1 favorite, weighed 197, seven pounds less than the challenger. Among the ex-champions introduced from the ring by announcer Harry Balogh was Schmeling, whose broad smile hid the resentment he felt at being side-tracked. If justice had been done, it would have been he, not Farr, who was getting first crack at the new champion. The crowd showed their sympathy by giving him a warm reception, although there was a sprinkling of boos and hisses.

In the first round, Louis nailed Farr with a solid right to the jaw. While others might have gone down, the tough Briton sprang to the attack, unleashing a flurry of lefts and rights that forced Louis to step back. At the end of the round, Farr patted the champion on the shoulder and walked back to his corner looking confident and strong. It was reported that he had sung Welsh songs in his dressing room while waiting for the call to the ring.

Farr's bobbing and weaving style bothered Louis all evening. He moved in on the champion, crowding him and giving him little room to unleash his power punches. Still, Tommy had to absorb plenty of Louis's jabs and hooks, leaving him with multiple facial cuts and a badly swollen nose. He proved his resilience and courage in the seventh round, when Louis beat him to the punch with a hard right to the jaw and went all out for a knockout, pouring on a barrage of heavy blows. The dogged visitor took it all, and it was Louis who looked more tired at the bell.

Despite the punishment he took, Farr never once went down and made nonsense of the oft-repeated slur of British "horizontal heavy-weights." He often beat Louis to the punch with his accurate jab and was never afraid to mix it with the heavier punching champion. At the end of the fifteen sharply contested rounds, the crowd rose to applaud his gallant effort.

Referee Arthur Donovan caused a bit of a stir by walking across to the Welshman's corner and shaking his hand immediately after the final bell. The implication that he thought Farr had won was soon dispelled when the scores were announced. Donovan gave Louis thirteen rounds, with one to Farr and one even. The crowd loudly voiced their disapproval. The two judges were more realistic, with William McParland scoring it nine rounds to six and Charles Lynch making it eight rounds to five, with two even. All the way back to his dressing room, Louis was subjected to the unfamiliar sound of booing, while the loser earned rapturous applause.

Though a unanimous winner, Louis was far from satisfied with his showing. On one of the rare occasions when he gave an excuse, he said he had hurt his right hand in the third round when he landed high on Farr's head. As a result, he couldn't punch with his usual power. Had he not suffered the injury, he said, he would have knocked out Farr in five rounds. After an examination by doctors, he was found to have aggravated bruising of the knuckles. The hand was put in a plaster cast, intended for a month, but he had it removed after two weeks.

"Tommy is one of the toughest men I ever fought," Louis confessed. "He fooled me. He didn't look too effective, yet he was puzzling, and his punches were annoying." Jack Blackburn paid his own tribute to the game Welshman: "Louis hit Farr with shots that would have dropped, yeah, flattened most other fighters in the world. Farr is a real tough man and he has an awkward style. He is a better fighter than people give him credit for."

Though the British radio broadcast made it seem as if Farr was an unlucky loser, Tommy said he would make no excuses and that Louis had earned the decision. "Louis is the best and cleanest fighter I ever met," he said. "He hits harder than all of them put together, but I would like to fight him again." His manager, Ted Broadribb, also had no complaints about the verdict. "I gave Farr five or six rounds," he said, "but had he not had his eyes bunged up, he would have done better." Twenty years later, in a radio interview, Farr said he wished people would stop referring to the Louis fight. "I've only got to hear his name and my nose starts bleeding again," he quipped.

Throughout his career, Louis earned credit for giving a second chance to any fighter who gave him a tough time. Invariably, he improved on his first performance, either by knocking out those who had previously taken him the distance, or by beating a stubborn challenger in quicker time. Farr was the only one who never got the opportunity to show if he could do better in a return match. The fault was his, not Joe's. In his next four fights, all of them in New York, he lost to Jim Braddock, Max Baer, Lou Nova, and Clarence "Red" Burman, thus eliminating himself as a leading contender.

Three days after the Farr fight, Louis and Schmeling reached agreement on a rematch for the following June. It took a certain amount of coercion by Mike Jacobs to get the German to agree to the terms. If Max held out for a 30 percent share of the gate, the promoter threatened to stage an elimination tournament, beginning with a Braddock–Baer bout, to find the next opponent for Louis. Eventually, Schmeling accepted the normal challenger's purse—20 percent of the box office takings, plus a percentage of the radio and film rights. A delighted Jacobs anticipated a financial bonanza. "I can see all those senators, governors, and mayors chasing me for a crack at the bout," he predicted. "They'll be in a line from here to San Francisco." Few cities, in fact, came up with suitable bids, and the fight was booked for New

York's Yankee Stadium, the site of the first Louis–Schmeling clash.

There was another condition in Schmeling's contract. Jacobs insisted that, due to his long period of inactivity, he must fight Harry Thomas to put himself back in the public eye and drum up ballyhoo for the Louis contest. So, on December 14, 1937, Max stepped into the ring for the first time since his win over Louis sixteen months earlier. A boycott staged by the Anti-Nazi League failed to affect the gate. The event, at Madison Square Garden, drew the biggest indoor fight attendance in New York for two years. Thomas, a game, if mediocre, heavyweight, was floored seven times by Schmeling's flashing right hand before the referee rescued him in the eighth round.

Both Louis and Schmeling kept in shape with two wins apiece in the first few months of 1938. The Brown Bomber put his title at stake against Nathan Mann and Harry Thomas. The Mann bout provided little more than mild exercise for Louis. He floored the challenger four times before finishing him off with a left hook in the third round. It was a significant win for the champion, for Mann had beaten clever Bob Pastor and difficult Arturo Godoy within the past year.

Thomas, who had lasted into the eighth round against Schmeling, failed to survive five with Louis. Indeed, it looked like the fight was over a round earlier when the challenger, groggy after taking a hard right to the head, started walking back toward his corner before the bell rang. Referee Dave Miller would have been within his rights in disqualifying him for turning his back on his opponent. But he could see the fighter was confused and allowed him to come out for the next round. He did him no favors. A hefty left hook sent Thomas crashing for the count.

Schmeling had his tune-up bouts in Hamburg. He beat South African Ben Foord, a former British and British Empire heavyweight champion, convincingly on points over twelve rounds and knocked out American Steve Dudas in the fifth.

Peter Wilson met Schmeling for the first time while he was training on the Bismarck estate for his bout against Foord. The *Sunday Pictorial* writer was impressed with Max's utter dedication to his profession.

> There is a rugged, primitive energy about Schmeling which is almost awe-inspiring. He lives a life which the Spartans would

have admired. He has never smoked or touched alcohol in his life.

When I saw him the first time, he had just finished his roadwork—eight miles slogging through the snow and mud— and he seemed to revel in the hard conditions. You can sense the "killer" in Schmeling when you see him. If the season were not ended, he would have been ranging through the dark woods, hunting stags or wild boars, with his hounds at his heels. As it is, he has been doing some clay pigeon shooting, to vary the monotony of training.

Six or eight rounds a day with his three sparring partners. Hours of skipping, punching the bag, and grueling foot-slogging through the forest. Heroic work for a man of thirty-two.

But, at thirty-two, Schmeling seems a living proof of the superman which has always been the German ideal.

While Schmeling tried his best to concentrate on the job ahead, without being distracted by the political spin reporters put on it, he recognized the growing anxiety of Americans about what was happening in Europe. Over the winter and spring of 1937–38, Hitler had increased the pace of German rearmament and territorial expansion. Germany's concept of obtaining more "living space" for its people was popular long before the Nazis came to power. The Führer, however, redirected the policy away from acquiring overseas colonies toward enlarging Germany within Europe itself. New territory to the east was essential "to enhance the area of the mother country." Hitler used a series of demands and threats to weaken the will of the Austrian government and annexed the country in March 1938. He next turned covetous eyes toward Czechoslovakia.

"World events made it increasingly difficult for Americans to disassociate Max Schmeling from his fascist homeland," wrote Chris Mead in *Champion Joe Louis*. "The swastika hugged Schmeling like flypaper."

12

BOMBER COMMAND

In the spring of 1938, Louis was in Washington as guest of honor at the Colored Order of Elks national convention. President Roosevelt, spotting a propaganda opportunity, invited the world heavyweight champion to the White House. During a brief conversation, the Harvard-educated aristocrat from New York said to the sharecropper's son from Alabama, "Lean over, Joe, so I can feel your muscles."

Having satisfied himself as to their steely quality, FDR said, "Joe, we need muscles like yours to beat Germany." Newspapers embellished the quote to read: "Joe, beat Schmeling to prove we can beat the Germans."

Julian Black, who accompanied his fighter on the visit, reported that Louis was hugely impressed on meeting the president and only his natural restraint kept him from going overboard in his enthusiasm. Black writer Earl Brown came away with a different impression after he had spoken to the man himself. Louis, conscious that Roosevelt had not fulfilled his preelection promises on racial equality, told Brown, "I didn't think nuttin' of it."

Schmeling's apprehensions were proved well founded when the SS *Bremen* docked in New York on May 9 after a six-day transatlantic voyage. A noisy group of picketers lined the quayside to jeer and shout abusive remarks. A banner proclaimed: Schmeling Go Home. Another urged: Boycott Nazi Schmeling. Pale and clearly disturbed, he was ushered to a waiting limousine by promoter Mike Jacobs and whisked by a circuitous route to his hotel, only to find more demonstrators waiting there.

Jacobs had tried to cushion Max from the hostile reception by hiring a tugboat so that reporters could interview Schmeling aboard the *Bremen*. It was evident, however, that the atmosphere in America had changed dramatically since his last visit. Newsmen, many of whom he considered friends, asked questions about boxing but were more concerned with Hitler and race issues. Did he, they wanted to know, consider himself a member of the "super race"? Was he afraid of what would happen to him in Germany if he lost?

Schmeling pleaded, "I am a fighter, not a politician. I am no superman in any way."

Whenever he stepped out onto Broadway or Fifth Avenue, he was greeted with insults and mock Nazi salutes. The memory was still vivid when he wrote nearly forty years later:

> I was desperate. It was only two years since the same city had congratulated me so enthusiastically. Now for the first time I began to realize it was no longer a matter of business. The goal that united all of them, promoters, editors, and boxing functionaries, was of a political nature. They had accepted a German champion in 1931, but a world champion that came from Hitler-Germany was unacceptable to all.

Of course, he could have made things much easier by taking the advice of American friends, including Jack Dempsey, to stay on and take U.S. citizenship. But, while reiterating that he was not a Nazi, he said he was proud of his nationality. "Once a German, always a German," he declared. In any case, Goebbels had ensured that there would be no likelihood of Schmeling defecting by barring his wife and mother from traveling with him.

The Ring's editor, Nat Fleischer, a Jew with a genuine admiration and affection for Schmeling, prepared a radio script for him to read, appealing to the sportsmanship of the American public. No radio station would put it on air. Disheartened, Schmeling checked out of his hotel and headed for his training camp in Speculator, New York, at the foot of the Adirondack Mountains, where the peace and quiet was a welcome antidote to the unpleasantness of the big city. Callers were surprised to find him so attuned to nature that he fed a friendly chipmunk from his outstretched hand.

Commencing his training stint with a week of roadwork, he progressed from eight to ten miles per day. His legs had never felt so strong, he said, and he "could fight a thousand rounds without feeling fatigued."

Although described as "sober and humorless" by one leading scribe, Max answered questions willingly and honestly. He was there to do a job, to regain the heavyweight championship of the world, and he aimed to show he was worthy of the honor. A good speaker of English, he occasionally annoyed listeners by lapsing into conversation with Max Machon in their native language. Inevitably, newsmen badgered him about Hitler and life under the Nazis. It wasn't all bad, he insisted. Not yet a critic of the regime, he pointed out that there were no strikes in Germany. Nearly everyone had a job. There was only one union, one political party. Life was good:

> Of course, Hitler and all Germany is interested in my attempt to win back the championship. I have had so much trouble getting my chance they are all rooting for me. But sport is sport in Germany, nothing more. Hitler is very interested in boxing. He devoted a whole page to it in *Mein Kampf.* That does not mean, however, he would put me in prison or even be seriously concerned if I was beaten.

Hugh Bradley, in the *New York Post,* sarcastically suggested that when Schmeling talked politics "he speaks pieces that might well have come out of a handbook of party discipline."

The perception that he was Hitler's messenger was deeply troubling to Max. "Whether I wanted it or not, I was a showpiece for the Nazis," he wrote in his autobiography. "Up to the day of the fight I received thousands of hate letters signed 'Heil Hitler' or 'Hit Hitler.' I didn't know what to do—only two years earlier this same city had cheered me wildly."

Louis, too, was irked with the political angles reporters constantly sought on the fight. He was a boxer, the heavyweight champion of the world, and his primary aim was to claim the irrefutable right to that title by beating the one man who held a victory over him.

To enable him to achieve that goal, Joe's handlers made sure that no stone was left unturned in his preparation at Pompton Lakes, New Jersey. Out went his beloved golf clubs, which had accompanied him everywhere, even to Kenosha, Wisconsin, when he was training to take the title from Jim Braddock. More important, there would be no sneaking off for dalliances with women. Even Marva, his wife, was advised to stay away. This was too important a mission to foul up with distractions of any kind. Peter Wilson noted that on several occasions he saw "rather flashy white women" being politely but firmly turned away from the entrance to the training camp. "There was, overtly at least, to be no repetition of the hatred which Jack Johnson, the first Negro heavyweight world champion, had engendered by his affairs with women not of his own color," he wrote.

For all its restrictions, Pompton Lakes seemed to Wilson to be the happier of the two training camps:

> Most of the spectators were youngsters and, from behind the wire netting which surrounded the ring on all sides, the black kids, grinning so widely that they threatened to cut off their ears, shouted their cries of encouragement to their idol Joe, like a troop of school kids at the zoo encouraging a favorite lion.

John Roxborough said Louis's mental attitude was the best he had ever known him to attain and that his eagerness had captivated the whole camp. "This isn't just another fight for Joe," said Roxborough, "it's a chance to catch up with Schmeling and square an account."

Hired sparring partners George Nicholson, Big Jim Howell, Basher Dean, Murray Kanner, and Willie Reddish, later to become Sonny Liston's trainer, were instructed to keep throwing right hands to get Louis used to what he could expect from Schmeling. After a while, he learned to block them so easily that it was instinctive. Unlike on other occasions, when Mike Jacobs had gotten him to knock out sparring partners to generate headlines, Joe concentrated on practicing moves and on ways of combating his opponent's strengths. Blackburn's strategy for the fight was for Louis to attack from the opening bell. In the 1936 fight, he noted, when Joe was on the offensive, following up jabs with combinations, Schmeling had been forced to retreat. When he neglected to maintain pressure and stood off to throw his jab, his opponent would counter with his devastating right. This time he must keep on top of Schmeling and not let him get set for his pet punch.

The policy of controlled aggression suited the champion's mood. He had waited two years to avenge his only defeat, and only a decisive victory would wipe out that bitter memory. Apart from professional pride, Louis felt genuine personal hostility toward the German. At another time he would say that he never hated any opponent, even Schmeling, but there was no denying he went into the fight determined to make Max pay for the beating he had inflicted in their first encounter and for the derogatory remarks he was reported to have made in the meantime. In one comment, Schmeling was alleged to have claimed that "the black man will always be afraid of me. He is inferior."

(In 2004, Joe Louis Barrow Jr. said that, although the period was certainly filled with animosity, there was no genuine hatred between his father and Schmeling. Both men were extremely focused on the fight, he said, with the German wanting a shot at the title that had been denied him by Jim Braddock, and Louis anxious to avenge his loss to Schmeling. "The full impact of Hitler's actions was finally being recognized and acknowledged, which created a higher level of intensity than most championship fights," he said.)

As the day of the bout neared, Louis spoke to newsmen with uncharacteristic venom: "I am out for revenge. All I ask of Schmeling is that he will stand up and fight without quitting. I'll give him enough to remember for life and make him hang up his gloves for all time."

Harvey Boyle wrote in the *Pittsburgh Post-Gazette*:

Usually Louis, on the side of diplomacy, and handled expertly in his public relations, has been pleasant with all foemen, stressing the virtues of his opponent, playing down his own part. Because of this attitude, whether sincere or posed, he has, in spite of his color, risen to eminence with a modicum of prejudice against him. He has, for the moment, however, dropped the old college spirit toward a fraternity brother, and he has been quoted several times as saying he would rather beat Schmeling than any fellow he has met. This is natural in view of the knockout he suffered and Schmeling's fouling charge.

As word reached the German camp that Louis was storing up a vengeful rage, Schmeling tried to play down any beliefs of mutual animosity. "Sport is sport, it has nothing to do with hate," he insisted.

Louis was not convinced by his rival's statement. "Maybe they put words in his mouth, but he didn't deny them," he said.

It didn't help Schmeling's case when various rumors gained wings. Hitler was going to make him minister for sport for the Third Reich if he won. His trainer, Max Machon, kept a full Nazi uniform, right down to swastika armband, in a closet at the Osborne Hotel. Storm troopers would join German fans sailing over on the SS *Hamburg* and SS *Europa*. A German correspondent, Arno Hellmis, informed his homeland that the Jewish governor of New York, Herbert Lehman, was part of a conspiracy to make sure Louis won. Schmeling knew he could dismiss the stories as the nonsense they were, but held back because he didn't want to cause more problems for his wife and mother, virtually held hostage by Goebbels.

The American press, in its attempts to predict and analyze the fight, constantly fell back on stereotypes in describing the protagonists. Louis was seen as a natural athlete with the strengths and guile of a jungle beast. Schmeling, on the other hand, was a more cerebral, methodical fighter but with fewer physical assets.

Bill Corum wrote in the *New York Journal*:

I don't believe anyone is going to teach Joe Louis how to fight. I do believe that he was born knowing and that he is the best and most exciting heavyweight of modern times when he is fighting by instinct, instead of trying to fight by numbers. How does anyone propose to make Joe a better methodical fighter than the Teutonic Schmeling, who is old Herr Methodical himself? There are certain gifts that the Negro race, as a race, and Louis, as an individual, have as a heritage. The ability carefully to work out a methodical plan, and adhere to it, is not among them. That's for Schmeling.

How much notice anyone took of what the pen pushers, most of whom had never pulled on a boxing glove, said was open to debate. Much more important were the views of the guys who had firsthand experience of the ring and knew the same joys, tensions, and pain with which Louis and Schmeling were so familiar. A United Press Agency poll of eight former world heavyweight champions had more than half forecasting a Louis victory. Jack Dempsey seemed to change his mind day by day.

Jim Braddock, after watching a Louis workout, said, "If Joe sets the same pace against Max as he did this afternoon, he'll murder the guy." Gene Tunney, another observer that day, said, "If Joe keeps it up, I don't see how he can lose. He's a much better boxer now. He is more compact, keeps his arms closer to his body and gets his right up to block punches. He still doesn't roll with a punch, which is too bad. But Joe can take a punch and counter—and when he does it won't be a fair exchange." James J. Jeffries, Jess Willard, Jack Sharkey, and Max Baer all went for Louis by a knockout.

Jack Johnson's contrary opinion was no surprise. Envious of the acclamation accorded to the only other black heavyweight to occupy the throne up to that point, Jack never gave Louis credit as a great all-around fighter. "Schmeling has the technique, and technique in fighting is more important than strength or punching ability," said Johnson. "Max, at thirty-two, should be right at his peak. I think Schmeling's cunning and strategy will win over Louis's poor craftsmanship." He had been one of the few to correctly pick Schmeling the first time, he reminded listeners, concluding, "You just watch. Louis is in for another mighty fall."

Dempsey appeared to cover his tracks by predicting both men would win. It depended on which report one read. A magazine article under his byline had him picking Schmeling as an easy winner. But when interviewed by sportswriter Jack Cuddy, he showed remarkable foresight by picking a first-round knockout by Louis. It didn't help Dempsey's credibility when both the newspaper article and the magazine piece appeared on the same day.

In a syndicated column, Dempsey recognized that Louis had developed into a well-poised, self-assured man of the world. He was "an altogether different person from the taciturn, shy young Negro of two years ago who spoke only when spoken to, and then only in mono-syllables." As for his fighting ability, he looked impressive when he cut loose on his sparring partners. His judgment of distance was good, and his timing sharp and accurate. However, he still had to prove he had the skill to avoid Schmeling's lethal right-handers and show his ability to "take it."

When he took a trip to Speculator, Dempsey found the German challenger relaxed and confident, and "looking a lot younger than his thirty-two years." In sparring, he made his partners earn their money, demonstrating the accuracy and power of his right hand. Dempsey's old nemesis, Gene Tunney, also dropped in, principally to assure Schmeling that there was no truth in stories that he had been coaching Louis on how to win.

Nat Fleischer foresaw an exact reversal of the first match, a win for Louis in twelve rounds. *The Ring*'s editor conceded that Schmeling had the psychological edge, due to his emphatic victory in 1936, but practically all the physical advantages, especially youth, were on the American's side.

Although Louis would enter the ring as a 2–1 favorite, many sportswriters preferred Schmeling, as he had several points in his favor. His deadly right hand had already bludgeoned Joe to defeat, and that would be a major psychological plus. Then there was his greater experience. He had almost twice as many contests as did Louis. Of his sixty-three fights, he had won fifty-two, thirty-five by knockout, with seven losses and four draws. He was considered an intelligent, calculat-ing fighter.

The wider opinion, however, was that Louis was a better boxer and a harder puncher than the challenger. No all-out slugger like other big hitters, he was gifted with probably the most accurate jab in heavy-weight history. It wasn't the type of flicking jab others used to build up points. Joe rammed his left hand straight and hard into his target, and it was a very difficult punch to avoid or block. Having opened up his opponent's defenses with a steady stream of jabs, Louis would then unleash powerful hooks and uppercuts that few could withstand. While his left hook was probably his most deadly weapon, he scored almost as many knockouts with his right hand. Also, although he was slow on his feet, he had fast hands. He could land three punches for every two of his opponent's. In addition to being nine years younger than Schmeling, Joe had a psychological edge of his own. He was so driven by his desire to beat the only man who had a victory over him as a professional that he refused to contemplate defeat.

Almost inevitably whenever there was a world heavyweight title contest in those days, there was a row of some sort. It could have been about the size of the ring, the thickness of the canvas, or the type of gloves to be used. Often it was just a publicity gimmick to boost ticket sales, but that was not necessary on this occasion. Most of the 70,000 tickets had long been snapped up. Schmeling had a genuine concern over the gloves chosen by the champion. Made in Chicago, they had much longer thumbs and thinner padding across the knuckles than the normal New York product. This, he felt, would give Louis, a noted left jabber, an advantage in that he could cause damage to the challenger's eyes. "If they get their way with the gloves, next they'll want to bring their own referee," snorted Max Machon.

Two days before the fight, Schmeling announced that he would pull out if the New York Athletic Commission did not insist on the use of regulation gloves. With less than twenty-four hours to go, he got his way. The commission ruled that Louis's gloves were stuffed with felt instead of the usual curled horsehair and therefore could not be used. First round to the challenger in the psychological battle.

Even happier was Mike Jacobs, guaranteed a million-dollar gate despite the campaign for a boycott by the Anti-Nazi League. New York was making preparations to welcome between 30,000 and 40,000 visitors for the fight, although hotel accommodations were almost impossible to find. Special trains from Chicago, Washington, and California, augmented by bus and air services, were fully booked. Jacobs sent a telegram to Schmeling "absolutely forbidding" him to take up an invitation from the American airman Dick Merrill to fly to New York City from Speculator. He remembered Gene Tunney's foolish act of bravado in taking an open-cockpit flight from Stroudsburg to Philadelphia on the day of his world heavyweight title challenge to

TOP: Flyer for the "Fight of the Century." (Mainstream)

ABOVE: Joe Louis, one of boxing's all-time greats, was world heavyweight champion for twelve years (1937–49) and defended the title twenty-five times. Neither record has ever been broken. (Hank Kaplan Archives)

TOP: What a way to become world heavyweight champion: Schmeling lies in agony on the floor as Jack Sharkey is disqualified for a low blow in the fourth round.

ABOVE: Louis is sent to a neutral corner by referee Tommy Thomas as he prepares to count out Jim Braddock in the eighth round and declare Joe the new world heavyweight champion.

Max Schmeling won the vacant world heavyweight title by beating
Jack Sharkey in 1930, and lost it to Sharkey in a rematch two years later.
(Hank Kaplan Archives)

Louis and Schmeling meet in 1935 as the German visits Louis's
training camp in New Jersey to see him prepare
for his fight with Paolino Uzcudun.

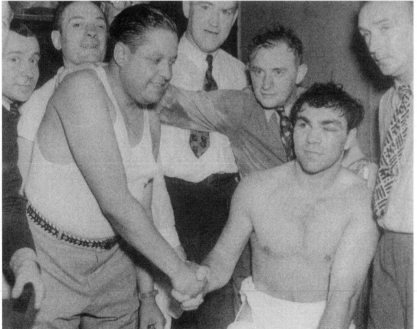

TOP: Schmeling celebrates as referee Arthur Donovan counts out Louis in the twelfth round of their nontitle bout in 1936.

ABOVE: Julian Black, Louis's co-manager, congratulates Schmeling, his left eye swollen shut, in his dressing room after his sensational victory. (Hank Kaplan Archives)

ABOVE: Adolf Hitler greets the conquering hero at a luncheon in the Reich chancellery on Schmeling's return from New York after beating Louis. Max is accompanied by his mother and his wife, the Czech film star Anny Ondra. (© Bettmann/CORBIS)

RIGHT: Schmeling with his American Jewish manager, Joe "Yussel" Jacobs. Max refused Hitler's demand that he split with Jacobs, whom he described as an honorable man.

TOP: The avenger: Louis, in the fourth defense of his world title, floors
Schmeling for one of three counts as he scores a brilliant first-round
victory in their 1938 rematch.

ABOVE: Louis shows no emotion as announcer Harry Balogh raises his hand as
winner against Schmeling. From the start of his career, Louis's managers told
him he must never celebrate after knocking out a white opponent.
(Hank Kaplan Archives)

TOP LEFT: A U.S. Army recruitment poster
issued during the Second World War.

TOP RIGHT: Joe and Max, now good friends, meet at a
New York function in 1960. (Hank Kaplan Archives)

ABOVE: Schmeling, at ninety, enjoys a meal at his home in Hollenstedt, near
Hamburg. He kept active and was looking forward to reaching
one hundred in September 2005. (Rinze van der Meer)

Dempsey in 1926. If his intention was to show his opponent how relaxed he was, it backfired. Tunney suffered airsickness and looked pale and shaken when the plane landed. He had to go and sleep it off for a few hours. As it happened, the escapade didn't do Tunney any harm, as he boxed the ears off the Manassa Mauler to take the title.

For Jacobs, the fight was a pot of gold beyond his wildest dreams. Even the fighters' training camps proved lucrative sources. As many as 5,000 people, paying a dollar a head, showed up twice a week to see Louis work out. For the actual contest, demand was so great that Jacobs upped the price of ringside seats from $30 to $40. In a typically imaginative trick, he added a number of ringside rows. The original rows ran from 1 to 37, but were now supplemented by rows 6A, 12A, and so on. He also put aside several thousand choice seats for the use of his ticket brokerage, selling them off for as much as $200 each. The fight was not the biggest gross gate of Uncle Mike's promotional career, but it was the one that made him most personal profit.

Jacobs also cleverly deflected the campaign for a mass boycott of the bout. Representatives of the American Jewish Committee had suggested that the world title, if it passed to the German, would be utilized by the Nazi propaganda machine as a weapon to weaken American morale. He responded by saying that to deny Schmeling his rightful chance would play into enemy hands by making him a martyr. Besides, he assured the delegation he met at his office, Louis was a cast-iron certainty to destroy his rival in the ring, thereby turning the event into a humiliating defeat for the Third Reich. As a pacifier, Jacobs also offered to hand over part of the fight receipts to a nonsectarian refugee group helping those fleeing German persecution. Although there were occasional warnings that thousands of brown-shirted German-American Bundists were standing by to create a riot at the Yankee Stadium, no major demonstrations of American Nazi strength occurred.

The political angles kept the fight on the front pages as well as the back pages. The much-trumpeted view of Germany as the archenemy was underlined, two days before the bout, by the arrest of eighteen people as alleged members of a Nazi espionage ring. The same day, the newspapers carried a report of a cable received by Schmeling: "To the coming World's Champion, Max Schmeling. Wishing you every success, Adolf Hitler."

Louis, interviewed after his final workout, said, "Don't you worry about me winning this fight. I'll try to finish it in two rounds. It's revenge I'm after."

Schmeling was equally confident of the outcome: "I'm going to win—and by a knockout. Louis is still an amateur. He goes to pieces when he's hit."

On June 22, the American nation heard, via a news agency report, Louis's concluding views, given the previous evening, on the significance of the event: "Tonight I not only fight the battle of my life to revenge the lone blot on my record, but I fight for America against the challenge of a foreign invader, Max Schmeling. This isn't just one man against another or Joe Louis boxing Max Schmeling—it's the good old U.S.A. versus Germany."

The statement, probably ghosted, drew a stinging response from across the Atlantic. The Goebbels-controlled *Der Angriff* accused the United States of "an organized campaign of lies" and of using the contest to raise racial and political issues. "Do Americans think so lightly of their world champion that even in the last hours before the fight they are trying to destroy Schmeling's morale with such attacks? Max would be wise enough to give the yelpers the cold shoulder and permit nothing to destroy his composure and optimism."

Louis was awakened by his bodyguard, Carl Nelson, at nine o'clock on the morning of the fight. An hour later, Nelson drove him, along with John Roxborough, Julian Black, Jack Blackburn, and three state troopers, to the offices of the New York State Athletic Commission for the official weigh-in. A crowd of interested onlookers joined reporters and newsreel cameramen as the champion, wearing sunglasses, a light suit without a tie, and white hat with black band, eased past. Inside, Louis stripped down to boxing shorts and found Schmeling already prepared. They exchanged polite nods, without speaking, but photographs of the event clearly showed the champion's animosity toward the German, whom he fixed with an icy stare. Schmeling looked grim-faced, but confident. Louis scaled 198¾, just over five pounds heavier than the challenger.

In the afternoon, Louis, after a rest at his friend Freddie Wilson's apartment, ate a salad and a steak, then went for a walk along the banks of the Harlem River with Blackburn and Wilson.

"How're you feeling, Joe?" Wilson asked.

"I'm scared."

"Scared?"

"Yeah, I'm scared I might kill Schmeling tonight."

That evening, when the Louis entourage approached Yankee Stadium, "there were cops everywhere you looked," Joe remembered. "When we got to the stadium, you could hardly get in. Going up, we didn't laugh much. Nobody made jokes. It was an important fight."

Amazingly, with so much at stake and with all that was happening all around him, Louis was so relaxed that he slept for two hours in his dressing room. Outside the arena, members of the Anti-Nazi League distributed leaflets urging a boycott of German goods. Communists handed out notes asking those in attendance to give three cheers for Louis and to boo Schmeling.

Blackburn woke the champion at nine o'clock and began the ritual of taping his hands, making sure the bandages were tight enough to form a rock-hard fist, while ensuring there was enough room for him to flex his fingers. Louis told his trainer that he was going all out for victory inside three rounds. "If I don't have Schmeling knocked out, you better come in and get me, because after that I'm through."

"No, it's all right," said Blackburn. "You can go fifteen rounds."

Mike Jacobs did his cheerleader bit by visiting the champion's dressing room to implore, "Murder that bum and don't make an asshole out of me."

"Don't worry about a thing," Louis replied. "I ain't going back to Ford, and you ain't gonna go back to selling lemon drops on the Staten Island ferry."

Jacobs didn't think it was the time or place to tell Joe that he had hedged his bets. He had got Schmeling to sign an agreement that he (Jacobs) would promote his future fights in the event of an upset. The world heavyweight title was his baby and he wasn't going to let it out of his reach.

Normally Louis shadowboxed for ten minutes before a fight. This night he spent half an hour flicking jabs and tossing hooks at the imaginary figure of his opponent until it was time to put on his blue silk robe. An escort of uniformed policemen surrounded Joe and his team as they stepped out into the arena to tremendous cheers.

In the other dressing room, Schmeling felt nervous—and lonely. In his autobiography, he recalled:

> A few days earlier the Boxing Commission had declared Joe Jacobs ineligible to work in my corner. Once again, he had had one of his public relations inspirations, when he had one of his other fighters, "Two Ton" Tony Galento (a.k.a. The Walking Beer Barrel), photographed in the ring with a keg of beer. What the commission would have normally accepted as a harmless gag was now grounds for punishment. They banned Joe Jacobs not only from my corner but also, to my amazement, from the locker room. Even Doc Casey, who had been in my corner so many times, wasn't there. The general hysteria and flood of threatening letters had both shocked and scared him. I had never before felt so alone before a fight. In the critical last few minutes even Max Machon was missing, as he had to go and observe the wrapping of Joe Louis's hands. So I was actually relieved when the door opened and an official came to bring me to the ring.

As soon as the crowd spotted him, the torrent of abuse began. Even with a police escort, he had to pull a towel over his head to protect himself from the stream of banana peels, cigarette packets, and paper cups aimed at him. Once both fighters were in the ring, policemen formed a square inside the ropes to block any more flying objects.

The referee, Arthur Donovan, called the contestants to the middle of the ring for their final instructions. He reminded both sets of cornermen that throwing a towel into the ring, the age-old token of surrender, was not recognized in New York. He, and he alone, would decide when the fight was over.

It may seem strange, in hindsight, that no objections were raised by the German side to Donovan acting as third man in the ring. He had certainly favored Louis in his fight with Tommy Farr the previous year by making him a more emphatic winner than did the two judges. He was almost a permanent fixture in Louis fights and ultimately took charge of no fewer than twelve of the Brown Bomber's twenty-five title defenses. But Donovan, son of Professor Mike Donovan, the noted American middleweight champion and boxing instructor, was scrupulously fair. He had officiated at the first Louis–Schmeling fight, and that was good enough for the German camp. Amazingly, Donovan and Louis never actually spoke to each other until 1963, when Joe almost knocked down the then-elderly pedestrian as he drove down a New York street.

After the announcements were completed, Donovan prompted Louis and Schmeling to touch gloves and called upon them to give the crowd "the greatest fight in heavyweight history." The fighters returned briefly to their corners. Schmeling, unshaven and with his black hair greased back, stood calmly while Louis shadowboxed twenty-five feet away.

The bell called them together for the first, and only, round.

13

SWEET REVENGE

The so-called Battle of the Century lasted little more than two minutes. Into that brief spell, however, was packed more drama, excitement, and controversy than in many a big fight waged over a hard fifteen rounds. It was enough time, too, for Louis to demonstrate that he was one of the most ruthless executioners in the history of boxing. He reduced the unfortunate Schmeling to a physical wreck.

The Brown Bomber was simply sensational. He hardly missed once as he tore the resistance out of Schmeling with powerful punches, scoring three knockdowns and making the German cry out in agony from a body punch before the referee rescued the helpless challenger. Max simply didn't know what had hit him.

Thrilling to the spectacle of the short, savage encounter was a gathering that included Postmaster General James A. Farley, the governors of several states, mayors of big cities, judges and lawyers, leading industrialists, famous stars of stage and screen, ring champions of past and present, and ordinary fans. Millions more around the world hunched around their radio sets to listen to broadcasts in four languages: English, German, Spanish, and Portuguese.

The 70,043 spectators packed into Yankee Stadium, producing a live gate of $1,015,012, could not claim that they were shortchanged, though it was one of the shortest heavyweight title fights on record. Rather, they could tell their grandchildren they were there when Joe Louis scored the greatest win of his brilliant career, on the night he reached a peak of fighting perfection.

At the opening bell, Louis, a study in concentration, advanced menacingly toward his foe. Eyes alert, arms poised, fists cocked, he met Schmeling just short of the ring center. The German backed warily toward his own corner, watching the champion intently, his right—the right that had sent Louis crashing to defeat two years earlier—ready to strike as soon as he saw an opening. He never got that chance.

Louis found his range with a sharp left jab that sent Schmeling's head snapping back as if it were on a hinge. A succession of similar blows had Max blinking his eyes and looking worried. Joe switched to left hooks, forcing the challenger backward to the ropes, which prevented Schmeling from countering. Back at long range, Schmeling saw his first chance to throw a right over the American's extended left arm. This was the punch that had started Louis's downfall the first time. Now, Louis was prepared, and the fist fell short of its mark.

Schmeling had more success with his second attempt, a right that struck Joe's head and brought a loud roar of encouragement from the German's supporters. It was to be the only punch he landed. Louis just scowled and stepped forward, smashing a terrific right to his rival's jaw to send him staggering against the ropes. Max grabbed the top strand with his right hand and held on tightly. The champion tried to hold Schmeling's chin in place with his left, but was unable to reach him with a right hand. He switched to the body, driving a left into Max's stomach. Schmeling bent over, still clinging to the ropes, so that his back was turned toward Louis. Joe ripped home a powerful right to the side, causing Schmeling to emit a loud groan. It was to provide a major postfight controversy, with the German camp alleging it was an illegal kidney punch.

Later, in an article published in *Life* magazine, Louis was quoted on the incident: "I just hit him, tha's all. I hit him right in the ribs and I guess maybe it was a lucky punch, but man, did he scream! I thought it was a lady in the ringside cryin'. He just screamed, tha's all."

As Schmeling hung on the ropes like a fly trapped in a spider's web, referee Donovan stepped between the fighters, giving Max a temporary respite. He then waved Louis on. The poker-faced champion let loose with a volley of lefts and rights that exploded against head and body. A solid right to the jaw sent the rubbery-legged Schmeling toppling forward to the floor. Though badly hurt and dazed, he regained his feet by the count of three. A merciless Louis slammed a left and two rights into Max's aching, puffing face and put him down again. Bravely, if foolishly, Schmeling got up before the count got past one.

There was no escape from the ruthless destroyer. As Schmeling tried to get his scrambled senses together, he was staggered by a succession of precision punches to the head. A final pulverizing right to the jaw sent him down for the third, and last, time. As Donovan waved Louis to the farthest neutral corner, Max Machon tossed a white towel into the ring. The referee refused to accept the trainer's signaled surrender and continued counting. He had reached five when, seeing Schmeling's distress, he spread his arms to indicate he had stopped the slaughter. The official time was two minutes, four seconds of round one.

Immediately, the police swarmed into the ring to keep out over-zealous spectators. Louis, as he had been programmed from the beginning of his career, showed not a trace of emotion as he was proclaimed the winner and still heavyweight champion of the world. The badly beaten loser, after receiving attention from his seconds, managed a smile as he walked across the ring to congratulate his vanquisher.

Back in his dressing room, Schmeling told reporters that he had no excuses, but the punch that had landed to his kidney had paralyzed him so he couldn't move. Joe Jacobs and Max Machon complained that their man had been hit with an illegal punch, and Schmeling, under pressure from further questioning, agreed that he had been fouled. He spent the night in hospital, where X-rays disclosed two fractured vertebrae in his back.

Referee Donovan said he saw no foul committed but added, "It must have been a murderous blow, for I heard Max scream. His seconds must have heard him, for they threw in the towel. The punch was quite fair."

In any case, Donovan would have been precluded from disqualifying Louis due to the no-foul rule that had been in existence for the past eight years. It had been introduced by the New York State Athletic Commission following the furor over Schmeling's winning of the title from Jack Sharkey, who was ruled out for a low blow.

Louis, who picked up $350,000 for his easy night's work, was as relaxed as if he had just returned from a short training run. Asked how he felt after his win, he drawled, "Something of a relief, I guess." He did allow a half-smile as he declared, "I'm sure enough champion now."

As soon as the radio broadcast was over, exultant blacks spilled out onto the streets to begin the celebrations. Harlem enjoyed a carnival atmosphere, with laughing revelers doing the goose step and mocking the Heil Hitler salute, while others jumped onto the running boards of passing cabs and private vehicles. At times, the partying spilled over into recklessness, as bottles and cans were thrown from tenement rooftops. Twenty policemen suffered minor injuries, and one mounted officer was taken to the hospital with a concussion after being knocked off his horse.

The rejoicing was echoed in towns and urban centers throughout the country. The citizens of Detroit, anticipating Joe's win, had pre-arranged with the police to have a section of Paradise Valley cordoned off for the victory party. They unfurled a prepared banner: JOE LOUIS KNOCKED OUT HITLER. A newspaper in Chattanooga, Tennessee, showed a photo of two chauffeurs and a doorman counting the $175 they had won on the result. The headline writer picked up a woman's happy cry: DAT BOY JOE LOUIS DONE WHUP 'EM ALL.

Murray Rose, of the Associated Press, quoted the unusually vocal champion:

> I don't usually get mad at anyone, but this time I was. This was one I wanted to win more than any other in my life. Maybe now those Nazis will stop bragging about how great they think they are. That Hitler is sure looking for trouble and he's gonna get plenty one of these days. He oughta remember what happened to Smellin'.

The badly hurt German spent ten days confined to the Polyclinic Hospital. One of his first visitors was Major General John J. Phelan, chairman of the New York State Athletic Commission. He wanted to know the extent of Max's injuries from the controversial body blow, but Schmeling believed the real reason for the visit was to determine if his purse should be held up for failure to continue the fight.

Louis, asked if he was going to visit Max, replied:

I was a little bit sore at Smellin' for some of the things that he said, but no, I'm not going over to see him at the hospital. I just guess he was the only man I ever been mad at. I'm sorry if he was hurt, tha's all. I don't like to hurt nobody.

The German ambassador in Washington, Hans Dieckhoff, dropped by to check on his countryman's condition. Though he knew nothing about boxing, he insisted on a full explanation of the alleged foul. Schmeling said that he had grabbed the ropes during the rain of punches, and as he turned, Louis threw the devastating right. It was his own fault for turning away, he explained, but Dieckhoff wouldn't be put off. It was an illegal punch, and he wanted to file an official protest. When the envoy saw that Max was eager to let the controversy die, he shrugged his shoulders and said, "Well, as you wish."

The Nazi Propaganda Ministry was not prepared to drop the issue. As Schmeling sailed for home after being delivered to the SS *Bremen* by ambulance, he learned that outrageous rumors were being circulated. Goebbels was claiming not only that Louis had intentionally landed a foul blow but that his gloves were padded with lead.

American reporters showed no sympathy for the beaten challenger and ridiculed the claims of a foul. They said it was poor sportsmanship by the German. Louis had made no excuses when he lost the first fight, they pointed out. Mike Jacobs invited the journalists to watch slow-motion footage of the fight, which showed that Schmeling was well on his way to defeat when Louis hit him in the side. It was clear that Max turned his back before the blow was struck.

When the film of the fight was shown in Germany, according to some accounts, it was edited to remove the sequence of punches that preceded the blow to Schmeling's side. All that would have been shown was Louis slamming home his paralyzing right as his opponent's back was turned. Another story that gained wide circulation was that the German radio broadcast was pulled off the air as soon as it became clear Schmeling was headed for defeat. People who had stayed up until 3 A.M. to hear Arno Hellmis's description got little more than a minute of the action before the power was cut off, it was reported. But Germans quizzed after the war insisted they had heard all of the fight.

One recalled how, as a thirteen-year-old Jewish boy attending a boarding school, he listened to the commentator pleading with Schmeling to get up from the canvas.

The Berlin Associated Press report made no mention of a power cut, deliberate or coincidental, but said that gloom enveloped the taverns where Schmeling supporters gathered for the radio transmission. They listened in silence as Hellmis addressed his closing words to the fallen hero: "We sympathize with you, Max, although you lost as a fair sportsman. We will show you on your return that reports in foreign newspapers that you will be thrown into jail are untrue."

Some German commentators were not so kind. *Reihe Der Sport* criticized Schmeling's lack of strategy and his weak defense: "One could have understood if the youth of the American prevailed after eight or ten rounds—that would have been a clear and understandable defeat, but the KO victory of Louis remains only the consequences of the carelessness of the challenger."

Nazi newspapers were eager to play down the significance of the result. Whereas two years earlier they had lauded Schmeling's win over Louis as a German victory, now "the defeat of a boxer does not mean any loss of national prestige." Images of a conspiracy to cheat Max out of regaining the world title were conjured up. *Völkischer Beobachter* alleged that boxing in America was "controlled by Jews," who had held back Schmeling for two years with "the dirtiest tricks." The editorial concluded: "Schmeling is undoubtedly the most dangerous opponent Louis could have in the world. The fact that he could not win in New York makes us consider whether it is worthwhile for us to look for another fight for the world's championship."

The American press, naturally, was in a celebratory mood. Even the most avidly racist writers proclaimed that it was a victory for America. O. B. Keeler, who had rarely said a good word about Louis in the past and had picked Schmeling to repeat his win, wrote in the *Atlanta Journal*:

> Joe Louis is heavyweight boxing champion of the world, and so far as this correspondent can see there is nothing to be done about it. Our fastest runners are colored boys, and our longest

jumpers, and highest leapers. And now our champion fighting man with the fists is Joseph Louis Barrow.

Syndicated columnist Hugh S. Johnson wrote:

The piteous flash I got of Schmeling, wrecked and out on his feet, was vivid pictorial disproof of this nonsense about Aryan physical supremacy.

The average of white intelligence is above the average of black intelligence probably because the white race is several thousand years further away from jungle savagery. But, for the same reason, the average of white physical equipment is lower.

If the black man had an opportunity to compete in athletics, there might not be any white champions at all. Certainly there would be fewer on a percentage basis . . .

It is nothing for us to weep about and seek white hopes. These black boys are Americans—a whole lot more distinctly so than more recently arrived citizens of, say, the Schmeling type. There should be just as much pride in their progress and prowess under our system as in the triumph of any other American. For all their misfortunes and shortcomings they are our people—Negroes, yes, but our Negroes.

Cartoonists jumped on the racial symbolism angle and made a mockery of Hitler. A *Chicago Daily News* sketch showed a plane labeled Brown Bomber flying off after dropping a bomb behind a distraught Führer.

The writers dug deep into their stores of superlatives to describe Louis's win. Bob Considine began his piece:

Listen to this, buddy, for it comes from a guy whose palms are still wet, whose throat is still dry, and whose jaw is still agape from watching Joe Louis knock out Max Schmeling. It was, indeed, a shocking thing, that knockout—short, swift, merciless, complete . . . He [Louis] was a big lean copper spring, tightened and retightened through weeks of training until he was one pregnant package of coiled venom.

Grantland Rice called it "the most sensational attack I've ever seen in the ring." Damon Runyon enthused, "That was beautiful. A great job." Royal Brougham told readers of the *Seattle Post-Intelligencer*: "Louis can be compared with Dempsey at his best, and maybe he's better." Jack Cuddy resorted to stereotype: "The Detroit Negro's mask-like face showed its hatred only through the eyes that gleamed at the former champion like those of an irate cobra." Bill Corum wrote in a similar vein, "When the animal in this placid, quiet Negro boy surges into his fists, then it's river, stay away from my door. When he's a tan tiger cat, he's the killer supreme."

Henry McLemore, of the United Press, also took up the jungle theme after watching the film of the fight:

The slow-motion picture of the 124 seconds of the Joe Louis–Max Schmeling fight is probably the most faithful recording ever made of human savagery.

The picture is much more terrifying to watch than the fight was. In Yankee Stadium, the rapidity with which the butchering occurred, against the background of noise and excitement, prevented anyone from getting a cold and objective view of it. In the quiet darkness of the small theater where I saw the fight pictures yesterday afternoon, I was appalled by the knowledge that this ruthless, unmerciful killer there on the screen was one and the same man who I had just left a few minutes before—a Joe Louis who talked of ice cream, and trips to Europe, and his new pin-striped suit.

I saw Joe again after I had seen the pictures, and although he was sitting in the same chair and talking in the same low voice, I didn't feel fully comfortable around him. It was as if I had seen a savage tiger behind the bar suddenly loosed to walk free among the people who had been watching him.

The Louis of the slow-motion pictures has no connection with ice cream and pin-striped suits and discussions of the weather. He is a jungle man, as completely primitive as any savage, out to destroy the thing he hates. Even the style of fighting he had been patiently taught was abandoned. He fought instinctively and not by any man-made pattern.

What such sensitive souls seemed to forget, or chose to ignore, was that Louis was simply doing a job, and doing it to the best of his ability. It's every boxer's intention to dispose of his opponent as quickly and efficiently as possible. If, in doing so, he appears cold and ruthless, that's the nature of the business. Reporters who feel queasy about what happens inside the ring might be better occupied sticking to the badminton beat. The reason they don't, of course, is that boxing provides more drama, more excitement, and more scope for delivering gripping prose than any other sport.

An aspect of the Louis–Schmeling fight that has been widely debated over the years is how much of an impact it made on political and racial issues of the day. It cannot be claimed with any real justification that, despite the intense nationalism surrounding the event, it had any noticeable effect on the march of events that would soon plunge the world into a war that ultimately cost many millions of lives. Nor did most white Americans' admiration for Louis galvanize them into demanding an immediate end to the widespread discrimination against their black fellow citizens. Possibly the most that can be said is that it helped, in some small way, to awaken people's minds everywhere to the evils that existed in their world.

Schmeling, commenting forty years after the event, was willing to concede that his defeat had a positive side. "A victory over Joe Louis would have made me forever the 'Aryan Show Horse' of the Third Reich," he said.

14

SPEND, SPEND, SPEND

Now, to his own satisfaction and everyone else's, the undisputed heavyweight champion of the world, Louis found himself in great demand. Offers of fights flooded in. Promoter Armaud Vincent sent a cable from London offering him a guaranteed $200,000, or 40 percent of the gate, for a return match with Tommy Farr at Wembley Stadium in London. A syndicate that included Gene Tunney and movie star Robert Taylor told Mike Jacobs they could guarantee one million dollars if he would promote a match between Louis and the leading contender during the upcoming San Francisco Exhibition. The ever-wary Jacobs said he would consider the offers when he saw the money on the table.

Jacobs, with Louis as his key player, had by now assumed a virtual monopoly over big-time boxing. The Brown Bomber was the top box-office attraction in the sport, and anyone who wanted to do business with the champion had to go through Uncle Mike. His control of the main asset meant he could reach out to the fighters in the lower weight divisions, offering them bigger purses than anyone else. Most of the champions and leading contenders signed up with Jacobs. On September 23, 1937, he staged an ambitious Carnival of Champions at New York's Polo Grounds, with no fewer than four world-title fights on the same bill. Jacobs lost money on the show, but he wasn't too worried. He had taken four more champions under his wing.

Any resistance to Jacobs's power grip disappeared when the Madison Square Garden Corporation leased the arena and the outdoor

Madison Square Garden Bowl to Mike's Twentieth Century Sporting Club. Jacobs then used pressure to force out his three secret partners at Twentieth Century—Hearst newspapermen Ed Frayne, Bill Farnsworth, and Damon Runyon—and become sole shareholder. He now had complete control of boxing in New York, the capital of the boxing world. Throughout the rest of the 1930s and into the postwar period, he was unmatched as a promoter, reaching his peak with the second Louis v. Billy Conn fight, which brought in almost two million dollars.

Meanwhile, Jacobs's main crowd-puller was enjoying a six-month vacation after beating Schmeling. To the dismay of Louis's management, that meant lots of golf. If Jack Blackburn constantly chided that golf was harmful to a boxer's muscles, other members of his team were concerned at how much money Joe lost betting on his game. He would play with entertainers like Tony Martin, Al Jolson, Bob Hope, and Bing Crosby, who were all better golfers than he was. There was even an unsubstantiated story that a former Pullman porter bought his house with money he had won from Louis at golf.

If that wasn't bad enough, Joe found plenty of other ways to get rid of his money. In one of his first investments, he started a chicken restaurant in Detroit. On the night of the opening, smartly dressed guests arrived to find that no one had thought of ordering any chicken. With management of that quality, the venture was doomed to failure. He also dropped about $30,000 in forming and touring with a black baseball team, despite attracting good crowds with himself as first baseman.

Not surprisingly for someone who didn't have two cents to rub together in his formative years, Louis, now that he had it, loved to spend. By 1940, he had bought his mother a house in Detroit and an expensive eight-room apartment in Chicago for himself and Marva. He owned twenty-five pairs of shoes and thirty suits costing a hundred dollars apiece. According to writer Earl Brown, Louis preferred "swagger models with huge square shoulders, ripples in the coat backs and cut-in waists. His taste in materials runs to checks, stripes and plaids with green predominating. In socks, he also liked bright colors." Other possessions included two apartment buildings, a large black Buick, and a 477-acre farm in Spring Hill, Michigan, where he kept two show horses, eighty Hereford cows, a hundred Poland China hogs, and a Chow dog.

Some of these could be considered investments, but he regularly splashed out money without thought of value or return. Many highly paid sportspeople and entertainers who came from deprived backgrounds were just as careless with their earnings.

Nightclub owners in Harlem were always happy when Louis was in town. "When Joe would walk into a place, the price of everything went up right away," said Billy Rowe, a long-time friend. "People would figure he could make the money, so why shouldn't he pay it out? And he would invite it. He had been a guy who had nothing and now suddenly he had millions, or at least thousands. So he would never look at a check, just put his hand in his pocket and pay."

Mannie Seamon, who became Louis's full-time trainer after Blackburn's death, said, "They should have called him 'Can't say no Joe.' He was his own worst enemy. He liked fun and laughter and guys clowning around, and he paid for all of it. Anyone could give him a hard-luck story, and as soon as it was over he'd reach in his pocket and pay."

Earl Brown said it wasn't unusual for Louis to start off a day with $2,000 in his pocket and by evening say to his wife, "Hey, Marva, have you got any money?" It wasn't a case of being taken in by sharp operators and tricksters. "Nobody cheated him of his money," said Marva. "He just spent it."

Much of his spending was done when Marva wasn't around. The Hotel Theresa in Harlem was a leading beneficiary of his payouts. The routine was that Joe would go to a nightclub, pick out one of the girls from the show, and spend a day or two with her at the Theresa. Whenever John Roxborough found out Louis was in New York, he would phone Mike Jacobs and tell him to find Joe. Their great concern was that he might get caught in an unsavory situation. White women were involved, and there was the worry of a Jack Johnson–type scandal. Jacobs would advise Joe to stay in a downtown hotel, but he preferred the Theresa.

Louis was making a lot of money in addition to his ring earnings, too. His popularity meant plenty of contracts from companies that wanted to associate his name with their products. He would endorse everything from clocks and radios to hair cream but was refreshingly candid about the items he backed. Asked by a reporter if he really used Castoria, a foul-tasting laxative, as a youngster, he said he had, but he "sure never cried for it."

He was adamant, however, that he would never endorse alcohol or tobacco. As a nondrinker and nonsmoker, he was conscious about preserving his healthy image and setting a good example for young-sters. Once, after he rejected an approach from a cigar company, the headline in the *New York Sun* read, "Louis turns down fortune."

For Schmeling, life wasn't proving anywhere near as full or productive. He lay in the hospital for six weeks after his worst ring loss as rumors circulated that he had been partially paralyzed and would never fully recover. Messages of sympathy and goodwill flooded in from friends and strangers alike. Rows of flowers filled his private ward. The *New York Times* reported that Hitler sent a message of sympathy to Max's wife and that Goebbels sent her a bouquet of flowers. Schmeling waited in vain for a call from his country's leaders.

Reminiscing many years later, he said, "I already knew, after this defeat, that I no longer existed for Hitler and Goebbels. The time for receptions in the Reich Chancellery and Daggers of Honor was over. For quite a while my name simply disappeared from the newspapers."

The one member of the Nazi hierarchy who showed any interest was Albert Speer, who phoned him in the hospital to ask how he was progressing. The two men, who were around the same age, had met briefly at a couple of receptions. Speer's design of the new Reich Chancellery in Berlin had been hailed as a work of genius, and he was regarded as Hitler's true favorite and confidant. After he left the hospital, Schmeling and his wife accepted an invitation to Speer's home. At the end of the visit, Max thanked his host for an interesting afternoon and said how much he had enjoyed the conversation. Speer seemed surprised by his guest's courtesy, in view of all that had happened. "I didn't tell him how isolated I had felt since my return from New York," Schmeling recalled.

For a while, Max thought about giving up boxing completely, but he still nourished a dream of regaining the world title and retiring as undefeated champion. To do so would mean having to return to the

United States, where he feared he would encounter even more hostility than before. That prospect became more of a certainty following a horrendous anti-Semitic pogrom that began on November 9, 1938.

German Jews were targeted in response to the fatal shooting in Paris two days earlier of the German diplomat Ernst vom Rath by a Polish-Jewish student. On what became known as *Kristallnacht* (Crystal Night, or the Night of Broken Glass), violent public demonstrations were widespread. Goebbels and the German press, which he controlled, maintained they were spontaneous reactions to the murder. Documents found after the war revealed that instructions had been issued to all headquarters and stations of the state police and the *Sicherheitsdierst* (security service) or SD for "spontaneous demonstrations" to be "organized and executed." Security chief Reinhard Heydrich instructed that synagogues might be burned down as long as there was no danger to German life or property. Jewish businesses and private apartments could be destroyed but not looted, public demonstrations should not be hindered by the police, and "as many Jews, especially rich ones, are to be arrested as can be accommodated in the existing prisons." Over two days and nights, more than a thousand synagogues were burned or otherwise damaged. Rioters ransacked and looted 7,500 businesses, killed at least 90 Jews, and vandalized Jewish hospitals, homes, schools, and cemeteries. Later, 30,000 Jews were taken to concentration camps to prepare for forced emigration. In a final act of humiliation, Jews were levied with a massive fine to pay for repairs to their own property. Hermann Göring, winding up a meeting of cabinet ministers that approved the measures, commented, "I would not like to be a Jew in Germany."

For over fifty years, Schmeling's act of heroism in sheltering two Jewish boys on that infamous occasion was kept secret. At a party honoring Max at the Sands Hotel in Las Vegas in 1989, a tearful Henri Lewin, a German-Jewish emigrant and now the hotel's president, disclosed how the boxer had risked his life to protect two frightened youngsters from the rampaging mobs. One of those youngsters was the speaker himself. The other was his brother, Werner. Schmeling had been a friend of the Lewin brothers' father, David, since the 1920s and had been a guest at their home. David ran a fashionable clothing store, where Max often bought his suits. He was also popular in show business and sporting circles, and dignitaries like the Prince of Wales had dined at his restaurant, the Gypsy Cellar.

On *Kristallnacht,* a frightened Lewin asked Schmeling if he would hide his two sons, aged fourteen and fifteen, from danger. Max agreed without hesitation and let the boys stay at his apartment in the fashionable Excelsior Hotel in Berlin. He informed the hotel reception that he was ill and gave orders that he didn't want any visitors. After two days, when the violence had died down, he escorted Henri and Werner to his house in another section of the city and later took them to the Lewin family apartment.

The Lewin family fled Germany in 1939 and spent the war years living with the Jewish refugee community in Shanghai. The brothers moved on to the United States in 1947. Henri, after some time working as a waiter in San Francisco, eventually acquired his own hotels in California and Nevada and was an occasional fight promoter.

At the Sands Hotel party in 1989, Lewin expressed belated thanks to the former world champion for risking his name, his reputation, and his life on behalf of himself and his brother. "If we had been found in his apartment, I would not be here this evening, and neither would Max," he said. An embarrassed Schmeling shed tears and said he didn't like being "glorified."

In an article in the January 1993 edition of *History Today,* Robert G. Weisbord, professor of history at the University of Rhode Island and author of *The Chief Rabbi, the Pope, and the Holocaust,* and Norbert Hedderich, assistant professor of German at the same university, wrote under a dual byline:

> While it is probably an exaggeration to suggest that Schmeling would have forfeited his life for his courageous deed, his standing as a national hero would surely have been undercut. Not surprisingly, it is Henri Lewin's opinion that Schmeling is "a man of the highest character—a champion outside the ring as well . . . a truly great German."
>
> Schmeling himself has never discussed the *Kristallnacht* incident: not in the countless interviews he has given, nor in his published reminiscences. He has modestly told the Lewins that what he did for them in 1938 was "the duty of a man." The

melancholy truth is that there were precious few real men in Germany in that era, righteous men, who fulfilled their moral duty. Max Schmeling, the reputed diehard Nazi, was one.

In 1992, an interview Dr. Laurence F. McNamee conducted with Schmeling appeared in *Boxing Illustrated*. Max, asked about the events of over half a century earlier, seemed slightly uncomfortable. He said, "It wasn't anything dramatic, like an underground [movement]. All my wife and I did was to let them hide at our home until they could get out. A lot of other Germans were doing the same thing, and I just had more to lose—especially because I was suspect."

Schmeling then requested that the discussion be turned back to boxing.

Since his summary dismissal of Schmeling, Louis wasn't exactly faced with a lineup of worthy contenders. His next title defense was a mismatch. John Henry Lewis had held the world light-heavyweight title for three years, but he was suffering from failing eyesight and wanted one big payday before he retired. Louis was willing to accommodate his friend, but Mike Jacobs feared a title fight between two black men wouldn't draw much of a crowd. There hadn't been an all-black heavyweight title fight since Jack Johnson and Jim Johnson boxed a draw back in 1913, and that was in Paris.

Jacobs arranged the fight for Madison Square Garden on January 25, 1939. He kept ticket prices low and, as a result, the arena was packed. Lewis, a good champion in his own weight class, conceded twenty pounds to the heavyweight king. He never stood a chance. John Henry was floored three times before referee Arthur Donovan called a halt after two minutes and twenty-nine seconds of the first round. Louis had decided to make it quick, rather than prolong the challenger's pain over several rounds.

Joe's next ring outing was another one-round job. Jack Roper, an awkward southpaw, staggered the champion with a left hook in the opening minute. Louis got over the shock and sent the 10–1 underdog crashing face down with a rapid combination. Roper made a valiant effort to rise but was counted out with his head stuck out between the ropes. He had lasted nine seconds less than the Brown Bomber's last challenger. Afterward, Roper gave a memorable explanation for his loss: "I zigged when I should've zagged."

Although the decisive victories over Lewis and Roper confirmed Louis's reputation as an awesome puncher, they didn't do much for his spending needs. He only made $34,000 apiece from the two fights, before expenses and taxes. With summer approaching, Mike Jacobs looked around for a capable opponent who could draw a big crowd for an outdoor fight with Louis. He settled for one of boxing history's most colorful characters, "Two Ton" Tony Galento.

Not exactly a candidate for a Mr. Universe contest, Galento was short, bald, and shaped like one of the beer barrels he stored at his saloon in Orange, New Jersey. He had been fighting for ten years and had never bothered with conventional methods of training and conditioning. He did no roadwork and ate and drank to his heart's content. Despite his lack of discipline, his short reach, and lack of mobility, he wasn't a bad fighter. He had beaten some respected heavyweights, including two of Louis's previous challengers, Nathan Mann and Harry Thomas. He was game, fearless, and he could hit. He was also one of the dirtiest fighters in history.

Galento was a publicist's dream, and he was aided and abetted by his seventh manager, Joe Jacobs, who hadn't been too busy with Schmeling recently. Two Ton Tony happily posed for photographers behind his bar, opening bottles with his teeth and lifting a full barrel over his head. Other publicity shots had his manager ironing his bulging stomach and using a syringe to disinfect his foul tongue. Not shy when it came to predicting the outcome of his forthcoming fight with Louis, Galento was quoted as saying in a mangled New Jersey accent, "I'll moider da bum."

Galento and Jacobs knew that their only chance of success was to get the champion riled, so that he would forget his natural skills and get involved in a brawl. That could leave Louis open to one of Galento's swings. The campaign went way beyond the accepted rules of fair play. Galento frequently insulted Louis, even phoning him at home to tell him what he would do to him in the ring and threatening to rape his wife.

Jacobs was almost as nasty as his fighter. He told reporters that Louis had a metal bar inside his right glove the night he knocked out

Schmeling. He would insist that Joe's gloves be carefully inspected before the fight began. Promoter Mike Jacobs ordered his namesake to retract the outrageous slur, which he did under protest. Galento, a notorious racist who had taken a few beatings from black heavyweights early in his career, told a reporter, "I'm going to knock that nigger out."

The press coverage of the prefight antics built up public interest in the fight. Most of the 34,852 spectators entering Yankee Stadium on June 28 saw it as another quick win for the champion, but there was plenty of sympathetic support for the 8–1 underdog. Galento's body fat helped give him a thirty-three-pound weight advantage, although, at 5 foot 9, he conceded four and a half inches in height.

Just before the opening bell, Jack Blackburn repeated the warning he had made many times: "He fights in a crouch and throws that left hook from the floor. If you leave yourself open, he'll tag you." Louis had only one thing on his mind: to make the little fat man pay for his abuse. He should have listened more carefully to his trainer.

Galento caught him with a sweeping left hook and shook him in the first round. Louis repaid his tormentor with interest in the second, pounding him ruthlessly with both fists and dropping him for a count of two. It was the first time Galento had ever been floored.

A sensational upset seemed to be in the cards in the third round, when Two Ton Tony knocked the champion to the canvas with one of his wide, looping left-handers. Louis avoided the full force of the punch since he was moving away, but the crowd was in an uproar as he rose at the count of four to face a furious attack. Galento was too undisciplined to make the most of his advantage, however, and the now wary champion was able to block and avoid his weighty but wild punches.

Fully recovered in the fourth, Louis drilled Galento with powerful, precise blows from both hands. The fighting saloon owner reeled like a drunk as the punches rained home on the inviting target. Galento, with blood spurting from his nose and mouth, bravely tried to fight back, but he couldn't do anything to stem the Brown Bomber's relentless onslaught. The challenger was being battered to pulp, and shouts of "Stop it" came from the crowd. Referee Arthur Donovan took a careful look at Galento but allowed Louis to continue his attack. A left hook to the jaw sent Two Ton Tony reeling. A right spun him halfway around. A fusillade of blows rendered him helpless, and Donovan, not before time, stepped in to rescue Galento. The far from grateful loser later complained, "If it hadn'ta been for that chicken-hearted referee, I'da moidered da bum."

Galento went straight home after the fight, feeling too ashamed to face the customers at his saloon. For the rest of his life, he insisted he could have beaten Louis if he had been allowed to fight in his natural no-holds-barred style. "The boxing commission scared me," he told writer W. C. Heinz. "They told me if I fought a foul fight they'd give my purse to charity. If I had the right manager he woulda said, 'Go out and hit him low.' I woulda butted him and thumbed him. I coulda been champion of the world."

Despite all the insults Galento had thrown at him beforehand, Louis had a lot of regard for the man he regarded as "a good street slugger." Years afterward, he said, "At first he got on my nerves, but later, you know, I got to like that son of a bitch. He had style and what they'd call 'charisma' nowadays." Joe was an occasional caller to Tony's bar, and they would laugh about how seriously they took things back then.

"The hardest punches I ever saw Louis throw were against Tony Galento," remembered Barney Nagler, one of Louis's biographers. "Every time he hit him it made little breaks in the skin as though [Galento] cut himself shaving." There was plenty of praise, too, for the bold showing of the underdog. "Tony Galento was more glorious in defeat than he ever was in victory," wrote Hype Igoe in the *New York Herald Tribune.*

In September, Louis fought in Detroit, his hometown, for the first time as champion. His opponent was Bob Pastor, who had made him look bad two years earlier by getting on his bike and backpedaling for the entire ten rounds. He could do that again, if survival was his only objective, but this time it was scheduled for twenty rounds, a long time to keep running. Anyway, Pastor knew that negative tactics wouldn't win him the world heavyweight title. He felt confident he could mix it with Louis. It was a foolish assumption.

The challenger came out fighting, only to be knocked down three times in the opening round and once more in the second. That was enough to convince Pastor of a change of plan. He reverted to the elusive style that had served him well in the first fight and managed to stay out of serious trouble until the eleventh round, when he was floored for the final time. Referee Sam Hennessey stopped the fight. When Pastor met former champion Jim Braddock the next day, he said he would have won except for being blinded by blood flowing into his eye. Braddock didn't buy the excuse, saying, "Yeah, he hits hard, don't he?"

Years later, Pastor admitted that the referee "probably saved my life. I couldn't see out of one eye, and he was hitting me pretty well. He was a terrific puncher."

For the third time in four years, *The Ring* honored Louis as Fighter of the Year. The magazine praised his "public relations and fine influence on the sport." Despite the well-earned plaudits, not everyone believed he was invincible. "He's not as good as they rate him," Galento said. "He can't take a punch." Jack Dempsey commented, "Joe Louis is a good, game fighter who boxes better than many critics think and punches like nobody's business. But his jaw is weak and eventually a puncher—a good, rough, tough guy who can take a punch and keep on punching himself—will take Louis's heavyweight title."

From the time of his loss to Louis to the outbreak of the Second World War, Schmeling fought just once. That was at the Adolf Hitler Stadium in Stuttgart on July 2, 1939, when he knocked out Adolf Heuser in the first round to capture the European heavyweight title.

Heuser, known as the Bonn Tornado, was a stocky, hard-punching fighter with a respectable record. Plenty of money was wagered on him to beat Schmeling, especially by those who considered Max washed up. The fight lasted only seventy-one seconds. Heuser started aggressively, trying to emulate what Louis had achieved, but Schmeling took the punches on his arms and gloves. When Heuser resumed his attack, Schmeling timed him with a perfect right cross to the jaw. The punch tore Heuser's legs from under him and sent him crashing down. He didn't move as the referee counted him out, or for some considerable time afterward. As a doctor was being summoned, Heuser's wife scrambled into the ring and threw herself on the canvas beside him, weeping hysterically and stroking his head. After a while, the doctors succeeded in bringing him around by means of artificial respiration. Schmeling had stayed in the ring, watching anxiously while his victim lay unconscious, and later visited him at his hotel. Heuser smiled ruefully and said, "If you had caught Louis with that punch, your fight would have turned out differently."

Because of the great interest in the fight, local newspapers rushed out special editions with reports from the ringside. In its haste, one paper came up with a classic howler. Its headline read: Max Schmeling KO's Adolf Hitler in Adolf Heuser Stadium.

Earlier in the year, Schmeling had journeyed to America to talk with Mike Jacobs about another fight with Louis. The promoter told him to get a few wins under his belt in Europe and then they could discuss a title fight in the summer of 1940. After his impressive dismissal of Heuser, the new European champion was lined up for a return match with Walter Neusel. The date was set for August 1939, but Max asked that it be put back for a month so he could gather the harvest at his farm. Events pushed the fight right off the calendar.

On September 1, Germany invaded Poland. Two days later, the British government, under Prime Minister Neville Chamberlain, informed Hitler that unless German troops were immediately withdrawn from the occupied land, Britain would declare war. When the Führer failed to respond, France allied itself with Britain and the Second World War began.

15

JOE GOES TO WORK;
MAX GOES TO WAR

Although most Americans were concerned at what was happening in Europe, there was a widespread hope that the war would stay "over there." They understood that the United States might become embroiled at some stage but hoped that day could be delayed as long as possible.

For Louis, life went on much as always. He fought often, so was in training for most of the time. Between fights he continued to spend money like it was going out of fashion. He patronized nightclubs, spent time with various girlfriends, had rows and reconciliations with his wife, and discussed with Mike Jacobs who he should fight next.

At the rate he was dispatching opponents, it was becoming more and more difficult to find anyone worthy of sharing a ring with him. One writer observed, only half-jokingly, "If Louis continues to fight himself out of competition, he will end up having to fight his own shadow."

Jacobs's search settled on a burly Chilean, Arturo Godoy, who had a reputation for durability if not much else. The fight was scheduled for Madison Square Garden on February 9, 1940. Louis, with some time to spare before going into training, was doing the nightclub rounds when he met up with an old flame, Lena Horne. She was singing with the Charlie Barnett orchestra and Louis claimed he met her by accident while he was out with some friends. The old magnetism was still there.

"She was more beautiful than she'd ever been," he recalled in *Joe Louis: My Life*. "Nice and sweet, but Lord, she had a filthy mouth. Could cuss better than any sailor wished he could. We started talking; next thing I knew, we were getting real serious. We were planning all kinds of places and ways we could see each other."

But there was work to be done. Affairs of the heart would have to wait until he got rid of Godoy. The South American proved an awkward customer indeed. Like Bob Pastor in his first encounter with Louis, Arturo was more preoccupied with finding a way to avoid the Brown Bomber's heavy artillery than on actually winning the fight. Whereas Pastor had succeeded by keeping his distance, Godoy's tactics were to cling to Louis like a frightened kid seeking his mother's protection. When he wasn't hugging the frustrated champion, he fought from a ridiculous crouch, his knees bent and his upper body arched forward so that his elbows were almost touching the canvas. Referee Arthur Donovan constantly badgered him to stand upright and to stop holding, but his words were wasted. Louis, in a lethargic mood, couldn't figure out a way to deal with such a unique style. He couldn't get his punches off as he was used to.

As the bell rang to end the tedious fifteen-rounder, a happy and unmarked Godoy grasped the unappreciative champion in a farewell hug and planted a kiss on his mouth. Louis considered the gesture acutely embarrassing. "I ain't never had no man kiss me," he said. While the contestants waited for the decision, the challenger's manager, Al Weill—who would go on to handle Rocky Marciano, the fighter who ended Louis's career—raised Godoy's left hand expectantly. There could be no real doubt as to the winner, however. It was Louis by unanimous decision. "It was my worstest fight," he said. The 15,657 spectators who shelled out $88,491 couldn't have agreed more.

As he had another ring date at the Garden the following month, Louis decided not to go home, but to hang around New York with Dickie Wells, the playboy pal who had introduced him to Lana Turner. One night at the Cotton Club, he met a glamorous dancer, Ruby Dallas, and fell head over heels in love with her. They saw each other as often as they could. Joe likened himself to an alcoholic who had fallen off the wagon. "I got drunk with all these beautiful, exciting women," he confessed.

Johnny Paychek, who had notched up a series of knockouts in the Midwest and was being touted by some as a white hope, was the sacrificial lamb for Louis's next title defense. Nat Fleischer said he had never seen any fighter more scared going into the ring than Paychek that night. The balding challenger spent the first couple of minutes circling away, until Louis backed him into a corner. A left hook dropped Paychek onto his knees, his right hand holding on to the middle rope. He waited until the referee got to nine before getting up and managed to keep out of danger for the rest of the round.

In round two Louis pursued Paychek until the challenger stopped to throw a weak left-hand punch. Joe's countering right landed flush on his opponent's jaw, snapping back his head and sending him crashing on his back. Donovan didn't bother to count, but pulled out the beaten man's mouthguard. One of Paychek's seconds threw a bucket of water over his head to revive him. Fleischer observed that "the field of championship contenders is the weakest in the last fifty years."

Mike Jacobs looked around for a worthy challenger for Louis to highlight his big summer promotion at Yankee Stadium. The best he could come up with was Arturo Godoy again. The first encounter had been such a bore that only 26,000 turned out for the rematch on June 20. True to form, Louis improved on his performance the second time around. He knew what to expect from Godoy and was better prepared. The Chilean challenger, encouraged by the fact that Louis had failed to floor him four months earlier, decided to be more daring by emerging from his crablike defense to throw some punches. That allowed the sharp-hitting champion to retaliate with short blows that opened up numerous cuts on Godoy's already pockmarked face. In the eighth round, Louis dropped his opponent twice, and the referee, Billy Cavanaugh, stopped the fight. A furious Godoy wanted to continue, and it took all of his cornermen's strength to wrap themselves around their man and save Cavanaugh from assault.

Nat Fleischer wrote in *The Ring:*

I wonder what more Joe Louis must show to prove to the skeptics that he is a great fighter! What did Jack Dempsey, Gene Tunney, Jim Jeffries, and other stars of the roped square exhibit in their public performances that the present champion lacks, other than quick thinking? What other titleholder was willing to face all comers and to place his title in jeopardy eleven times in three years?

Louis has clashed with sluggers, clever boxers, combination fighters, rugged, strong men, weavers—in fact, every possible variety of opponent, and the result has been the same. In short, even though he failed to stop his opponent in their first engagement, he solved the riddle in a return bout and proved that as he now stands, he is a well-rounded performer, able to cope with any style elected by the opposition. That is what makes him so invincible.

Other writers weren't quite as complimentary. While recognizing his outstanding qualities as a fighter, they felt he wasn't doing much to establish his claim to ring immortality by disposing of a succession of mostly mediocre opponents. Between December 1940 and June 1941, Louis disposed of seven challengers, one for every month. It was Jack Miley of the *New York Post* who coined the phrase "bum of the month club" to describe Louis's ritual slaughter of the innocent. It was a cheap shot. True, most of his challengers weren't in his class, but that wasn't his fault. Throughout his record twelve-year reign as world heavyweight champion, he never ducked a deserving challenger. Anyone who gave him a hard fight was always guaranteed another chance, unless, like Tommy Farr, he hit a losing run. Invariably, Louis figured out a difficult opponent's style and made an easier job of it the second time around.

It is worthy of note, too, how focused he remained throughout his prime years. Ring history is chock-full of instances where an outstanding champion grew complacent and dropped his guard long enough for a hungry challenger to take advantage. Even Sugar Ray Robinson, considered by most experts to be the best pound-for-pound fighter of all time, won the middleweight title five times, the welterweight title once, and lost in six other championship fights, including a bid for the light-heavyweight title against Joey Maxim. Louis, though he had his off-nights, never let anyone topple him from the championship throne, even temporarily.

★   ★   ★

Germany's relentless advance across Europe continued throughout 1940. Denmark was too weak to put up much resistance. The Netherlands surrendered, followed by Belgium. Norway put up a fight and was supported by British and French forces, but the Allied troops were forced to withdraw when France was invaded. In Britain, dissatisfaction with the campaign led to the fall of the Chamberlain government, making way for a coalition headed by Winston Churchill. From August to October, the Luftwaffe crossed the English Channel to launch mass daylight raids but lost nearly two thousand aircraft in the Battle of Britain. The German attacks switched to the hours of darkness, and the major cities suffered massive loss of life and destruction of property. By May 1941 the raids had subsided, the aggressors having failed in their objective to break the stubborn resistance of the British people.

At the outbreak of the war, Schmeling was told to report for a physical at his district Wehrmacht headquarters. The summons surprised him, as prominent sportspeople, along with artists, actors, and the like, were considered to be exempt from callup. Besides, he was thirty-five years old, beyond draft age. Waiting for his turn outside the examination room, he saw so many boyish faces that he felt he belonged to another generation. Pronounced fit, despite his protestations that he had several sports injuries, he was told by the doctor, "Don't worry, by the time you're inducted it will all be over."

The medic had given him false hope. Within weeks, Schmeling received an order to report for army induction. Still convinced there had been a mistake, he soon learned that he was the victim of a conspiracy. The Reich's sports minister, Hans von Tschammer, had not forgotten their earlier disagreement and had waited patiently for the chance to get his revenge. Now, with Hitler's personal approval, he bent the callup rules to force the former world champion into uniform. Schmeling was assigned to an antiaircraft unit in East Prussia.

Shortly afterward, he got the sad news from America that Joe Jacobs had died from a heart attack at the age of forty-one. Max recalled the happy times they had together and how his loquacious manager would gesticulate madly while making his point, all the time gasping for breath as he chomped on his everpresent cigar. Although

Schmeling had split from Jacobs toward the end of his career, it had nothing to do with the fact that his manager was Jewish. The split was over money. Max claimed that some of his entitlements from the long-term partnership never reached him.

"I thought the world of Jacobs," he said many years later. "He was very religious, and every Friday night he would go to the synagogue. Many times I went with him. I sat right next to him through the whole service."

In the summer of 1940, Schmeling was ordered to report for duty in the Wehrmacht's parachute regiment. After doing some jumps and learning the basic skills, he naively assumed he would be utilized in training recruits. The battalion commander kidded him along, telling him he would have to complete the full training program in order to pass on his knowledge to others. Excused from weapons training, he spent most of the eight weeks lying in sand bunkers gazing at rabbits and birds while his colleagues roughed it out in open terrain. At the end of the course he was promoted to corporal.

Italy, having entered the war as an ally of Germany, invaded Greece in October 1940, only to be driven back far into Albania. Germany, in order to consolidate its control of the Balkans, attacked both Greece and Yugoslavia, and, in less than a month, overran both countries. British forces sent to the assistance of Greece were forced to withdraw but held on to the island of Crete. It was there, in May 1941, that Schmeling's parachute unit got its first taste of real combat. Max got no preferential treatment and was required to take his turn jumping over the defending British emplacements.

The German Ju52 planes zoomed in low over the Greek islands to avoid enemy radar. By the time they reached Crete they were flying at an altitude of only about five hundred feet. This was supposed to minimize the amount of time the parachutists would be left hanging in the air as defenseless targets. Many failed to make it, plunging to their deaths as their chutes were torn to shreds by machine gun fire. Some of the planes that dropped them were also hit, their engines spluttering out before they made deadly descents in trails of black smoke. The German casualty count was heavy.

Schmeling was lucky to land in the middle of a vineyard, which gave him cover, but it prevented him from using the rolling technique he had so often practiced in training. As a result, he crushed muscles in his knee and aggravated the back problem that had stayed with him since the Louis fight. Barely able to move, he managed to crawl some five hundred feet to his supply container, a white barrel with red stripes. Spotted by the enemy, he was under heavy fire as he inched forward before falling unconscious from pain and fatigue. It was the following night by the time he found his unit and he was taken to a field hospital.

There was to be no rest. Hobbling about on a couple of canes, he was given the duty of escorting a wounded English prisoner to the nearby town of Khania. To his surprise, as they linked arms to give each other support, the captive soldier recognized him. When they sat down to rest, Max gave the prisoner a cigarette and got to share an orange in return. The Englishman said he was an avid boxing fan and a friend of Tommy Farr. When the pair eventually reached their destination, after spending time flattening themselves on the ground to avoid flying debris from high-caliber British shells, the Englishman was taken to a makeshift prison stockade. Before parting with his escort, he said that when he met Tommy Farr again he would have quite a story to tell. They shook hands and wished each other good luck.

The world outside Germany got a more sensational account of what had happened to Schmeling in the island invasion. MAX SCHMELING KILLED IN CRETE ran the stark headline in the *Times* of London on May 30. Quoting New Zealand sources in Alexandria, the paper said the boxer had been slightly wounded during the fighting and was being treated by German field ambulance men when British troops appeared and made prisoners of the group. Schmeling, who was "truculent," declared his identity and was handed over to an escort to be taken to a prison camp. Along the way, more German paratroopers dropped down, and in the confusion, according to the report, Schmeling picked up a rifle and tried to escape. Before he had time to do anything, he was shot and killed. The *Times* of the following day printed a German wireless service denial of the story, adding that Schmeling had been taken ill but was progressing favorably. When American reporters informed Louis of the turnabout in the story, his response was succinct: "Smellin' said some bad things about me and my people, but I'm glad he's not dead."

Goebbels used the opportunity to highlight the "lies" one could expect from enemy newspapers. He presented Schmeling before a press conference to give a correct interpretation of the events. As the United States was not yet at war with Germany, American papers were still represented by correspondents throughout occupied Europe. The propaganda minister's plan backfired badly.

Schmeling, speaking from his field hospital bed, disclosed that he was suffering from dysentery, probably brought on by drinking chocolate left behind by the British that had turned sour. When asked about alleged British breaches of international war conventions, he said he knew of no instances of cruelty toward prisoners and described the British as good fighters. "Some of my comrades who were captured said they were treated well," he explained. As nearby German officers showed their discomfort, Max concluded that he hoped for an early end to the war so he could once again meet his many American friends.

While Schmeling's widely reported views were positively received in Britain and America, they raised a storm in Berlin. A furious Goebbels tried to have him brought before the National Socialist People's Court, but as Max was a serving member of the *Wehrmacht*, only a military court had jurisdiction to hear the case.

Upon his recovery, Schmeling was sent to Berlin to face trial before a military court. After interrogating him at length, the judges found that there was no case to answer. His declaration that he favored American neutrality did not amount to criminal action, they ruled, and other members of his parachute company had confirmed they had seen no examples of British atrocities. Goebbels found another way to punish the former pride of the Third Reich. He ordered that Schmeling's name never again be published in a German newspaper.

Louis did his patriotic duty and registered for army service in June 1940, just before the second Godoy fight. The move panicked Mike Jacobs into organizing the monthly series of title defenses before he lost his main meal ticket.

"Al McCoy, the top heavyweight in New England, was the first to be handed a blindfold and a cigarette," as Richard Bak, author of *Joe Louis: The Great Black Hope*, wittily described Joe's title defense the week before Christmas. A badly gashed eye prevented McCoy from answering the bell for round six. On the last day of January, Red Burman bit the dust in the fifth. Gus Dorazio got no farther than the second round in mid-February.

On March 21, big Abe Simon made Louis work a lot harder for his $19,400 purse. Simon, an amiable giant who outweighed the champion by fifty-two pounds, was floored in the first round. As he lay on his back, ringsiders were surprised to see him grinning widely before climbing to his feet. Asked afterward about his strange behavior, he replied, "It was the first time I'd ever been knocked down cleanly, and the thought struck me, 'Abe, what a funny looking sight a big hulk like you must be to those people sitting out there.' " He made another couple of trips to the canvas before Louis finished off his incredibly game opponent in the thirteenth round.

Joe got the smallest pay package of his championship career ($17,468) for knocking out Tony Musto in the ninth round in April. He more than doubled that the following month in an incident-packed match with Buddy Baer, younger brother of Max, at Griffith Stadium in Washington, D.C. Buddy, at 6 feet 6½ the tallest man Louis ever met in the ring, had fought on the same bill the night the Brown Bomber destroyed his brother. He, too, lost on that occasion, but he had built up an impressive knockout record and ruined the American campaign of flamboyant Irishman Jack Doyle by stiffening him in the first round. His short-route victims also included three Louis opponents, Abe Simon, Nathan Mann, and Tony Galento.

The fight got off to a sensational start when Baer, after several exchanges, landed a three-punch combination to send the off-balance Louis plunging backward through the ropes. The champion landed on his elbows and shoulders on the ring apron. Unlike the occasion in 1923 when helpful reporters pushed Jack Dempsey back into the ring against Luis Firpo, Louis needed no illegal assistance in recovering from his embarrassment. Back in the ring at the count of four, he traded punches with the fired-up challenger and then took complete control in the second round, when Baer absorbed considerable punishment.

Buddy, showing tremendous spirit, had a good third round and left Louis with a swelling by his left eye. Two rounds later, a trickle of blood appeared underneath his right eye. No one was used to seeing Joe so marked up. After conceding the fifth to Baer, Louis upped his tempo in the sixth, pounding the Denver-born giant with accurate punches until dropping him with a cannonball right to the head. As Baer rose at seven, Louis let fly with both fists and the challenger collapsed again. What followed was the subject of major controversy.

As referee Arthur Donovan's count reached nine, a bemused Baer somehow struggled to his feet. The bell rang at that instant, but neither fighter nor the referee heard it in the tumult. Louis loaded up a right and sent his opponent down for the third time in the round. Baer looked like he was out cold. His seconds, Ray Arcel and Izzy Klein, jumped into the ring and hauled him to his corner. When the bell rang for the seventh round, Baer's manager, Ancil Hoffman, stood in front of his fighter and refused to move. He demanded that the referee disqualify Louis for hitting after the bell. Donovan refused and warned Hoffman that he had no right to be in the ring as the fight was still on. When Hoffman stood his ground, Donovan declared that Baer was disqualified for failing to answer the bell for round seven. While Louis had not fouled his opponent deliberately, it was an unsatisfactory way to win what had been an unexpectedly tough title defense. Buddy would get another chance nine months later.

Clearly, Baer was no bum, and neither was Louis's next challenger, Billy Conn. The talented Irish-American from Pittsburgh had been chasing a fight with Joe for quite a while, but was considered too small. While Conn had been world champion at light-heavyweight from 1939 to 1940, he was cocky enough to think he could take on and beat the best of the big men, including Louis. He did, in fact, gather some impressive heavyweight scalps, including those of Louis foes Bob Pastor and Al McCoy.

Mike Jacobs was all for pairing the Pittsburgh Kid with Louis. He knew Conn, with his fresh, dimple-cheeked good looks and his outgoing personality, would attract huge popular support. Louis's fight-a-month campaign had not been the financial success the promoter or fighter had hoped for, so Conn looked like the obvious lucrative candidate for Joe's eighteenth title defense. Contracts were signed for the fight to take place at the Polo Grounds in New York on June 18.

So much had been written about Louis that there was little new to say about him. It was Conn who filled most of the newspaper column inches, especially when he provided a couple of stories that were guaranteed to tug at readers' heartstrings. First, he revealed that he was in a fix with regard to his sweetheart, Mary Louise Smith. Her domineering father, "Greenfield Jimmy" Smith, a former major-league baseball player turned bar owner, hadn't taken kindly to her relationship with a prizefighter. He sent her off to a convent college, so that the nuns could keep a close eye on her. Love, as always, found a way, and the young couple ran off with the intention of getting married. Greenfield Jimmy found out and got the Catholic bishop to issue a ban on any priest in Pennsylvania conducting the wedding ceremony.

While all this was going on, Conn's mother, Maggie, an Irish immigrant who had toiled hard for her family, was dying of cancer. Billy had used much of his recent ring earnings to pay for her treatment. After being foiled in his attempts to marry Mary Louise, he visited his mother in the hospital. He wanted to give her a diamond bracelet, but Maggie, knowing the end was near, told her son that he should give it to his sweetheart. Furthermore, he should ignore Greenfield Jimmy and marry the girl he loved.

As he kissed his mother and got up to leave, Conn said, "I gotta go now, but the next time you see me I'll be heavyweight champion of the world."

"No, son," she said, "the next time I see you will be in Heaven."

Louis was aware of the public sentiment for Conn but was more concerned with the challenger's speed and how the physical differences between them would be perceived. He wondered if he, with something like a thirty-pound weight advantage, would be seen as a bully beating up a smaller man. The issue troubled him to the extent that, against his trainer's advice, he made himself come in below two hundred pounds. Usually he gradually scaled down his training, but this time he worked hard on the road and in the gym right up to the day before the fight. He also ate and drank sparingly so that, at the weigh-in on the morning of the bout, he tipped the scales at 199½, the lightest he had weighed in a year. Conn weighed in at 174, just under the light-heavyweight limit.

Ring legend informs us that Louis, when asked how he was going to deal with the fleet-footed challenger, replied, "He can run, but he can't hide." Writer Shirley Povich insisted that Joe had already made that remark before his second fight with Bob Pastor. If so, why did it take more than a year to be regarded as a good quote?

Close to 55,000 people passed through the turnstiles to see the fight. They included thousands of Pittsburgh Irishmen who had chartered a train, known as the Ham and Cabbage Special, to New York. Back in Conn's hometown, the Pittsburgh Pirates interrupted their evening game at Forbes Field to let fans listen to the radio broadcast over the public address system. They, and the millions more gathered around their radios across the world, were treated to one of the most exciting fights in heavyweight history.

Conn, with a tremendous display of skill, aggression, and courage, came closer than any man previously to knocking the Brown Bomber off his championship perch. Only Conn's cockiness in electing to go all-out for a knockout, when he could have settled for a clear points win, prevented him from scoring a mighty upset.

Conn, the 4–1 underdog, started cautiously and conceded the first few rounds as Louis methodically stalked him, looking for the openings for his heavy artillery. Then Conn picked up the pace and began to score with fast shots as he flitted around the ring, keeping well out of reach of his bigger, slower opponent. The champion looked tired and unable to fathom Billy's elusive style. In a clinch, Conn said, "You've got a fight on your hands tonight, Joe."

"I know it," Louis admitted.

Conn, his confidence growing, daringly attacked in the fifth round but was staggered by a left hook to the jaw. Immediately, Louis went for the kill, drilling lefts and rights to the head and sending his rival lurching backward. By the end of the round, Conn had picked up a cut over his right eye and another on the bridge of his nose. Yet he had survived the storm without going down.

The Pittsburgh Kid kept out of harm's way for the next couple of rounds but realized he would have to go for it if he wanted to be heavyweight champion of the world. He launched a thrilling attack in the eighth round, making Louis's jaw the target for right-hand smashes that landed straight and often. The blows lacked steam and merely served to fluster the titleholder. More important, however, the success of his offensive boosted Conn's confidence even more.

Repeatedly in the ninth, Conn connected with full-blooded rights to the head and body. His stinging left jabs brought blood from the champion's nose. A left hook to the body clearly hurt Louis just before the bell. Joe returned to his corner looking puzzled. He had expected problems countering Billy's speed, but he hadn't banked on him being so aggressive.

Infuriated, Louis mounted an attack in the tenth and Conn, in his haste to get away, slipped on the wet canvas in his corner. Joe, faced with a wide-open target, refused to take advantage and allowed Billy to regain his composure. The act of good sportsmanship was much commented upon afterward as further evidence that Louis was a clean fighter.

The momentary slip did nothing to affect Conn's surging belief that the heavyweight title was his for the taking. He rained home combinations in the eleventh round, forcing the nonplussed champion to cover up before the onslaught. In the twelfth, after an exchange in which Conn suffered a cut under his left eye, he suddenly rocked the champion on his heels with a full-strength left hook to the jaw. Louis dove into a clinch to avoid going down, while Conn went all out for a knockout. The crowd was in an uproar.

It was now clear to all that Conn had the fight won. All he had to do for the last three rounds was to keep dancing and sniping away, and he would be world heavyweight champion for sure. But Billy wanted to do it in style. He wanted to win by a knockout. He had taken the best Louis had to offer and had repaid him with interest. He had the great Joe Louis hanging on for dear life. This was going to be easy.

Coming up to the bell for the thirteenth round, manager Johnny Ray urged Billy to be cautious. He knew how dangerous Louis was up to the last seconds. "Just stick and run, stick and run," Ray pleaded, "don't take chances." In Louis's corner, Blackburn was telling the weary champion, "You're losing on points. You've got to knock him out."

The Polo Grounds resounded to the cheers from 55,000 fans as Conn stood his ground and mixed it with one of the most deadly punchers of all time. The desperate champion slammed home power-ful lefts and rights. Though hurt, Conn lashed out with a furious burst of punches that stopped Louis in his tracks. Suddenly, in the last minute of the round, Louis connected with a right flush on Conn's jaw. The challenger's knees buckled. He swayed backward. He was hurt, and

Louis knew it. Once again, Louis showed what a deadly finisher he was as he closed in for the kill. He rained lefts and rights on his helpless victim as Conn tried desperately to cover up. Louis switched to the body, ripping in vicious blows that sapped the speed from Billy's legs and took away his last ounce of endurance.

The final combination of a left to the body, a right uppercut, a left hook, and a right cross caused Conn to pitch over onto his right side, his curly head bouncing off the canvas. Somehow, he managed to get himself up on one knee, and then stand up, but it was too late. Referee Eddie Joseph had counted to ten and waved the rubbery-legged fighter out. There were only two seconds left in the round.

A relieved Louis said in his dressing room, "I knew I had to knock him out to win. I was waiting for him to lose his head. He's a real smart fighter, and you got to admit he's faster than I am."

Sportswriters blamed Conn for letting his Irish blood fire him up, so that he foolishly went for a knockout instead of settling for a points decision. Billy's manager agreed, telling Conn, "If you had a Jewish head instead of an Irish one, you'd be heavyweight champion now."

Sometime later, when Conn discussed the fight with Louis, he said, "Gee, what a tough break I got. I had your ass beat. I could have won the title, been the champion for six months, then I'd let you win it back."

"How was you gonna keep the title for six months," Joe retorted, "when you couldn't keep it for twelve rounds?"

At least Conn was comfortable with the knowledge that his good showing guaranteed him a return match. Mike Jacobs, delighted with the $450,000 takings from the fight, knew that a second Louis–Conn encounter would do even better. But it was becoming increasingly probable that major sports events would have to take a backseat for a while. While Louis was preparing for another title defense in September, German troops were pushing to within 220 miles of Moscow. Nazi U-boats torpedoed American-owned freighters with cargoes of war materials destined for Britain. Aviation ace Charles A. Lindbergh was among the pacifists urging his country to stay out of global conflict. He told a rally of America First, "The three most important groups who have been pressing the U.S. toward war are the British, Jewish, and Roosevelt Administration."

The United States held its first peacetime military draft, and among those classified 1-A was Joseph Louis Barrow. As sole supporter of his family, which included his mother and several close relatives, he might have sought a deferment, but he raised no objection to his classification.

His last ring opponent in 1941 was Lou Nova, a tough Californian who had established himself as number-one contender by twice knocking out Max Baer. Nova claimed an extra dimension to his fighting ability—a mysterious "cosmic punch." A keen student of Far Eastern metaphysics, which included yoga, Nova intended to use that knowledge to overcome Louis's more basic skills. A good old-fashioned left hook to the jaw in the sixth round made nonsense of the challenger's theory.

16

WE'RE ON GOD'S SIDE!

Most Americans were enjoying a normal relaxing Sunday when the shocking news broke on December 7, 1941, of a Japanese bomb attack on Pearl Harbor. Early that morning, Japanese planes operating from aircraft carriers swooped over the naval base at Oahu, the main island of the Hawaiian group. They dropped their deadly cargoes, killing 2,403 servicemen and destroying warships, naval and military aircraft, and installations.

Americans expressed outrage that the offensive had occurred while Japanese diplomats were talking peace in Washington. The sneak raid was likened to a boxing sucker punch, delivered while the victim had his guard down. After the war, an inquiry held the local commanders responsible for the fact that the base, despite warnings, was totally unprepared for the attack.

Four days after Japan declared war on the United States and Britain, the German-Italian alliance announced that it was also at war with America. The conflict in Europe, and the Sino-Japanese War that had been fought since 1937, had escalated into the Second World War.

Like many celebrities from the worlds of sports and entertainment, Louis was quick to commit himself to the cause. Commenting on the Pearl Harbor raid, he drew a boxing analogy: "I was mad, I was furious, you name it. Hell, this is my country. Don't come around sneaking up and attacking it. If a fighter had done that to me, I would have smashed him. I'm strictly for fair deals and open fighting."

While preparing to undertake his patriotic duty, Joe was given a sharp reminder of the perilous state of his finances. On top of the results of his extravagant spending habit, he owed $81,000 in taxes. Not wanting to be bothered with matters he didn't understand, he told his accountant, Ted Jones, to pay the bill. But Jones advised him to hold out, let the taxes build up some more, and then he could probably do a deal with the Internal Revenue Service for less than the total amount due. Louis thought the suggestion made good sense.

Though relieved that he could shelve his tax worries, Joe had gotten himself into even deeper debt by borrowing from Mike Jacobs against future ring earnings. He pestered Uncle Mike for money so often that he felt almost ashamed to ask for more. On one occasion, when the cash-strapped fighter accompanied the promoter to the airport, he was trying to pick the appropriate moment to ask for another large loan. When Jacobs was called to board his flight, Joe offered to carry his topcoat to the departure gate. Just before they parted, Louis plucked up the courage to ask for the money. "For $10,000," Jacobs joked as he made out a check, "I could've carried my own coat."

With Louis's immediate future uncertain and the prospect of boxing being forced into limbo for the duration of the war, however long that might be, Jacobs came up with a bright idea. He asked Joe if he would agree to take part in a charity boxing match, with all of his purse going to the Navy Relief Society, an organization that helped families of sailors killed in combat. Without hesitation, Joe said yes. To make sure the fighter knew what he was letting himself in for, Jacobs emphasized that he wouldn't get a cent for putting his title on the line. "That's fine with me," Louis told him.

The public applauded the fighter's generosity, which even won over those who regarded all fighters as nothing more than heartless brutes. The press lined up to pass out the plaudits. Jimmy Powers, writing in the *New York Daily News,* said that for a champion to risk a personal asset worth one million dollars for no return was truly a magnificent gesture. Powers pointed to the comparison with Jack Dempsey, who had dodged the draft in the First World War and caused further outrage by posing as a shipyard worker for a publicity photograph. This showed the former heavyweight champion wielding a sledgehammer while wearing striped trousers and shiny patent-leather shoes. In the Second World War, Dempsey was a lieutenant commander in the Coast Guard.

Louis said all the right things. "I ain't fighting for nothing," he told one reporter, "I'm fighting for my country."

Some black Americans expressed misgivings about Joe's choice of charities. The *Pittsburgh Courier,* a black newspaper, urged him to use his position to make a statement about discrimination in the navy. He refused, believing that his agreement to fight for Navy Relief was in itself enough to embarrass the top brass and bring the issue to public attention.

Madison Square Garden was bedecked in red, white, and blue bunting on the night of the fight, January 9, 1942. The challenger was once again Buddy Baer, who had knocked Louis out of the ring and given him so much trouble eight months earlier. Jack Blackburn, who was battling arthritis, rheumatism, and a weak heart, told Joe he didn't think he would be able to make it up and down the ring steps for round after round. "Don't worry," Louis told him, "I guarantee you won't have to climb those steps more than once."

With war fever in the air, the occasion was used to present a long drawn-out program of introductions and speeches. Wendell Willkie, the Republican presidential candidate in 1940 whom Louis had supported because he felt FDR had not fulfilled his promises to American blacks, took the microphone to address the 16,689 in attendance and the millions of radio listeners. "Joe Lou-ie," he began, with the common mispronunciation of the champion's name, "your magnificent example in risking for nothing your championship belt, won literally with toil and sweat and tears, prompts me to say, 'We thank you.' And in view of your attitude, it is impossible for me to see how any American can think of discrimination in terms of race, creed, or color."

Louis proceeded to make good his promise to his ailing trainer. He tore into his towering challenger with both fists flying, knocking him to the floor three times. The last time, Baer used the ropes to haul himself aloft, but too late to beat the count of ten. The fight had lasted just two minutes fifty-six seconds.

Joe, after deducting training expenses from his $65,200 purse, handed over $47,500 to Navy Relief. Baer donated $4,078, a portion of his earnings, while Mike Jacobs reportedly contributed $37,229. The promoter's generosity was not all it seemed, according to Truman Gibson, a close friend of Louis and a high-ranking War Department aide. He said Jacobs failed to disclose that he had held on to his share of the revenues from radio and film rights.

Baer realized he had no future in boxing and hung up his gloves after his swift demolition. He later confessed, "The only way I could have beaten Louis that night was with a baseball bat." Buddy went on to a successful movie career, appearing in such diverse productions as the biblical epic *Quo Vadis?* and the somewhat less memorable *Snow White and the Three Stooges.*

The day after the fight with Baer, Louis enlisted in the army. Useful publicity was generated by the champion taking his physical while photographers' flashbulbs popped and reporters fired questions at the new recruit. It was the same the next day, when Joe, driven up in a chauffeured limousine, reported for duty at Camp Upton on Long Island. In what looked like a prepared scene, the clerk typing out the form asked Louis for his occupation. "Fighting," Joe replied, "and let's at them Japs!"

Louis was assigned to Company C, an all-black unit, for basic military training. Segregation was very much a reality in the U.S. armed forces throughout the Second World War. Most black servicemen worked in supply or construction units, where they were mainly under the command of white officers. High-profile figures like Louis could expect special treatment and were granted passes to attend fund-raising dinners and recruitment rallies.

Unlike Max Schmeling, forced to take an active part in the war by the vindictive Nazi hierarchy, Louis was able to perform his military service helping boost troop morale through personal appearances and exhibition bouts with servicemen. Usually, these sparring sessions were harmless enough, but occasionally Joe forgot himself, or wanted to teach an overeager opponent a lesson, and delivered a knockout punch.

Having fought for free to benefit Navy Relief, Louis was pressured to do the same for the Army Relief Fund. He agreed to put his title at stake against another former opponent, Abe Simon, at Madison Square Garden on March 27. Transferred to Fort Dix, in New Jersey, Louis undertook token military duty while spending most of his time training under Mannie Seamon in a specially constructed gym. Jack Blackburn was now too ill to play his part and was in and out of hospitals and convalescent homes.

The Boxing Writers Association of America awarded Louis its highest honor, the Edward J. Neil Memorial Plaque. The award was made annually by the association and was named after the Associated Press reporter and war correspondent who died in 1938 covering the Spanish Civil War. Former New York mayor Jimmy Walker, making the presentation at a swanky dinner, told the champion:

> Joe, all the Negroes in the world are proud of you because you have given them reason to be proud. You never forgot your own people. When you fought Buddy Baer and gave your purse to the Navy Relief Society, you took your title and your future and bet it all on patriotism and love of country. Joe Louis, that night you laid a rose on the grave of Abraham Lincoln.

Joe, in his reply, spoke from the heart, as always:

> You don't know how good you make me feel. The way I feel is good. I'd never have thought I'd feel so good as when I won the heavyweight championship of the world, but tonight tops them all. I feel better than I ever felt in my life. Thanks for what you did for me. I want to thank Mike Jacobs for what he did for me. I want to thank the boxing commission for what it did for me. I hope I never did anything in the ring I'll be sorry for in the years to come. I'm a happy man tonight.

If that speech drew sustained applause, it was nothing compared to the reception he got a few weeks later at a dinner given by the Navy Relief Society at Madison Square Garden. Wearing his private's uniform, he nervously stepped up to the dais to say a few words. He finished his short address by saying, "I have only done what any red-blooded American would do. We gonna do our part, and we'll win, because we're on God's side. Thank you."

The line about being "on God's side" might have been intended to come out somewhat differently, but President Roosevelt liked what he heard. He sent Louis a telegram congratulating him on his choice of words. Billy Rowe, a columnist with the *Pittsburgh Courier* and someone who was close to Louis, suggested that Joe had misread a sentence that had been written for him as "We'll win because God is on our side." In his autobiography, Joe said bandleader Lucky Millander gave the script to him. At any rate, "We'll win, because we're on God's side" proved a powerful rallying call for Americans facing the biggest fight of all.

The patriotic fever carried over into the ring at Madison Square Garden, as Louis disrobed to face Simon. Radio broadcasters Don Dunphy and Bill Corum identified him as "Private Joe Louis of the United States Army" and informed listeners that the champion had bought $3,000 worth of tickets to give away to servicemen. Undersecretary of War Robert F. Patterson climbed between the ropes to tell the 15,367 in attendance that Louis was "a truly great champion, a credit to the ring and a credit to the army."

The Brown Bomber didn't show much charity toward his opponent, hammering Simon to defeat in the sixth round. Dunphy signed off his broadcast by telling the nation, "We won't stop punching, just as Louis does, until we win."

After the fight, Joe was given a five-day furlough to go and see Jack Blackburn, who was confined to Chicago's Provident Hospital with pneumonia. On his daily visits, he would talk with his longtime trainer about all the good times they had shared. Just after Louis returned to camp, Blackburn died. Joe returned to Chicago for the funeral, where he was among nearly 10,000 mourners. Louis reflected on how his old team was disintegrating. John Roxborough, his comanager, along with Julian Black since the start of his career, was serving time in prison for running a numbers operation. Black looked set for a similar fate when charged with income tax evasion, but the case against him was dismissed.

Joe's management team wasn't the only thing that was breaking up. So was his marriage. Marva accused her husband of neglect and of hitting her on two occasions. Joe responded that the only time he used his hands near her was to "peel off dough" to feed her extravagant spending habit. He took out a newspaper advertisement declaring that he would no longer be responsible for her debts. Marva was awarded temporary alimony of two hundred dollars a week, pending the outcome of divorce proceedings. On the day the divorce was to become final, Joe was photographed carrying a smiling Marva out of the courtroom. All thoughts of parting were forgotten.

Mike Jacobs, meanwhile, was working on another fight between Louis and Billy Conn. Though the match was announced as being for the Army Relief Fund, it soon became clear that there would not be much left of the charity cake by the time it was handed over. The promoter and both fighters were not prepared to settle for leftover crumbs. Louis, who owed Jacobs nearly $60,000, sought to have the sum written off before his purse was calculated. Conn, in debt to Uncle Mike for $34,500, expected similar treatment. Jacobs demanded control of the first twenty rows of seats, which would net him a tidy sum. Even after all the deductions, there would have been around $750,000 for Army Relief, but Secretary of War Henry L. Stimson had grown tired of the shenanigans. He put a ban on the fight, declaring that it would be unfair to the millions of other servicemen who had no such opportunities to work off their debts while serving their country. Even when Louis and Conn relented and offered to fight for free, Stimson refused to budge. He prohibited all similar projects for Army or Navy Relief, declaring that both agencies were sufficiently funded.

The rather unsavory background to the abortive charity fight did not harm Louis's public image all that much. He was held in such high esteem that people were prepared to show understanding. What the publicity had served to highlight was just how badly the champion had handled his finances. As well as what he owed Jacobs, he had borrowed $41,000 from Roxborough. In early 1942, the Internal Revenue Service assessed him for a tax bill of $117,000 on his previous year's earnings. He didn't have the money to pay anyone.

At least the IRS wasn't pressing him for immediate payment. Servicemen were allowed to freeze outstanding tax bills until they got out of uniform. The day of reckoning was still some way off. Besides, Louis reasoned, he was still world heavyweight champion, and when the war was over, he could get back to what he did best—fighting—and the money would start rolling in again.

What he didn't want to think about was the fact that even great fighters cannot go on forever.

★   ★   ★

Germany's forgotten man, Max Schmeling, was under no illusions that he could pick up his boxing career where he had left it once the war was over. He was already well into the veteran stage for a fighter in 1940 when a plan was drawn up to have him fight Walter Neusel. The Reich Ministry of Sports put a firm jackboot through that proposal by banning Schmeling from boxing. It soon became evident that he had been singled out for biased treatment when Neusel was given clearance to fight someone else. Max saw there was no point in arguing. He relinquished his European title and announced his retirement from the ring.

Still, his status as one of Germany's great sporting icons meant he wasn't completely without influence in important circles. This was proven when the reigning German heavyweight champion, Heinz Lazek, sought his help. Lazek, an Austrian, was in love with a Viennese woman of Jewish descent. Every attempt he had made to get permission to marry was refused. The situation became even more problematic when Lazek's girlfriend had a baby, leaving the couple open to prosecution under the mixed-race laws. The woman was arrested and thrown into prison. Her lover looked likely to follow her.

Schmeling promised to do what he could. He got in touch with Philipp Bouhler, the member of Hitler's staff responsible for dealing with clemency petitions. They had met at the Führer's country home some years earlier. Bouhler, after hearing Max's plea on behalf of the couple, reacted angrily.

"Whenever anyone hears from you, it's always about Jews," he raged. "As if there weren't enough important matters at the moment." After considering the matter further, however, he softened his stance and got the charges dropped.

A little while later, Schmeling was again called upon to help a boxer in trouble. Paul Noack, the German light-heavyweight champion, had sought shelter with his wife under a highway bridge during an air raid. Many other people were there, and, during the crush, the fighter's wife complained that someone had molested her. Noack picked out the presumed perpetrator and beat him up. He was charged with assault.

Schmeling was reluctant to test Bouhler's patience so soon after his last approach, so he went to see another former acquaintance, Count Wolf von Helldorf, the police commissioner for Berlin. He pleaded that Noack had overreacted in defending his wife's honor. Von Helldorf, who later would be hanged as one of the conspirators who attempted to assassinate Hitler in 1944, was able to help Noack, but Max was increasingly being seen as an irritating meddler. An official from the Ministry of the Interior berated him for only using his name to help criminals and Jews. The tone of these remarks was plainly threatening.

The granting of such favors didn't come without a price. Schmeling was requested, and he agreed, to undertake several important missions for the Nazis. In one, he was required to dispel a rumor, broadcast by the BBC, that Primo Carnera, a member of the Italian partisan resistance, had been captured by the Germans and put before a firing squad. The State Department in Berlin thought that if Max could track down Carnera, a photo of them together would serve to highlight the inaccuracies of enemy propaganda. To Schmeling's surprise, he found Primo at his home at Sequals. For some reason, no one had bothered to check if he was there. So eagerly did the giant Italian embrace his visitor that Max thought he would be crushed to death. The two former world heavyweight champions drove to Venice, where they spent the evening discussing boxing, their current lives, and the awful effects of the war.

The success of his trip encouraged the Nazis to send Schmeling back to Italy on a more urgent mission. His assignment was to help patch up a rift between the Third Reich and Pope Pius XII. SS officers had committed a diplomatic gaffe by arriving unannounced at the Vatican and greeting His Holiness with raised right arms and a resounding "Heil Hitler." The Vatican demanded an apology for the lack of respect shown by the officers.

Schmeling was told that, as an apolitical man, he could help restore good relations between the two sides. This was vital before talks commenced on declaring Rome an open city to protect it from war damage. A private audience with the pope was arranged, and Max received a warm welcome. The pontiff, speaking excellent German, talked of his time spent in Berlin and of his interest in sports, and recalled that he had been a keen mountain climber. He said he had followed his guest's boxing career with interest and asked after Max's wife and mother.

Although Schmeling had been advised not to discuss politics, he had to listen to the pope remark on how the war had brought so much tragedy to people all over the world. Two small gifts, rosaries for Max and his wife, were handed over, along with a signed photograph of the pontiff. The donor said he knew the couple were not Catholics, but the items were mementoes of the meeting. As he ended the half-hour audience, the pope said, "My greetings to Berlin. We can do so little. We pray for peace soon."

When Schmeling returned to Berlin to report on his trip, a Foreign Office official asked him if he had heard the pope correctly. Hadn't he said that he was praying for a German victory? Max told him there was no mistake and he repeated the pontiff's message. The Vatican meeting was reported in *Osservatore Romano* and was picked up by newspapers around the world. The German press ignored it.

In April 1943, Schmeling's stint with the *Wehrmacht* ended as unexpectedly as it had begun. He was discharged with the rank of corporal and awarded the Iron Cross, Second Class. Of his three and a half years in uniform, he had spent just two days at the front.

Louis, too, was constantly on call to use his name to help people and causes. The most pressing issue for black people serving in the U.S. armed forces during the Second World War was segregation. President Roosevelt had promised much but delivered little in tackling the ingrained racism. Black troops were trained and housed in separate units. Most were placed in labor or service battalions. Only after losing a court action was the army forced to set up a special air corps training facility for black pilots. And it took a military emergency, in the Battle of the Bulge in December 1944, for black troops to be used in combat in any large numbers. Their limited involvement was distinguished by their courage and sacrifice.

Although Louis was engaged in selling the war to his country's nearly 13 million blacks, the government was not quite sure how best to use him. In June 1942, while plans for a second Conn fight were being discussed, he succeeded in getting himself assigned to Fort Riley, in Kansas, a cavalry post. An accomplished horseman, he said he "couldn't be happier" than he was there. Now as Corporal Joseph Louis Barrow, he was able to use his relationship with Truman Gibson, a black lawyer and civilian aide to Secretary of War Henry L. Stimson, to secure better conditions for black soldiers on the base.

At least once a week, he called Gibson to discuss the various problems facing blacks. On more than one occasion, the talks involved future baseball Hall of Famer Jackie Robinson from UCLA. Robinson and several other blacks had applied for courses at Fort Riley's Officer Candidate School, only to find the doors closed to them. Under official army policy, they should have been eligible for training in integrated facilities, but the camp's white command chose to ignore the ruling. Louis spoke to Gibson about the issue, and within days of his hearing the objectors' case, Robinson and eighteen other blacks were enrolled in the school.

This didn't mean that all the camp's racial problems were suddenly resolved. One day, Gibson received an urgent call from Louis. Robinson had gotten involved in a fight with a white officer. He had heard the officer calling a black soldier "a stupid nigger son of a bitch" and voiced his objection. "Sir, that's a soldier in the U.S. Army," Robinson said. The officer retorted, "Nigger, that goes for you too." Robinson jumped on the agitator and knocked him to the ground. After Gibson's intervention, and the passing of gifts from Louis to the officer, no more was heard of the incident.

Louis and Robinson teamed up to achieve several successes in integration at Fort Riley. They exerted pressure on the base commander to extend the seating area of the canteen sectioned off to blacks, for instance. It might have been a small victory, but it wasn't without significance, considering the times. Robinson, who had a short fuse, got into another fight with a bus driver who told him that "the place for niggers is at the back of the bus." When Jackie hesitated, the driver pulled a gun. Robinson grabbed the weapon and used it to smash the owner in the mouth, breaking several of his teeth. After that incident, the army thought it might be better off without Robinson and gave him an honorable discharge.

It was another Robinson, the future world welterweight and middleweight champion known as Sugar Ray, who seconded Louis in a dangerous situation involving a white military policeman. It happened while the boxers stood waiting for a bus at Camp Siebert in Alabama. Fed up with the delay, Louis said he was going to call a cab. He went over to a phone booth where the white troops were waiting. The MP, twirling his club, told him, "Soldier, your color belongs in the other bus station."

"What's my color got to do with it?" Louis asked. "I'm wearing a uniform the same as you."

"Down here, you do as you're told," the MP barked as he poked the heavyweight champion in the ribs with his club.

"Don't touch me with that stick," Louis warned.

"I'll do more than touch you," said the MP, drawing back his arm as if to strike him.

Before that could happen, Robinson jumped on the policeman's back and wrestled him to the ground. Some other MPs were about to intervene when one shouted, "Hey, that's Joe Louis."

The two boxers were taken away to face the provost marshal, who bawled them out for disobeying an MP. When the officer refused to consider their side of the story, Louis said, "Let me call Washington." The realization that the heavyweight champion had friends in high places served to smooth things over, but Louis feared the incident, once it was reported in the newspapers, would reflect badly on Robinson and himself. In fact, it had a positive effect. Soon afterward, the army ruled that all military buses should be desegregated.

While serving with the Special Services Branch, Louis was part of a troop of prominent boxers, including Robinson and Bob Montgomery, that toured army bases in the United States, Europe, and Africa. Joe regularly reported to Gibson on what he saw and learned of segregation problems. From England, he called to reveal that, along with other black American soldiers, he had been shepherded into an improvised black section of a movie theater. An investigation resulted in the ban being removed.

Gibson, interviewed by Joe Louis Barrow Jr. for a biography of his father, said,

> I know what Joe did and experienced during the war. He had a great capacity for feeling. He was a deep person and he resented the way Negroes were treated. You have to live through it to know what black soldiers put up with during the war. Every bus driver in the South was deputized and armed. His

sole mission in life was to make Negro soldiers get to the back of the bus. It might be only a slight exaggeration to say that more Negroes were killed by white public bus drivers in the South than were killed by the Nazis.

Louis did a lot of growing up during his army years. With his wife in Chicago and his mother in Detroit, he had to make a lot of his own decisions. They weren't always wise decisions, however, especially where money was concerned. With no fights to fund his irresponsible spending habits, he found his meager army salary totally inadequate. To continue treating his fellow soldiers to lavish meals and handing out expensive gifts all around him, he had to go on borrowing from Mike Jacobs. By the end of the war, he owed the promoter more than $150,000.

Early in 1943, Louis learned he had extra responsibilities. His wife was expecting a baby. He bought an apartment near Fort Riley with the aim of keeping them together, but Marva was uncomfortable in the Kansas heat and missed her friends and family in Chicago. She returned home to give birth to a daughter. The proud parents named her Jacqueline, in honor of Jack Blackburn.

Even the new arrival could not patch up a rocky marriage. It wasn't helped when Joe spent six months in Hollywood while Irving Berlin's stage hit *This Is the Army* was being turned into a war propaganda movie. His minor role consisted of punching a speedball as background to a musical number and making a short patriotic speech. So he had plenty of spare time between shoots. This gave him the chance to get together with some old flames, as well as form new relationships.

He linked up again with Lena Horne, who was on the Twentieth Century Fox lot filming the all-black musical comedy *Stormy Weather*. She sang the title song, which couldn't have been more appropriate for what was happening in her life just then. In the middle of a divorce, she plunged into a new relationship with Louis. In his memoirs, Joe admitted he thought seriously of divorcing Marva to marry Lena, but the idea made him "feel like a dog." At the same time, another former lover, Lana Turner, was pestering him to visit her on the set of a movie she was making. According to Louis, he resisted the Sweater Girl's approaches. He had enough to handle in Lena and her fiery temperament.

In one of his many tiffs with the singer, who accused him of neglecting her while seeing other women, Joe lost his temper. He hit her and began choking her. Her screams brought her aunt running into the hotel room, threatening to call the police. Louis left the hotel, shaking with emotion. He later confessed, "I got chills because I realized I could have committed murder. I had never known such a feeling. I'm not that kind of person. Passion can mess you up." When he phoned Lena to apologize, she hung up on him. It was the end of their affair.

On March 28, 1945, as General George S. Patton's Third Army surged through Germany and U.S. Marines prepared to attack the heavily fortified Pacific island of Okinawa, Marva was granted a divorce. Joe didn't contest her accusation of desertion.

In Europe, six years of unprecedented death and destruction were mercifully nearing a climax. Mussolini was captured and executed by Italian partisans as he was trying to escape from Como to Switzerland. The Allied forces took control of most of Germany, and Russian troops occupied Berlin. On the last day of April, Hitler, together with Eva Braun, whom he had just married, committed suicide in his Berlin bunker. Seven days later, Germany surrendered unconditionally. On September 2, the Second World War ended officially when Japanese Emperor Hirohito, his nation completely demoralized after atomic bombs were dropped on Hiroshima and Nagasaki, signed surrender documents.

As America rejoiced, Louis, back in civvies after his formal discharge in October, basked in the glow of his impressive army record. He had traveled more than 70,000 miles, boxed ninety-six exhibitions, visited countless hospitals and bases, and had been seen in person by about five million servicemen. Almost the entire nation had seen him featured regularly in newsreels, on recruitment posters, and in propaganda films. Not forgotten either was his generosity in donating his purses from two fights to Army and Navy Relief, nor his uplifting statement about America winning the war "because we're on God's side." He was awarded the Legion of Merit Medal "for exceptionally meritorious service" and won glowing praise in *Life* magazine as "a quiet parable in racial goodwill."

17

THEY NEVER COME BACK!

The war over, Louis and Schmeling took stock of their lives. The outlook looked rosier for the American. He was still heavyweight champion of the world and, at thirty-one, young enough to cash in further on his talents. The matter of his accumulated debts rarely cost him a second thought.

For Schmeling, the future was more uncertain. Like most Germans, he had lost almost all of his possessions, and, at forty, he was too old to consider picking up his boxing career. But what else could he do?

A modest business venture with two old friends got him into deep trouble with the occupying British military authorities. Together with John Jahr and Axel Springer, he set up a publishing company in Hamburg with little more than hope, a couple of rented rooms, a typewriter, and a worn-out Opel P4 that had been hidden under a haystack for years. While awaiting a license to begin publishing, the three directors sat around the telephone waiting for printing orders that never came.

When word got out of Schmeling's involvement with the fledgling company, an English military correspondent thought it would make a good story for the *Daily Express*. She wondered how a former boxer had become involved in the publishing business. Foolishly, Max exaggerated his influence with the British and gave the impression that the granting of a license was a "sure thing." Three days after the interview was published, Schmeling was arrested and imprisoned. A fortnight later, he appeared before a British military court, charged with "making a false statement to a member of the Allied Forces in a matter of official concern."

The prosecution alleged that he told the reporter the firm had been given permission to publish books for the reeducation of German youth. Max claimed he was misquoted and that his association with the company was really just a friendship with Springer, one of the partners. He did hope to get involved in a sporting capacity with young Germans sometime in the future, he added. After a hearing lasting five hours, Schmeling was found not guilty. As he left the building, the relieved reporter threw her arms around him and apologized for causing him so much trouble.

No sooner was he free from those proceedings than he was back up before the military court. This time he wasn't so lucky. He had bought a small house and started building work before getting planning permission. Sentenced to three months in prison and fined 10,000 marks, he served every day of his term.

Still, his troubles were not over. On a visit to a circus, he was spotted by the ringmaster, who turned the spotlight on him and introduced him to the audience. The warm reception he got wasn't echoed by the British, who regarded it as a demonstration of approval for a sporting idol of the Third Reich. Soon afterward, word filtered out that the publishing firm of Springer, Jahr, and Schmeling would never get a license as long as Max was involved. On the same day that he announced his withdrawal, the two remaining partners got their license.

Mike Jacobs lost no time in finding work for Louis. That meant putting his title on the line for the twenty-second time, and it was obvious that his first postwar opponent would be Billy Conn. The memory of their epic battle in 1941 was still relatively fresh in the public mind, and a return would be a sure money-spinner. Because it was too late in the year to stage an open-air bout, the fight was scheduled for June 19, 1946, at Yankee Stadium. Jacobs set ringside seats at $100, an unheard-of price up till then. There was an early rush for the top tickets, but demand then petered out.

If Jacobs was a familiar presence, the rest of Louis's entourage had changed considerably. Jack Blackburn was gone, and Mannie

Seamon had taken over as trainer. John Roxborough and Julian Black, whose original ten-year contract with Joe had expired during the war, were no longer in the picture. Roxborough honorably stood aside because he didn't want to harm Joe's good image by linking him with someone who had done time in prison. Louis dropped Black when he reportedly refused to lend Joe the $25,000 he needed to settle his divorce. Instead of trying to pay off Marva with money he didn't have, Louis agreed to take her on as a comanager along with Marshall Miles. This arrangement meant that she was entitled to a percentage of his purses.

After a cosy four years doing nothing more strenuous than three-round exhibition bouts with servicemen, it was hard for the champion to knuckle down to serious training. Especially torturous was getting up around 5:30 A.M. for five-mile runs, but Joe, always a conscientious trainer, accepted the regimen without protest. By the time of the fight, he was down to 207, just seven pounds more than he weighed for the first bout with Conn.

"Nobody can expect him to be quite the fighter he was when he polished off Schmeling in their second fight," Seamon told reporters, "but I'll go on record that he'll be 90 percent of the best Louis you ever saw. And that will be more than enough."

If the long layoff had softened Louis and blunted his reflexes, Conn was in even worse shape. Almost eight pounds heavier than he was the first time, the Pittsburgh Kid was no longer a kid. He was much slower and clearly lacked the will to engage in another long, hard championship battle. As early as the opening round, hurt by a stinging burst of punches, he grabbed his opponent and whispered, "Take it easy, Joe, we've got fifteen rounds to go." Louis laughed before getting back to business.

A revelation to the spectators was how easily Louis out-jabbed the supposed master craftsman. More than a points-scoring weapon, the stiff left hurt every time it ripped through Conn's guard. Apart from landing a hard right in the second round that stunned the champion, Billy hardly made an aggressive move, being content to keep his distance from his relentless pursuer. The crowd had grown restless long before the Brown Bomber applied the finisher in the eighth round. A hard overhand right set the challenger up for a left-right combination that sent Conn crashing on his back. He struggled up to a sitting position as referee Eddie Joseph finished the count.

Mike Jacobs was disappointed with the crowd turnout of 45,266, way below his prediction of 70,000. Nevertheless, the gate receipts ($1,925,564) were topped only by the second Tunney–Dempsey encounter in 1927. Louis's share, $625,916, was by far the highest earnings of his career, almost doubling what he got for the second Schmeling fight. By the time he paid Jacobs, Roxborough, and the IRS what he owed them, however, he had just $70,000 to take home. And he still owed taxes on what he had just earned.

As well as forming a business partnership with Marva, Louis fell in love with her all over again. He proposed and they got married for the second time a few weeks after the Conn fight. Although she knew it wouldn't be easy, she resolved to do her best to stop him straying from the nest. Joe made promises, too, but soon returned to his old habits.

As soon as the honeymoon was over, Joe was back in training for a September fight with Tami Mauriello, a hard-punching Italian-American but not considered much of a threat to the champion's long reign. The 9–1 underdog almost caused a sensation when he sent Louis staggering into the ropes with an overhand right in the first minute. Mauriello tried to follow up his advantage, but Louis covered up, clinched, and soon regained his bearings. Within a minute, Tami was down from a left hook. He was no sooner on his feet than another left hook left him draped over the middle rope. He was still in that position when referee Arthur Donovan completed the count after two minutes and nine seconds. It was to be the last one-round win of Joe's career.

Louis's $100,000 purse quickly disappeared, as usual, so he went on a couple of exhibition tours in a bid to maintain his extravagant lifestyle. After expenses, most of what he earned went into paying taxes. Marva had wisely kept her money separate and, with her share of the Conn payout, set up a trust fund for their daughter, Jacqueline. Now she was expecting another child. Typically, Joe was out on the golf course when Joseph Louis Barrow Jr. was born on May 24, 1947. With a growing family to provide for, he felt under increasing financial pressure.

Clearly, the only way to make good money was in a championship fight. The heavyweight division was not exactly overflowing with talent, and the choice of veteran "Jersey Joe" Walcott as next challenger didn't cause any great swell of excitement. Walcott was a capable fighter, but he had a patchy record and had retired several times. He believed the fact that his being black stopped him from getting the important fights he deserved. Since teaming up with shrewd manager Felix Bocchicchio, however, he had notched up impressive wins over the likes of Joe Baksi, Jimmy Bivins, Lee Oma, and Joey Maxim to establish himself as a legitimate contender. Still, most experts believed his best days were behind him. Aged thirty-three when he got his first title shot, he was actually four months older than Louis.

On December 5, 1947, the first all-black world heavyweight-title fight since Louis fought John Henry Lewis almost nine years earlier turned out to be much more competitive than anyone expected. Indeed, the 10–1 underdog showed no respect for Louis's reputation and came might close to taking the title.

A crafty fighter with a disconcerting habit of turning and walking away from his opponent, he befuddled the slow-moving champion with his tactics. Before the first round ended, he had dropped Louis with a sneak right. Up quickly, more angry than hurt, Joe went after his tormentor in a bid to repay the indignity. Walcott was too cute to be caught.

In the fourth round, Jersey Joe again nailed Louis with a right and floored him for a seven count. But Walcott probably threw away his best chance by being too cautious. He allowed Louis to regain the initiative. Walcott's biggest achievement was making the champion look like an old man. Louis, the beginnings of a bald patch showing, was too slow to pin down his elusive opponent. Missing were the old combinations that had gunned down so many worthy challengers over the past decade. He could see the openings, but his reflexes had eroded so much that he couldn't capitalize. The Brown Bomber was more like a jaded First World War biplane.

At the end of the fifteen rounds, Walcott looked like the deserving winner. Louis, convinced he had lost and feeling disgusted with his performance, had left the ring by the time Harry Balogh took the microphone to announce, "Judge Frank Forbes scored the fight eight rounds to six, one round even . . . Louis! Referee Ruby Goldstein scored seven rounds to six, two rounds even . . . Walcott!" The cheering was replaced by a chorus of boos and jeers as Balogh got to the deciding vote: "And Judge Marty Monroe scored it nine rounds to six . . . Louis! The winner by split decision and still the heavyweight champion of the world, Joe Louis!"

Goldstein said of his decision to favor Walcott, "Some will agree with me, some won't." Asked to comment on the champion's poor showing, he said, "It appeared to me that Louis was in the same position as any other man who stays away from his trade too long. He wasn't sharp, and he was missing punches he wouldn't have missed had he been boxing more often."

Others took the criticism a step further, suggesting that Louis was in irreversible decline. They noticed that he could still spot the openings and have his fists cocked and ready, but he couldn't let the punches go quickly enough. His reflexes simply didn't measure up anymore.

Over three decades later, Walcott was still convinced he was robbed. "Like thousands of people who saw it, I thought that I won the fight. I thought I won it very big. But out of my respect and admiration for Louis, I never felt bad about not getting the decision. He was such an idol to the world. I think that anyone that dethroned him would be the most hated guy in the world."

Louis wanted to retire but felt he couldn't leave on such a sour note. A return match with Walcott was set for June 23, 1948. First, he undertook a twenty-six-day exhibition tour of Europe. In London, he was scheduled to box three times daily at the Health and Holiday Exhibition. He was promised $80,000, but the organizers hit financial difficulties and he had to settle for half that amount. Moving on to Paris, he was enthusiastically greeted whenever he stepped out of his hotel. After additional exhibition bouts in Brussels, he canceled the Swedish leg of his tour when he learned that the promoter wanted to pay him in ice skates!

What money Joe did get was spent on regular shopping sprees. Marva filled her travel trunk with fashionable Paris clothes and other expensive goodies. She didn't discover that her husband had an extra trunk until customs officers asked him to open it. It was packed mainly with bottles of perfume. She turned to Joe and said sarcastically, "Do you plan to supply all the chorus girls up and down Broadway with perfume?"

The Walcott fight was postponed for two days because of rain in New York. Much of the talk, as fans filed into the Yankee Stadium on June 25, was about how much of the old Louis was left, and whether he still had the ability to keep up his tradition of always doing better in return bouts. Walcott was still feeling bitter about the decision in the first meeting and was determined he would win beyond doubt this time.

Louis's plan was to box the challenger until Walcott tired. Jersey Joe's tactics were to keep his distance and frustrate his opponent, hopefully causing him to leave openings for sharp counters. The result was a lackluster fight with only occasional flashes of excitement. In the third round, in an exchange reminiscent of their first fight, Walcott dropped the champion onto his haunches with a left and right to the jaw. Taunting Louis throughout the bout, he bobbed and weaved, did his trademark "walkabouts," and hit his gloves together before launching little bursts of punches. Louis had his occasional successes, such as when he rattled Walcott with a left hook and a series of jabs in the eighth round. In the tenth round, referee Frank Fullam, conscious of the spectators' boredom, urged, "Hey, one of you guys get the lead out of your ass, and let's have a fight."

Louis was the one who responded best. In the eleventh round, he maneuvered Walcott up against the ropes and landed three successive rights to the jaw. Though hurt, Jersey Joe recovered quickly and, rebounding off the ropes, stung the champion with a left and right to the head. He made the same mistake Billy Conn had made in 1941, thinking he could stand in front of Louis and beat him in a slugging match. Joe was fading, but he wasn't that far gone. Seeing his opportunity, he momentarily became the Brown Bomber of old as he whipped home a flurry of punches. Walcott crumpled to the canvas, and, though he got to his knees by seven, he was unable to beat the count. There were only four seconds left in the round.

After his record-breaking twenty-fifth successful defense of the world heavyweight title, Louis took the microphone to announce, "This was for you, Mom. This was my last fight." Although his decision to retire was genuine, he knew his greatest challenge was finding something to replace the buzz of boxing.

Businessmen eager to use his name made many approaches, and, encouraged by Marva, he agreed to get involved in the setting up of the Joe Louis Insurance Company. It had offices in downtown Chicago, but he lost interest just as the firm was making headway, and failed to turn up at directors' meetings. Eventually the company was sold and the name was changed. The same lack of application had resulted in the winding up of other business ventures, such as the Brown Bomber Bread Company in New York, the Rumboogie cabaret spot in Chicago, a New York public-relations firm, and a soft-drink company making Joe Louis Punch.

While all this entrepreneurial activity was leaving him frustrated and bored, his second marriage was falling apart. Fed up with his insatiable appetite for extramarital affairs, Marva filed for divorce. Joe pleaded for another chance, but in vain. Years later, he admitted that he had "no intention of being faithful—too many pretty girls out there."

Even after the divorce became final in early 1949, Marva tried, for the sake of their two children, to maintain some sort of family relationship. Joe Jr., in his adulthood, recalled how tenuous that link was: "When birthdays came, and no present arrived from my father, she asked friends from other parts of the country to send us a gift signed 'From Dad.' It didn't take much for us to realize that we weren't Dad's top priority."

One of the oldest sayings in boxing is "They never come back." What it really means is that they always come back but never successfully. The number of world champions who hung up their gloves and stayed retired is tiny in the long history of the game. Of the heavyweight kings, only Gene Tunney and Rocky Marciano resisted the temptation to give it another go. At the time of this book's writing, Lennox Lewis was swearing he would be the third to retire as undefeated heavyweight champion, but only time will tell if he meant it.

The reasons so many pull on the gloves again usually fall into two categories—money and boredom. Fighters mainly come from under-privileged backgrounds and are not used to handling big money. Having failed to make wise investments during their peak earning years, they find it hard to maintain their free-spending lifestyles after they quit. All too many, indeed, end up flat broke. Boxing is what they know, so that is what they return to. They convince themselves they can take up where they left off, or at least make enough money to keep them comfortable for the rest of their days.

Finding something to do that adequately replaces the buzz they got from boxing is equally difficult for ex-fighters. In truth, nothing can replace the thrill of combat and having their hand raised at the end of a fight. Many still go to fights as spectators and enjoy being introduced from the ring or having their hands shaken by fans. But watching boxing can be agony for them. They have to smother the urge to get in there and show "those clowns" how it's done. Others stay in the sport as trainers or cornermen, or continue to train to stay fit. Such close proximity to boxers only increases the pull to become part of it all again. "Marvelous Marvin" Hagler, the legendary former world middleweight champion, said the secret of staying retired was to avoid the gym. "Once you get the smell and start punching the bag, you get tempted to get back in the ring," he said. Hagler retired in 1987 and stayed retired.

Far more often than not, ring comebacks end in pathetic failure.

For some time after the war ended, Schmeling didn't know which way to turn. He later confessed that he and Anny lived a hand-to-mouth existence and had to sell most of their possessions to survive. The stark fact was that his boxing career was over, his savings had evaporated, and he didn't have another occupation.

His name still meant something in boxing, however, and when promoter Heinz Schuble inquired whether he might be interested in becoming a referee, he gratefully accepted the offer. Boxing was enjoying something of a revival in Germany, with prewar stars like Walter Neusel and Gustav Eder engaged in comebacks and lots of talent emerging from the amateur ranks. Schmeling's name on a bill, even as a referee, added to the box-office appeal. But the payment he received was meager.

Around this time, Schmeling met up again with Max Machon, who was back working as a manager and trainer. They discussed the boxing resurgence and Machon expressed the opinion that, whenever a country was defeated in war, the people were overcome by sports frenzy. After talking further about the phenomenon, Schmeling startled his former trainer by stating, "Don't call me crazy, but I want to fight again."

Machon laughed at the idea, reminding Schmeling that he was in his forties, hadn't fought for eight years, had undergone several operations, and would be up against young fighters eager to make a name at his expense. Max insisted he had no other choice but to pull on the gloves again. Before they parted, he told Machon he would commence training, see how his legs bore up, and when he had reached his old fighting weight, he would contact him again. When Machon got the call, he put Schmeling through an exhaustive series of tests and was impressed by his condition. Though remaining skeptical about his comeback plans, he agreed to work with him again.

For several months, Schmeling lived a Spartan existence at his Hamburg training camp, working with intense determination, while accepting that he no longer had the gift of youth. Finally, the time came to prove if he still had something to offer, or if he was being a complete fool. His comeback opponent was Werner Vollmer, who boasted he was younger, bigger, and faster than the ex-champion, and would win. Besides, he had once hurt Schmeling in a training spar, he claimed.

Schmeling looked fit when he arrived in Frankfurt for the fight. He voiced quiet confidence, telling reporters that victory would earn him a tilt at the German heavyweight title, held by Hein Ten Hoff. After that? "I will go as far as I can," he said.

The date of the comeback fight was September 28, 1947. It was Max's forty-second birthday. As he ducked between the ropes, the crowd broke into an enthusiastic chorus of "Happy birthday to you."

The open-air bout, which was scheduled for ten rounds, drew a crowd of 40,000, which included many American GIs. Right from the opening bell, Vollmer went on the attack, eager to overwhelm the ring-rusty veteran. He soon realized that, whatever else Schmeling had lost, he still packed power in his punches. A hard right knocked Vollmer off his feet. It was the first of his seven visits to the canvas. Only his courage and endurance kept him going. By the seventh round, Vollmer's right eye was badly swollen, and he was bleeding from the nose and mouth. An accurate right put him out of his agony.

The warm ovation he received reminded Max of earlier, greater victories. The gamble had paid off, and even Machon was amazed at how well he performed. Ringside experts were convinced that, given the chance, he could still be an important player on the European scene. Schmeling resolved not to get carried away on the new wave of adulation. He was happy that his legs had proved strong, his punching power was almost as good as ever, and his fight strategy had paid off. But, in the exchanges with Vollmer, he noticed how his reactions had slowed. Whatever the backslappers might be saying, he knew his glory days were in the past.

Though he followed up the win over Vollmer by beating Hans-Joachim Drägestein on points over ten rounds, he sensed that reality would soon come knocking. And it did. Nonetheless, it was a bit of a shock to drop a points decision to Walter Neusel, who was almost as old as himself. For the winner, there was the added satisfaction of avenging his knockout loss to Schmeling fourteen years earlier.

Max had just two more fights. He repeated his win over Drägestein, this time on a ninth-round knockout, and was beaten on points over ten rounds by Richard Vogt on October 31, 1948. Before the referee gave his decision, Schmeling made up his mind to hang up his gloves for good.

His return to the ring might not have been covered in glory, but it did provide the springboard to better times. With the money he earned from his five fights, he bought a house and forty acres of land in Hollenstedt, near Hamburg. There he bred mink for the fashion industry, raised bees to produce honey, and became Europe's top producer of Virginia tobacco. In his leisure time, he indulged in his favorite pastimes of hunting and bird watching on the lands around his home. As his business enterprises prospered, he and Anny looked forward to spending the rest of their lives in well-earned comfort.

Schmeling's financial status got a massive boost when he linked up with the Coca-Cola Corporation. It was thanks to his friendship with Jim Farley, the one-time president of the New York State Athletic Commission, that the opportunity arose. Farley, who had sympathized with Max at the time of his phantom fight with Jim Braddock in 1937, now headed the American soft-drink company. Coca-Cola was looking for a way to establish a foothold in the German market. Farley came to an agreement with Schmeling, awarding Max the franchise to bottle and distribute the product throughout what was then West Germany.

Schmeling became a very rich man.

18

LIFE AFTER BOXING

If Louis had shown just a fraction of his old rival's business acumen, he might have avoided the financial and personal grief that dogged him in retirement. But Joe never gave a thought to tomorrow. "It didn't make any difference how much money I could have made," he once acknowledged, "I would still have ended up broke."

Despite having told his mother after the second Walcott bout that he wouldn't fight again, Louis still hadn't officially announced his retirement. He looked for some kind of financial arrangement that would provide him with a regular, guaranteed income when he was finished with boxing.

Truman Gibson, his legal adviser, took a proposed deal to the Twentieth Century Sporting Club. Joe would have one last championship fight against one of the leading contenders, but he would demand more than his usual 40 percent of the gate. According to a memo that Sol Strauss, Mike Jacobs' lawyer, helped prepare for the Madison Square Garden board, $100,000 would have to be passed to Louis "under the table," hidden from the grasping fingers of the taxmen. The negotiations fell through when Joe asked what would happen if he lost. He was told he would be put on Twentieth Century's payroll to help with publicity and promoting fights for a salary of $20,000 a year.

"You mean I will have to work?" an incredulous Louis asked. Told this would be the case, he responded, "Then I will work one day a year.

I want to play golf, not work."

Another proposal, the brainchild of Harry Mendel, a New Jersey press agent, seemed much more attractive. It was envisaged that a corporation would be set up to control the destiny of the world heavyweight title once Joe formally retired. The corporation, with Louis as front man, would sign up the four leading contenders: Walcott, Ezzard Charles, Lee Savold, and either Joey Maxim or Gus Lesnevich, who were due to fight soon. The contracts would be sold for cash and a share of future earnings to whoever was interested in promoting the contests.

Jim Norris, a multimillionaire with wide business interests, took a positive view when approached to join the corporation. Together with his partner, Arthur Wirtz, Norris agreed to form the International Boxing Club in partnership with Louis, with Norris taking 80 percent of the stock. Joe reportedly was paid $350,000 for relinquishing his title, although some sources said it was as low as $150,000. He kept the remaining 20 percent of IBC stock and was guaranteed an annual salary of $20,000.

On March 1, 1949, Louis officially announced his retirement in a letter to Abe Greene, commissioner of the National Boxing Association.

The IBC had been set up in direct opposition to the Twentieth Century Sporting Club, and Louis wondered how Mike Jacobs would react to the severing of their longtime partnership. He need not have worried. When they met, Uncle Mike, now a sick man, threw his arms around him and said, "Joe, I ain't got a kick coming. You were always great with me." Jacobs accepted $150,000 to give up his role as promoter at Madison Square Garden.

Controversy dogged the IBC, which had links with underworld figures eager to make inroads into boxing. It would go on to monopolize the sport in America for the best part of a decade. With most of the world champions under its control, deserving challengers wouldn't get a title chance unless they and their managers played ball with the IBC. It took a courageous stand by Cus D'Amato, manager of heavyweight champion Floyd Patterson, to finally break the stranglehold. His adamant refusal to do business with the IBC was largely instrumental in forcing the U.S. government to act. The organization was eventually found to be in violation of antitrust laws and was dissolved.

For the first time in twelve years, there was a new world heavyweight champion when Ezzard Charles outpointed Jersey Joe Walcott over fifteen rounds in Chicago on June 22, 1949. Charles was a clever boxer and hard puncher but lacked the crowd-pleasing appeal of his illustrious predecessor. It didn't help matters that only the National Boxing Association recognized him as titleholder. The New York State Athletic Commission and the British Boxing Board of Control adopted a wait-and-see stance. When, the following summer, only 6,298 people turned up to watch Charles defend against Freddie Beshore in Buffalo, New York, the clamor grew for Louis to come out of retirement.

Joe warmed to the idea. No heavyweight had ever come back to win the world title for a second time, and he believed he could be that record-breaker. Also, the money would help meet the demands of the IRS. The measure of his tax debt in 1950 was more than $500,000. Against the best advice of those closest to him, he announced that he would return to the ring to face Charles.

Charles wasn't eager to fight the man who had been his boyhood idol, but his managers, Jake Mintz and Tom Tannas, convinced him that if he wanted to be recognized as the true heavyweight champion of the world, he would have to beat Louis.

The IBC scheduled the fight for September 27 at Yankee Stadium. It gave Joe just six weeks to reach peak fitness, although he had kept reasonably sharp with a series of exhibition bouts since his retirement. On the night of the fight, he scaled 218, outweighing his opponent by thirty-five pounds.

Charles had started his professional career in 1940 as a middle-weight but was at his best as a light-heavyweight. His outstanding feat was beating the legendary Archie Moore three times, once by knockout. *The Ring* rates him the greatest light-heavyweight of all time. He might have been a more ruthless fighter but for the tragic outcome of one of his fights. In 1948, Sam Baroudi died after being counted out in the tenth round, and Charles seemed to tone down his aggression from then on. Still, he took the scalps of some of the best light-heavies and heavyweights of the period, including Joey Maxim, Joe Baksi, Jimmy Bivins, Charley Burley, Lloyd Marshall, and Gus Lesnevich.

Although Charles was the reigning champion, Louis was obviously the main attraction. This entitled Louis to 35 percent of the gate, leaving Charles with a 20 percent share. Joe was installed as 2–1 favorite to regain his old title. The fight was televised live across the nation, with New York surprisingly not blacked out, and this accounted for a low turnout of 13,562 fans. Most people chose to watch it in the comfort of their homes or in their neighborhood bars.

It was sad viewing for all but fans of Charles, as Louis, looking old and slow, was unable to cope with the champion's speed and skill. Even when Charles stood his ground and traded punches up close, Joe was unable to find his old payoff power. He landed often enough to bruise one of Ezzard's eyes, but he was the one who suffered the most damage. Charles, sniping away with an impressive variety of blows, cut the old warrior over both eyes, bled his nose, and almost knocked him out in the fourteenth round. Louis was so exhausted when he returned to his corner that his seconds had to lift him off his stool for the final stanza.

Tears flowed down Joe's bruised cheeks when the unanimous decision went to Charles. He refused to speak to a radio interviewer and hurried back to his dressing room, a loser for only the second time in his career. He kept reporters waiting for quite a while before he sat down, holding ice bags to his face, to answer their questions. "I enjoyed the fight," he said, none too convincingly, "and I want to thank you all. I done the best I can. I'll never fight again."

Younger people who had watched Louis's sad performance wondered why their elders had made such a fuss about the great Brown Bomber. "Many of them never saw Joe, in the flesh or in the movies, when he was young, quick and lethal," observed Tim Cohane in *Look* magazine. "To that huge TV audience, the dominant visual image of Joe Louis must be a raked, swollen hulk, wearily, if gallantly and proudly, groping for the top ring rope."

The section of the population that felt the hurt most deeply were those American blacks who had seen their great idol reduced to a battered hulk by one of their own race. In the ghettos, where Charles would have expected praise for his historic win, he found himself an antihero. Even in his own Cincinnati neighborhood, some people actually booed him when he returned as undisputed heavyweight champion of the world.

Jimmy Cannon understood the sentiments: "Louis was proof that a Negro could escape the slums. They yearned for him to last forever. It made them ache because he could be defeated. It didn't matter that Charles was black, he had beaten Louis, and they would not forgive him. He had stolen something from their lives."

Two weeks after his statement that he had positively retired, Joe said he would continue his comeback. His disappointing $103,529 gross earnings from the Charles fight would go nowhere near satisfying the IRS demands. And, after deducting expenses, he still owed taxes on his purse from the fight.

Like most fighters who find themselves at the end of the road, Louis was in denial. He found excuses for his defeat. Charles had caught him at a bad time, when he was inadequately prepared. He could work his way back into contention by beating some of the leading contenders. A series of fights would sharpen up his reflexes, help rekindle his former enthusiasm, and allow him to show Charles he hadn't beaten the real Joe Louis. And hadn't he always done better in return fights?

As the first step on his rehabilitation strategy, Joe stepped into a Chicago ring against Cesar Brion. It was two months after the Charles fight. Brion, a tall Argentinian with a decent record against mostly mediocre opposition, was no match even for the faded Brown Bomber. Louis was a clear winner on points over ten rounds but didn't cause any great ripples of excitement.

Joe looked much more impressive the next time out. In his first fight in Detroit since knocking out Abe Simon almost a decade earlier, he gave Freddie Beshore a pasting, forcing the referee to rescue the bloodied ex-sailor in the fourth round. It was a performance of some merit, as Beshore had lasted into the fourteenth round against Ezzard Charles in a title fight some months previously. Louis, who said he had trained harder than at any time since the second Conn fight, was unmarked and barely breathing hard at the finish. Observers said it was his best showing since he knocked out Tami Mauriello in 1946.

Keeping busy, Louis had Omelio Agramonte wobbling on his heels and bleeding, but failed to stop the stubborn Cuban. Sixteen days after scoring a tenth-round technical knockout over Andy Walker, he had a return match with Agramonte. Although he floored his opponent in the second round, the first knockdown he had scored in his comeback, he couldn't finish him off and had to settle for a wide points victory. The result showed how far Louis had slipped. For the first time in his career, he had been unable to halt a fighter who had previously taken him the distance.

His next opponent, Lee Savold, looked capable of giving him some real problems. Although, at thirty-five, he was only two years younger than Louis, Savold was a crafty, experienced veteran with power in his fists. He was recognized by the British Boxing Board of Control as world heavyweight champion after disposing of British champion Bruce Woodcock in four rounds, although the claim wasn't taken seriously elsewhere.

For one night, something of the old Brown Bomber was miraculously restored as he battered Savold to bloody defeat in six rounds. Fans excitedly debated the way he put together those lethal combinations and were convinced that, with this form, he was a certainty to regain the world title. Few suspected that they had witnessed the last knockout victory of Joe's career.

Louis supporters had further grounds for optimism when, the month after he beat Savold, Jersey Joe Walcott took occupation of the world heavyweight championship throne. In his fifth title attempt, Walcott sensationally left-hooked Ezzard Charles to defeat in the seventh round. Louis, with two wins over Jersey Joe, felt justified in thinking that, given the chance, he could make it a hat trick against his old rival.

While waiting his turn, Joe took on Cesar Brion for the second time in nine months. Though a clear winner after ten rounds, he once again failed to halt the Argentinian. Two weeks later, Jimmy Bivins, who had reigned as "interim" world heavyweight champion while Louis was in uniform during the war, also took him the full distance. It was evident that the Savold knockout had been a flash in the pan. He no longer had the ability to pin down opponents whose main ambition was to say that they shared a ring with Joe Louis and were still standing at the final bell.

Around this time, fight followers' attentions began to switch to an exciting twenty-eight-year-old Italian-American from Brockton, Massachusetts, named Rocky Marciano. The Rock, as he was known, was a crude brawler and short for a heavyweight at 5 foot 11, but there was no doubting the power he packed in his stumpy, muscular arms.

Most ring observers agreed that a new crowd-pleasing contender was just what the moribund heavyweight scene needed. It didn't harm Marciano's appeal that he was white.

Jim Norris, fully aware of Marciano's market value, offered Louis $300,000 to fight Rocky at Madison Square Garden on October 26, 1951. For Joe, who had been averaging $15,000 for his new edition of the Bum of the Month campaign, it was too good an offer to refuse. His handlers were apprehensive, however, and advised him not to take the fight. Louis told them they had nothing to worry about.

"I didn't figure on any problems with Marciano," he said years later. "He was strong, sure, but he fought like a street brawler. Figured I could outbox him any time, and I needed the money too much to turn him down."

As a fourteen-year-old boy, Marciano had sat with his pal Izzy Gold beside a radio, listening in rapture to the commentator describing Louis's annihilation of Schmeling. "We had about fifty cents in our pockets," remembered Gold, "and we were thinking about all that money that Louis made. We never dreamed that some day Rocky would be fighting Louis in Madison Square Garden. We had wild imaginations in those days, but not that wild."

Going into the fight, Marciano had an unblemished record of thirty-seven straight wins, thirty-two by knockout. Still, the bookmakers installed Louis as a marginal 6–5 favorite. The 17,241 spectators were solidly on the side of the former champion, cheering loudly as he rammed stinging jabs into his rival's face. Marciano, on the attack from the outset, missed as often as he landed, with ponderous swings. When his blows did land on target, however, they clearly hurt.

As the bell rang for round eight, there was little anticipation that what had been a dull contest was about to change dramatically. Marciano, slightly ahead on all three official scorecards due to his constant pressure, weaved inside Louis's guard and bustled him to the ropes with a barrage of punches to the head and body. A solid left hook to the jaw sent Joe sagging to the floor. Almost immediately, he got himself up on one knee, where he waited until the count reached eight before rising.

Rocky, going straight for the kill, missed with a fast flurry, then composed himself and leveled his punches at Louis's jaw. Two lefts landed with authoritative impact, forcing Louis back to the ropes. He stood there with his eyes glazed and his arms dangling at his sides. Marciano couldn't miss the wide-open target. A tremendous right to the jaw sent Louis tumbling backward through the ropes onto the ring apron. Referee Ruby Goldstein, saving the old warrior the indignity of being counted out, spread his arms to indicate the fight was over.

Over, too, was Joe's fighting career. It was only his third defeat in sixty-seven contests spread over seventeen years, and the first time he had failed to last the distance since Schmeling knocked him out in 1936. After the fight, he was full of praise for his conqueror: "He hits harder than Schmeling. The better man won. It was a beautiful left hook that started it. This kid is tough enough to beat anyone."

Marciano said he was happy to have won but felt sorry for his victim. The victory sprung him into the top-contender spot. His unshakeable fighting spirit and bludgeoning punches enabled him to come from behind to knock out Walcott in the thirteenth round and become world champion in September 1952. After six defenses, he retired with a record of forty-nine wins in forty-nine fights, all but six by knockout. He remains the only undisputed world champion in history with a perfect record.

During the Labor Day weekend in 1969, when Louis was in Charlotte, North Carolina, to referee a wrestling match, he was told that Marciano had been killed in an airplane crash near Des Moines, Iowa. A few days later, he was among the mourners at the funeral of the man who had brought down the shutters on his boxing career eighteen years earlier.

In the immediate aftermath of the Marciano fight, Louis was at a loss as to what to do next. Like all retired fighters, he missed the cheers of a packed arena and the thrill of having his hand raised one more time. At the same time, he was happy at the prospect of not having to go running at the crack of dawn, or never again having to take punches to the jaw.

With America now at war in Korea, Joe was asked to do a tour of military installations around the Far East. In one month toward the end of 1951, he sparred a dozen exhibition bouts. They were his last appearances in the ring.

His main income during this period was the $20,000 annual salary he earned from the International Boxing Club, topped up by his takings from the small public relations company he had started with Billy Rowe after the Billy Conn fight in 1946. While Rowe looked after the principal business, Joe's undemanding role was to take clients out to dine. This left him plenty of time to play golf with friends, make personal appearances, and visit his mother in Detroit and his two children in Chicago. Marva allowed Joe, who was obliged to pay $5,000 a year in child support, to see Jackie and Joe Jr. whenever he wished. He looked back on it as a good time, with no worries—except taxes.

A grim reminder of passing time was the deaths, at opposite ends of 1953, of his mother and "Uncle Mike" Jacobs. "If it weren't for Mike, willing to take a chance on a black boxer, I would never have gotten to be champion," admitted Joe. "Mike opened the door so other black fighters could get a better chance. He helped break down a lot of prejudice in the fight game." Lillie Reese Barrow left a small estate to be divided between her family. Joe's share came to $660. The tax people seized it.

Most Americans felt that the IRS was unduly hounding one of the country's greatest sports idols, someone who had done so much to boost national morale during the war. By 1956, his tax debt stood at $1,243,097. According to one estimate, he would have to earn an average of at least $310,000 annually for the next twenty years to clear what he owed, including accumulated interest, and to keep pace with current income taxes.

Still, no one thought he was desperate enough to take up an offer to reappear in the ring—as a professional wrestler. A promoter guaranteed him $100,000 for a series of bouts. Friends begged Joe to turn it down. They felt it was beneath the dignity of a great boxer to get tangled up in the shady grappling business.

Louis swallowed his pride and togged out for his wrestling debut in Washington, D.C., on March 16, 1956. The 41,000 spectators at the Uline Arena didn't know whether to cheer or cry as the balding Brown Bomber, the fat bulging over the waistband of his tights, struggled to escape from the clutches of ex-cowboy Rocky Lee. The referee was Joe's old boxing rival Jersey Joe Walcott, also clearly in need of a buck. After about ten minutes, Louis ended the farce with a forearm smash to his opponent's jaw.

His new career was not to last. As Louis and his regular partner, Lee, were going through the motions in Columbus, Ohio, Rocky momentarily forgot the script. Instead of seizing Louis in a headlock, he slammed him to the floor, breaking two of his ribs and bruising his heart. Joe took time off to recover, but when he tried to return to the ring, he was refused a license. The ban came as a relief to his admirers, who couldn't bear to watch him humiliating himself in these freak shows. When someone likened Louis wrestling to the president of the United States washing dishes, Joe's comeback was "Well, it ain't stealing."

His domestic life seemed to take a turn for the better when he married Rose Morgan, a tall, attractive businesswoman. She ran a chain of hairdressing salons. It wasn't long into the marriage that Rose realized her mistake. Her husband showed no commitment to changing the habits of a lifetime, which meant spending most afternoons on the golf course and hitting the night spots with his friends later on. He went on seeing other women. After lasting less than two years, the marriage was annulled.

Louis's sorry record as a husband didn't discourage Martha Malone Jefferson, a successful lawyer, from falling in love with him. A year older than Joe, Martha was the first black woman to practice law in California. She was married for seven years to Bernard Jefferson, who later became a California Superior Court judge, but she felt the union had exposed her "to books, not life." Louis fulfilled her need for that missing experience. They got married in 1959.

Joe's penchant for disastrous business ventures continued. He joined an old friend, Leonard Reed, in a nightclub comedy act, but he fumbled his lines and the act flopped. His public relations company then got involved in promoting Cuba as a prime tourist destination for black Americans. Once again, Louis's timing was off. The U.S. government was at that point engaged in cutting off diplomatic relations with Cuba's Communist ruler, Fidel Castro. The outcry over the Louis venture forced him to drop the $287,000 account.

At least Joe's tangled tax affairs finally got sorted out to a large extent, thanks to his wife's skill as a negotiator. Martha found a sympathetic ear when she explained his ongoing problems to Dana Latham, commissioner of the IRS. Louis was supposed to be paying the agency

$20,000 a year, plus taxes on his current income. Martha instanced the government seizure of all but $500 of the $40,000 he got for the nightclub act. At that rate, she told Latham, Joe might decide he would do just as well not working at all. The IRS, though never officially writing off his massive debt, agreed to tax him just on his current earnings. In 1961, these amounted to no more than $10,000.

While undoubtedly relieved to be free of his biggest burden, Louis didn't exactly repay Martha's sterling work by resolving to be a faithful husband. He put her patience to the ultimate test when, on his return from a business trip to New York, he confessed that he was the father of a baby whose mother was a drug user. Martha immediately booked a flight to New York to confront the woman, and a few days later, in December 1967, returned home with the child in her arms. She persuaded Joe that they should adopt the boy, who was named after him.

Louis's association with the New York woman had reacquainted him with drugs, which he had first experienced in a Milwaukee hotel room in 1958. On that occasion, according to Joe, he was leaning over the side of the bed when his companion, an actress in pornographic movies, jabbed him in the buttocks with a syringe. When he jumped up in alarm, she told him it was just something to relax him. After that first taste of heroin, he admitted that the woman "had me good." He was saved from a rapid descent to destruction by the intervention of the FBI. Agents told him they had been keeping close tabs on the woman, who was running drugs for the Mafia, and that he was being used as a shield. Joe hightailed it back to Los Angeles and Martha.

In 1966, Louis entered a period of tranquillity when he was invited to join the public relations department of the Thunderbird Hotel in Las Vegas as a casino greeter. His job was to roam the gaming hall, meet and greet clients, and encourage them to try their luck at the tables. Later, he moved on to a similar role at Caesars Palace Casino, run by his friend Ash Resnick. He was given a daily allowance to join customers at the gambling sites. In a city populated by so many show business personalities, it gave him a lift to be instantly recognized everywhere he went. Martha and his young son joined him to live in a suite provided by the hotel.

Although freed from the pressures of trying to keep the IRS

satisfied, Joe never felt he had enough money for his everyday needs. He also felt trapped in his family environment. Having a wife and a small child around all the time didn't fit in with his newfound independence. He drifted back to drugs.

After an operation to remove his gall bladder, Louis got into the habit of sniffing cocaine. It was 1968, and the Olympic Games, taking place in Mexico City, were engulfed in a political storm. Black athletes were planning to boycott the event in protest at racial discrimination in the United States. Reporters badgered Louis for his views. He said he didn't agree with the proposed boycott. "What can you do, have a Black Olympic Games of the world?" he asked. "Who is going to sponsor it? Who is going to come to it? There are times you have to be practical and find another way to fight."

Emerging from a bad session with drugs, Joe collapsed and was admitted to hospital to have his stomach pumped. Martha stuck by him and encouraged him to beat the habit. Around this time, the New York woman who had presented him with a son became pregnant again. Although Louis could prove he wasn't the father, Martha decided they should adopt the boy as a companion to Joe's young son. Wishing for an even larger family, this remarkable woman then gained guardianship of two young girls when their father, a client, died. Joe never grew close to his foster daughters. Candice, one of the girls, recalled that he "never disciplined us or corrected us. Most of the time he was playing golf or he was upstairs in bed." Martha would serve him lunch and dinner in bed. He would come down for breakfast and watch *Captain Kangaroo* on television with Candice's younger sister, Amber.

It was around this time that Martha noticed her husband had begun to act strangely. He had always been particular about his hygiene and clothes, but now he was going days without showering or changing. He hung around the house and rarely took his golf clubs out of the closet. Gradually, he slipped into paranoia, believing Mafia hit men were out to get him. He refused to eat Martha's meals, fearing they were poisoned. He put tape over air conditioning ducts and heaters, convinced that the Mafia was trying to pump poisonous gas into his room. He complained that hotel guests were following him, waiting for a chance to harm him.

Martha consulted with Joe Jr., now a banker in Denver, and he signed commitment papers to have his father admitted to Colorado General Hospital's psychiatric ward. Louis was upset at his son's action, and Joe Jr. feared it would cause an irreconcilable split between them. In time, Louis saw that Joe Jr. had acted in his best interests and they remained close.

When word of his mental illness got into the newspapers, hundreds of letters flooded into his hospital ward. Doctors determined that his condition had nothing to do with boxing. (There could have been a hereditary link. His father, who never boxed, had been confined to a mental institution in Alabama.) After five months of treatment, Louis was well enough to be discharged, on the condition that he returned twice weekly for therapy on an outpatient basis. He obeyed instructions for a while but stopped going when his physician became ill. He never returned to Colorado.

In 1971, Louis was put back on the payroll at Caesars Palace as a full-time greeter at a salary of $50,000 a year. He would make himself available to chat to visitors, sign autographs, and pose for photographs. The house-money allowance he was given to join customers was quickly lost or given away. Many longtime fans were saddened to see the national hero reduced to such a role, but Joe Jr. felt this view of his father was unfair.

He explained:

> Those who criticized him didn't understand him. He was in his element again. He was earning a salary, traveling, and meeting people. He was loved by Caesars Palace and the people who visited there. Those who felt Las Vegas somehow demeaned his stature have got it wrong. They wanted him to retire in some pristine house, but that's not the way he lived his life. He'd always had an exciting, worldly life, and Las Vegas was just an extension of that life. It might not be what you or I would do, but it clearly made him happy. Las Vegas doesn't take away anything that he had accomplished before.

In 1977, Louis developed a heart condition called a dissecting aneurysm. The prognosis was grim: he had several days to a few weeks to live. Frank Sinatra, a friend of Joe's since the 1940s, called Michael

De Bakey, a renowned heart surgeon who had developed a treatment for the disorder. Louis was flown to Houston for the operation, with Sinatra providing the plane and paying all the medical bills. Joe came through the surgery well and spent three months in the hospital. In spite of intensive physical therapy, however, he was confined to a wheelchair from then on.

Sinatra hosted a benefit for Louis at Caesars Palace in 1978, with 1,500 people paying $500 a plate. Among the guests were Los Angeles Mayor Tom Bradley, movie star Cary Grant, Muhammad Ali, and two of Joe's former opponents, Billy Conn and Max Schmeling. Max, who flew over from Germany for the occasion, recalled, "It was the last time I saw Joe. He was brought in by wheelchair. I spoke to him, and he recognized me. He said 'Max,' but he was in very bad condition."

As a result of heart irregularities and severe high blood pressure, Louis suffered a slight stroke. He was fitted with a pacemaker, but his heart was too weak for it to be of major benefit. On April 11, 1981, he was wheeled to ringside at Caesars Palace to watch Larry Holmes defend his World Boxing Council heavyweight title against Trevor Berbick. Though too ill to enjoy the fight, he waved in appreciation of the standing ovation he got from the 4,000 people in attendance. Early the following morning, he collapsed while walking to his bathroom. Within half an hour of being admitted to Desert Springs Hospital, he died from cardiac arrest. He was a month from his sixty-seventh birthday.

The funeral service was held at Caesars Palace, where Reverend Jesse Jackson delivered a touching eulogy, ending with the prompt to the gathered mourners, "Let's hear it for the champ!" The people rose to their feet, clapped their hands, and slowly waved their arms in the air in a final farewell to the great man. Some at the time criticized the placing of his body inside a boxing ring at the hotel's sports pavilion as disrespectful, but his family felt it was what he would have wanted.

Eight days after his death, Louis's body was flown on an air force jet to Washington, D.C., where it lay in state for two days at the Nineteenth Street Baptist Church. On April 21, some eight hundred mourners watched as the body was finally laid to rest in Arlington National Cemetery, normally reserved for heroes of war. President

Ronald Reagan, waiving the regulations, said it was "a fitting place for a man whose instinctive patriotism and extraordinary accomplishments have made him one of the most unforgettable Americans of our time." Joe's last wife, Martha, was buried alongside him on her death in 1991. The gravestone makes no reference to Louis's boxing fame, merely describing him as "Technical Sergeant, U.S. Army."

In complete contrast to his old rival's sad decline after he finished boxing, Schmeling continued to enjoy a happy marriage, financial security, and excellent health. His idyllic lifestyle suffered a severe jolt, however, when his beloved Anny died following a stroke on February 28, 1987. She was eighty-five. They had been married for fifty-four years.

Max buried his sorrow in his many business and leisure activities. A terrific advertisement for a life in which he never smoked or drank, he exercised regularly and kept up with the sports scene. Into his late eighties, he still went jogging and, on wet days, rode an exercise bike placed in front of a television set at the same Hollenstedt house he had lived in since 1949. "I don't need a big villa," he told those who asked.

As head of the board of directors at Coca-Cola in Germany, he called in at the offices three times a week to sign papers and deal with other business, and every month he met with fellow directors of the other companies in which he was involved.

"I am a rich man, so money is not important to me any more," he said. His wealth was used to help those he considered less fortunate than himself. In 1991, he set up the Max Schmeling Foundation, with the proceeds going toward organizations representing children, handicapped people, churches of various denominations, the Red Cross, and old folks' homes. He donated a large sum of money to his birthplace village of Klein-Luckow. The German Boxers' Union got an annual donation. When he heard that one of his former opponents, Mickey Walker, had hit hard times and was in a New York hospital, he sent $500 a month to help pay his medical expenses.

Joe Louis, too, had found out how real a friend his former opponent was in his time of need. Though Schmeling tried his best to keep it quiet, it emerged that he had sent Joe money from time to time to help pay his medical expenses. When Louis died, Max got his friend

Henri Lewin to represent him at the funeral and pass a check for $5,000 to Joe's widow. After their 1954 reunion, Max had never visited the United States without trying to see his former ring rival. When ABC Sports sent Louis to Germany in 1966 to act as co-commentator with Howard Cosell during the television broadcast of the Muhammad Ali v. Karl Mildenberger world heavyweight title fight, Schmeling invited him to his home. "I'll always remember our car ride to our villa," Max told Joe Louis Barrow Jr. "I was driving on the German autobahn. I was going at over 120 kilometers per hour. Joe went lower and lower in his seat. Here was the fearless Joe Louis, afraid of my driving. In America, I later remembered, you have speed limits."

As he grew older, Schmeling's health caused him no great concern, although a bad case of pneumonia in 1994 nearly killed him. While he no longer went hunting, he enjoyed watching the wildlife on the grounds of his forty-acre estate. On this occasion, he sat for some time without a coat and caught a chill. He became very ill, losing more than thirty pounds, but his great resilience enabled him to recover. The illness, however, prevented his attending the laying of the foundation stone for the 7,000-seater Max Schmeling Arena in Berlin. He would also have liked to have been present at the funeral of his old American ring rival, Jack Sharkey, in August that year.

Inevitably, frailty began to take hold as he progressed through his nineties, and he needed the care of two long-serving housekeepers. At times, his pride would get the better of his judgment and he would neglect to use his cane, get dizzy, and fall. But his diabetes appeared to be under control, and successful cataract surgery on both eyes allowed him to continue reading his daily newspapers and sports magazines. Wednesdays were set aside for playing cards with his land tenants. It helped him keep his mind sharp.

"Even though I have no children, I don't feel lonely," he said. "I was very happily married to Anny for fifty-four years. Just months after her death, I got proposals from society ladies wanting to marry me. Unbelievable."

On how he would like to be remembered, he said he hoped it would be as "a good man." He had no fear of death, did not believe in religion, and wished to be buried "next to my dear wife."

On his ninety-ninth birthday in 2004, he spent the day quietly with a few close friends. "I am getting older," he said. "It's not a reason to celebrate." Asked if he still followed boxing, he replied, "When there are big fights, I try to watch them on TV, but I no longer get up at four o'clock in the morning to see a fight."

A few weeks later, the German public television channel ZDF announced its "best German sports stars of the century" at a Berlin ceremony. Schmeling came in sixth, behind motor-racing ace Michael Schumacher, eight times Olympic rowing champion Birgit Fischer, World Cup 1974 soccer captain Franz Beckenbauer, and tennis stars Steffi Graf and Boris Becker. Movie and television actor Joachim Fuchsberger read a letter from the former boxing champion, who expressed his regrets at not being there but said he had promised his doctor he would not travel or take part in any public appearances. When Fuchsberger finished reading the message, the audience gave Schmeling a standing ovation.

This remarkable man, born in the reign of the kaiser and survivor of two world wars and a boxing career that spanned two and a half decades, said he had one remaining ambition. "I want to make one hundred," he announced. Unfortunately, he missed out by seven months. Over Christmas 2004, he caught a bad cold and never recovered. He fell into a coma and died at his home on February 2, 2005. True to his wishes, he was buried next to his wife in a private ceremony attended by a small circle of friends. Despite his admission that he was not a religious man, he had explicitly asked the town pastor, Hans-Joachim Krause, for a Christian burial. His last wish was granted. German chancellor Gerhard Schröder said, "He was a star, but he didn't let fame go to his head."

Even though he didn't quite make his centenary, Schmeling had lived longer than any world champion, at any weight, in boxing history.

19

CONCLUSIONS

JOE, MAX, AND THE ALL-TIME GREATS

Schmeling beat Louis. Louis beat Schmeling. Two fights, one win apiece. Even Steven. Of course, it's not as simple as that. Would any true student of boxing dare to suggest that Max was Joe's equal?

Louis was, without question, one of boxing's all-time greats. Schmeling was a gifted fighter who earned his place, along with his American rival, on the illustrious list of heavyweight champions of the world, but he falls short of being a legend.

The main knock against the German is that he won the title in controversial circumstances. Even he felt so bad about being declared world champion while writhing on the canvas in agony from Jack Sharkey's low blow that he didn't want to accept the honor. No other heavyweight champion, before or since, won the title on a disqualification. Public sympathy swung Schmeling's way when he was cheated of victory, according to most observers, in his return match with Sharkey.

It is his sensational knockout of Louis in their first meeting that is rightly regarded as his greatest triumph. On that memorable occasion, Schmeling reached the peak of his twenty-four-year career. Even if it was somewhat fortuitous that his principal fighting tool was his powerful straight right, and that Louis's greatest weakness was that he left himself exposed to that particular punch, the result was still a triumph for Max's ingenuity and planning. He could never have beaten the "unbeatable" Brown Bomber but for his unshakable belief in his own ability.

That being said, the way Louis wiped him out inside a round in their return match, and scaled such great heights in the ring, left no doubt as to who was the superior fighter.

In any legitimate poll of boxing's all-time greats, Louis is way up there with the best. In 1997, *The Ring* magazine voted him the hardest puncher in history. It attributed his power to his perfectly proportioned build, with powerful back, shoulder, arm, and leg muscles. Also, he was blessed with superb coordination and the ability to put his weight behind every blow.

The Ring article gave an excellent summary of his strengths:

Weapons: Jab, hook, uppercut, cross—you name it, he had it. There was kayo power in every one of the Brown Bomber's punches, but the most important of all was his battering ram of a jab, which was equal in power to an ordinary heavyweight's best right cross. His jab, the lead weapon in Louis's spectacular arsenal, was always used to correctly set up the rest of his powerpunches. His double jab–right cross combination, one of his favorites, was a thing of beauty, as was everything else about this truly remarkable athlete.

Watching Louis on film, one cannot help but marvel at the accuracy of his punching. While many big hitters throw lots of blows, unconcerned that many will miss, and confident that others will land and do damage, Joe picked his punches to perfection. Nothing was wasted. Writer Paul Gallico said, "He could drive his fists through a knothole and never touch the sides."

Critics maintain that he was a slow thinker and a slow mover, and always had trouble with clever, mobile fighters. They also point to the knockdowns he suffered, indicating he couldn't take a punch as well as he delivered one. Another suggestion is that he was robotic, programmed to do what his trainer, Jack Blackburn, told him.

Certainly, he was no dazzling dancing master. But, as Billy Conn learned that he could run but couldn't hide, Louis invariably caught up with faster opponents before the fifteen rounds were up. Weak chin? Against Schmeling, he stood up to terrific punishment from the German for round after round before collapsing in the twelfth. It was another fifteen years before Rocky Marciano knocked him out, in the last fight of Joe's career. Those were the only occasions when he failed to last the distance.

Knockdowns? Yes, he was decked by James J. Braddock, Tony Galento, Buddy Baer, and Jersey Joe Walcott (three times in their two fights), but he was not badly hurt and recovered to win all of those bouts. His strategy was to get close to his opponents so that he could unleash his deadly short punches, and this inevitably put him in the danger zone with good counterpunchers.

If the allegation that he couldn't win without Blackburn guiding him from the corner had any substance, how come Chappie didn't produce a batch of Joe Louis clones? The talent had to be there in the first place. While no one can deny that Blackburn was a master technician who played an important part in perfecting Joe's style, it was the fighter who did the business when the bell rang. He had to react immediately in a crisis situation, not wait until he got back to his corner and ask his trainer what he should do. It was Louis who took or ducked the punches, sized up the opponents, and capitalized on spotting the openings for his explosive fists.

Nat Fleischer, recognized as the foremost authority on boxing for many years, thought Louis was the best finisher and had the best straight right of all the heavyweight champions. *The Ring*'s founder and longtime editor saw them all in action, from James J. Jeffries to Joe Frazier. His top ten, drawn up in 1958, has a decidedly eccentric look about it. Louis was rated No. 6, behind Jack Johnson, Jeffries, Bob Fitzsimmons, Jack Dempsey, and James J. Corbett. His final four places went to Sam Langford, Gene Tunney, Schmeling, and Marciano.

Of course, Fleischer's selection was made before Muhammad Ali came on the scene, but he never grew to share the general adulation of the man who insisted he was "the Greatest." Right up to his death in 1972, the one-time Mr. Boxing stuck by his conviction that Johnson had the all-round ability to beat them all. Fleischer rated Louis on a par with Dempsey as a big puncher but considered him "an exceedingly

slow starter," a strange judgment of someone who scored twenty-eight knockouts inside three rounds.

Nigel Collins, current editor in chief of *The Ring,* rates Louis just behind Ali as the all-time outstanding heavyweight, with Schmeling languishing in the lower reaches of his top twenty. "Both Louis and Ali's fame went beyond the ring and into the cultural fabric of their times," he said. "Imagine how barren the heavyweight landscape would have been without Louis and Ali, and you have a pretty good idea of how significant they were—and still are to those with a sense of history."

In a *Boxing Illustrated* study by Herbert G. Goldman, published in 1989, Ali headed the list of the top one hundred heavyweights of all time. Louis occupied second place, with Schmeling slotted in at No. 15.

Gilbert Odd, who reported on boxing for over sixty years and was a longtime editor of the British weekly *Boxing News,* ranked the heavyweight champions for his 1985 book *Kings of the Ring.* Ali came out tops, for his "superb defense, speedy footwork, punching power, and durability." Louis came second, for his "superb, if methodical, boxing skill." He thought Joe's career was spoiled by having to spend four years in the army and that his record was "built mainly on older men and second-raters." Schmeling, a "resolute fighter and strong right-hand puncher" came tenth on Odd's list. Max's career, too, was hampered by the war, he concluded.

Most contemporary experts are in agreement that Louis emerges as runner-up to Ali on the all-time list. The consensus is that, when both men were in their prime, Shufflin' Joe would never have caught up with the Louisville Ghost. Even if pinned down, Muhammad's granite chin would probably have gotten him through the emergency. His long-range slashing punches would most likely have cut up Louis and readied him for a late-round stoppage. By the time of his so-called second coming, however, a much slower Ali would not have been as clear a favorite. Could he, for instance, have afforded to perform his rope-a-dope trick against such a deadly finisher as Louis?

Archie Moore, a light-heavyweight legend who, at forty-six, was outclassed by a twenty-year-old Ali, or Cassius Clay, as he then was known, gave his opinion to Thomas Hauser on who was the better fighter between Ali and Louis: "I believe in my mind and heart that Ali would have beaten Joe. If they'd fought five times, I believe Ali would

have won four." The only heavyweight who might have beaten Ali, thought Moore, was Jack Johnson, "a hard hitter and a master boxer."

Ernie Terrell, not just beaten but humiliated by Muhammad in a 1967 title fight, told Hauser, "This guy [Ali] has a style all of his own. It's far ahead of any fighter's today. How could Dempsey, Tunney, or any of them keep up? Louis wouldn't have a chance; he was too slow."

One man with a different view on the outcome of the mythical showdown was respected trainer Eddie Futch, a one-time sparring partner of the Brown Bomber. "I'd rank Ali with Joe Louis and Jack Johnson as the three greatest heavyweights of all time," he said. "Maybe I'm prejudiced because I came along with Louis, but I think he would have beaten Ali. People remember how hard Louis punched; what they don't remember is what a good boxer he was. I always thought Joe would have seen the flaws in Ali's style and been able to take advantage of them."

When, in the early 1960s, Ali began enlightening the world about his greatness, he was hurt to discover that his boyhood idol, Louis, was among his main critics. Just as bad, Louis refused to call him by his Muslim name.

Louis told reporters:

Clay has a million dollars' worth of confidence and a dime's worth of courage. He can't punch. He can't hurt you, and I don't think he takes a good punch. He's lucky there are no good fighters around. I'd rate him with Johnny Paychek, Abe Simon, and Buddy Baer . . . I would have whipped him. He doesn't know a thing about fighting on the ropes, which is where he would be with me. I would go in to outpunch him rather than try to outbox him. I'd press him, bang him around, claw him, clobber him with all I got, cut down his speed, belt him around the ribs. I'd punish the body, where the pain comes real bad. Clay would have welts on his body. He would ache. His mouth would shut tight against the pain, and there would be tears burning his eyes.

Ali's response was scathing:

Slow-moving, shuffling Joe Louis beat me? He may hit hard, but that don't mean nothing if you can't find nothing to hit. I'm no flat-footed fighter . . . Joe Louis had a thing called the bum of the month club. The men that Joe fought, if I fought them today in Madison Square Garden, they'd boo them out of the ring. Fat bellies, out of shape, awkward, had no stance, no stamina, no footwork . . . How would Joe Louis have knocked me out? What's he gonna do when I'm jumping and sticking and moving? And don't say I can only do it for a minute, because I can keep it up for fifteen rounds, three minutes a round. Now, how is Joe Louis gonna get to me? I just can't see slow Joe Louis, who is shorter than I am, fought at a lighter weight than I did, and wasn't half as fast, knock me out. Would I just quit dancing that night and stand there and let him hit me?

In time, Louis recognized Ali's skills as a fighter, reckoning that he would still have beaten him but not as easily as he disposed of Johnny Paychek. Ali, for his part, rediscovered his respect as Louis grew weaker. In the mid-seventies, he invited the old champ to his training camp and offered him a gift of $30,000. Reminded by a reporter of his earlier criticism of Louis, he refused to acknowledge that he had said those bad things.

"Everybody loved Joe," Ali said after Louis's death. "From black folks to redneck Mississippi crackers, they loved him. They're all crying. That shows you. Howard Hughes dies, with all his billions, not a tear. Joe Louis, everybody cried."

SCHMELING AND THE NAZI CONNECTION

When American writer Paul Gallico was in Berlin for the 1936 Olympics, he took the opportunity to visit Schmeling for a *Saturday Evening Post* interview. In the ex-champion's study, he observed a large glass cabinet displaying prizes won for amateur boxing as well as trap and skeet-shooting competitions. On a shelf stood a large bronze bust of the boxer, "not a very good one," and a plaster head of Jack Dempsey, "an excellent one."

Taking an equally prominent position was a large framed photograph of Adolf Hitler, signed by him and dedicated to the fighter in recognition of his recent sensational win over Louis. On the floor stood an enormous basket of fast-fading flowers decorated with red ribbons and swastika emblems, a gift from Hitler to Frau Schmeling. "It must have taken three men to lift it," noted Gallico.

Hitler was immensely proud of what Schmeling had done for Germany and lauded his achievement as proving the doctrine of Aryan superiority. Max, for his part, was flattered by the dictator's attention. Although the relationship would be soured by Max's refusal to ditch his Jewish manager and damaged beyond repair after his crushing defeat by Louis in the return match, it is clear that there once was mutual admiration between fighter and Führer.

Schmeling admitted he was initially pleased with Hitler's rise to power. Like most Germans, he came under the almost hypnotic spell of the Nazi leader and was caught up in the spirit of optimism that lifted the country in the early 1930s. The outside world, feeling threatened by the Third Reich's soaring ambitions and denouncing its treatment of Jews, found it hard to disagree with America's proposal to boycott the Berlin Olympics. Schmeling, upheld as apolitical and an internationally popular sportsman, agreed to present the German case to the American Olympic Committee. His plea undoubtedly helped influence the decision to drop the boycott.

It wasn't the only time Schmeling ran errands for the Nazis. During the war, he accepted a mission to search for Primo Carnera, reportedly the victim of a German firing squad. Propaganda Minister Goebbels was delighted when the Italian boxer was found safe and well. It gave him the ammunition to denounce the enemy's trumped-up story. Schmeling was rewarded with another trip, to meet the pope and help heal a rift between Berlin and the Vatican.

Though Schmeling's actions caused him to be branded a Nazi collaborator, it was never a one-way thing. In return for his cooperation, he was able to obtain valuable favors, including gaining clemency for Jews under threat of imprisonment or death. While the party hierarchy came to regard him as something of a nuisance, they could not afford to be dismissive of someone who remained a national icon.

Abroad, Schmeling's insistence on keeping Joe Jacobs as his

manager in a face-to-face meeting with Hitler won him widespread praise. His uncompromising stand was certainly brave. It was also pragmatic. He knew if he dumped Jacobs he would be finished with the American people. Keeping their respect would be vital in re-establishing valuable links when the war was over.

Looking back today, over half a century since the end of the war, it is hard to escape the conclusion that Schmeling was an opportunist. Undoubtedly, he was in a difficult position. His home, his family, and his roots were in Germany, while his boxing interests could not flourish without American support. The logical thing was to keep a tentative foot in both camps.

It was 1954 by the time Schmeling made his first postwar visit to the United States. He was invited to Wisconsin to referee some preliminary bouts on a bill headed by German middleweight champion Hans Stretz against Alabama's Billy Kilgore. The promoters rightly calculated that the former champion's appearance would entice many of the city's large German population to buy tickets.

Max used the visit to look up some old acquaintances and mend a few bridges. Happy to find that Louis was prepared to let bygones be bygones, as already described, he next tried to contact Paul Damski, to whom he owed an everlasting debt for introducing him to Anny Ondra. The former boxing promoter and his wife, Sonia, had fled Germany in 1933, the same year Max and Anny got married. Damski arrived in England filled with hatred for Germany and all things German. That included his one-time friend, Schmeling.

"He was a German. A Nazi. He was no different from the rest," Damski told Stanley Weston, editor and publisher of *Boxing Illustrated,* in 1964. "That was how I felt at the time. I came face to face with him a year later, by accident, in a London sports arena. It was on May 12, 1934. But I turned my back on him and left him standing there."

When Schmeling was in the United States for his return match with Louis, he had tried to phone Damski, then living in New York. His messages were left unanswered. Damski took his wife to see the fight "praying to see him get his head knocked off."

Now it was 1954, and Max still hadn't given up his quest for reconciliation. Damski's son answered the phone but couldn't persuade his father to take the receiver. Later that day, Damski got a call from

Harry Markson, managing director of the Madison Square Garden Corporation, whom he knew and respected. Markson said Schmeling was with him and desperately wanted to set up a meeting. Damski softened a little and had a short conversation with Max. Fifteen minutes later, a cab pulled up outside Damski's diamond store. Schmeling stepped out, entered the shop, and threw his arms around Damski's neck. Damski, however, was still doubtful. He did not hug back. After talking for about an hour, it was agreed that they should dine together at Jack Dempsey's restaurant. They sat down at three o'clock in the afternoon and were there until four o'clock the next morning.

Damski recalled:

> At first Schmeling did all the talking, and I just listened. But after a few hours he convinced me I had made a terrible mistake. He was never a Nazi and, in fact, he had risked his life working against Hitler. Max mentioned the names of at least a hundred Jews he claimed he helped save from the gas chambers. Of course, he could have made up those names. I was still skeptical, very skeptical. But later he mentioned three names I knew well. They were friends of mine in Germany, and I knew the circumstances under which they had escaped the Nazis. Schmeling also knew those circumstances down to the smallest details. Everything he said fitted together like the parts of a watch. He couldn't have known those things unless he was speaking the truth.

Saul Goldsmith was one of the names mentioned. He was sentenced to death, but Schmeling intervened to get him transferred to another camp where he would be safe. There was John Braude, an old friend of Damski's, whom Max sneaked out of a truck that was taking him to a concentration camp. Walter Friedman, another friend, was saved when Schmeling arranged to have his records switched from one file to another at Gestapo headquarters.

Schmeling explained that he was able to pull off these daring feats because of his association with a group of insurgent officers on the German General Staff. This was the same group that planned an assassination attempt on Hitler in 1944. Max told Damski that he always hated Hitler: "I wanted to poison him because I knew he was mad—like a wild dog."

There were other poignant things said by Schmeling during that marathon conversation at Dempsey's, things that convinced Damski he had sorely misjudged his dining companion. Max said he had not spoken to his younger brother, Rudolph, since the end of the war because he was a Nazi.

Then there was Anny. "She is a Czech," said Schmeling, "and everybody knows the Nazis hated the Czechs as much as they hated the Jews. How could I ever be part of something that killed my wife's people?"

In December 1960, when Max returned to the United States to appear in a *This Is Your Life* television tribute to Joe Louis, he spent considerable time with Damski. He also granted an interview to *New York Post* columnist Leonard Shecter. The writer was not as receptive to Schmeling's plea for understanding. He wrote:

> There is an air of unreality about Max Schmeling, as though he duels in an old silent film, scratchy and full of jerky, puppet-like movements. Somehow, it's a feeling he cultivates, begging belief that there was no Nazi Germany, no war, no blood, nothing but a time when men spent themselves gloriously only in the square arena of boxing . . . The truth is that the first time Schmeling dropped on Crete he ruined both his knees and that was the end of the war for him. This is no apology for Schmeling, who wore the uniform of the enemy. It may even be true that, as has been written, he stood by and watched riflemen take target practice against Jewish children burrowing out of the Warsaw ghetto.

Shecter also quoted a columnist, whom he did not name, of writing about a proposed visit by Schmeling just after the war: "I trust that he will give an exhibition, not of boxing, but of how he dropped as a paratrooper on Crete and helped obliterate an outnumbered British garrison."

Schmeling was furious when he read Shecter's column. "How can he say things like that?" he complained to the now sympathetic Damski.

"I never saw Max as angry as he was that day," remembered Damski. "His face was flushed and he kept clenching and unclenching his fists. Then he reached into his inside pocket and pulled out a letter."

The letter was written by a Munich businessman, a friend of Schmeling's, and told of a meeting with General Delmar T. Spivey, head of the Culver Military Academy in Indiana. Spivey spoke very highly of the ex-boxer and told how he had got to know Max while he was a prisoner-of-war in Berlin in 1944. Schmeling deserved a lot of credit for the way he helped captured Americans, said Spivey, who gave details.

Damski said, "If there remained the slightest doubt in my mind about Max being a Nazi, that letter wiped it out."

Some of the damage done by Shecter's vitriolic article was repaired when another prominent New York reporter, Bill McCormick, interviewed the German and learned about the letter. Not prepared to accept the details at face value, McCormick checked it out with Spivey. The general confirmed everything and extended an invitation to Max and his wife to be his guests at Culver. McCormick wrote an objective piece about the incident. He neither confirmed nor challenged Schmeling's statements, but concluded, "The evidence is now before the jury."

As late as 1991, *American Heritage*, in an article penned by Joseph D. O'Brien, denounced Schmeling as "vehemently pro-Hitler." Two years later, the English periodical *History Today* published an article under the dual byline of two Rhode Island University academics, Robert G. Weisbord and Norbert Hedderich. It read, in part:

In 1936 Schmeling allowed himself to be used when he wrote a one-page foreword to a book on German boxing which was published by the Nazi party. The author, Ludwig Haymann, was a former amateur boxing champion and sometime professional fighter. Subtitled *Boxing as a Race Problem*, the book made the case for Germans to develop a unique style of boxing in line with Nazi racial ideology. Ultranationalism permeated the text which contained a few anti-Semitic slurs. Schmeling's brief foreword was generally inoffensive and bland in tone, although it did refer to "our leader, Adolf Hitler" and to the Führer's belief that boxing built character. Max also wished the book the success it deserved.

The writers were convinced that Schmeling never joined the Nazi party. Nor did they believe he was ever a spokesman for the party in the United States or in Germany. They quoted "a clearly hostile remark about Hitler" made by Schmeling when he met Harry Markson, then a newspaper reporter, in 1936. Max was shown a copy of the *New York World Telegraph* bearing a photograph of Norman Thomas, the perennial Socialist Party candidate for the presidency. He was curious about Thomas, but Markson assured him that Thomas was not taken seriously and had no chance of making it to the White House. Schmeling replied that they had a fellow like that in Germany who wasn't taken seriously and now he was running the country.

In 1992, after Schmeling had been inducted into the International Boxing Hall of Fame, Dr. Laurence McNamee went to Hamburg to interview the eighty-six-year-old former champion for *Boxing Illustrated*. He asked about the old newspaper reports that he became Hitler's darling and that he and his wife had dinner with the Führer. Schmeling told him:

It's normal for a head of state to have a reception for a successful athlete. The papers were correct. I wonder, though, if they mentioned how many times I turned Hitler down? Did they ever mention that I had dinner with President Roosevelt? That he used to come to my training camp? That I used to correspond and exchange stamps with Roosevelt and Jim Farley, his campaign manager? No. Hitler really embarrassed both me and my wife.

There is no doubt Schmeling could have offset much of the negative publicity had he chosen to disclose how he had helped Jews during the war. It was left to others to reveal his heroism on *Kristallnacht*, when he sheltered and helped the young Lewin brothers escape to safety. Modesty might have played a part in his reluctance to talk about such incidents, but there could also have been an element of that old pragmatism at play. Better not to boast about deeds that some of his fellow countrymen, even after the war, would have considered unacceptable.

Today, there is no clear consensus on where Schmeling stands in relation to his dealings with the Nazi regime. American boxing historian Tracy Callis thought that the reception Max got from Hitler after beating Louis encouraged him to be tolerant of some Nazi policies, but the fact that he put his own life at risk to help others showed he valued humanitarian principles. Boxing archivist Hank Kaplan suggested that Schmeling was a victim of circumstances. On his travels, he would have seen democracy at work but could not opt out of living in a police state. "My impression remains that most Americans who know Max speak favorably of him," said Kaplan.

Niels Thorsen, a Dane with one of the world's largest collections of boxing books, said,

> Many Germans who did not sympathize with the policies of the Nazis had to be smart to survive. One obvious thing to do was to play it a bit in both directions, and Max was a master at that. He knew that Hitler could use him after his victory over Louis. That gave him leeway to such an extent that he could work openly, even with Jews. Hitler would close his eyes as long as Max remained in the public eye, a person who furthered the vision of the Aryan race and the 1,000-year Reich.

Others will not hear a bad word said about Schmeling. Rinze van der Meer, Dutch correspondent for the British weekly *Boxing News*, said that the afternoon he spent in Max's company in 1995 was "one of the best days of my life." Arrangements had been made for him, along with a few others, to visit the ex-champion's home. "Be on time, as Herr Schmeling is very punctual," he was warned. He was there at noon on the dot. Initially overawed in the presence of such a famous man, the visitor was put completely at ease as Schmeling went to great pains to ask about his life, his work, his family, and his interests. A 2004 television documentary that attacked Schmeling's association with the Nazis was described by van der Meer as "below the belt."

Boxing News assistant editor Tony Connolly agreed: "It was poor. As if Max could denounce Germany while in America to box . . . he could never have gone home—and he had family back home to think about."

LOUIS AND THE CIVIL RIGHTS ISSUE

Joe Louis had enough on his plate, especially trying to cope with persistent health and financial problems, without being badgered by questions like: What did you ever do for the black cause? It hurt especially that a fellow fighter, Muhammad Ali, was among those who accused him of being grateful, compliant, and undemanding in his attitude to white people, that he was an Uncle Tom.

It was the early 1960s, and the American civil rights movement was gaining momentum. In southern states, what started out as non-violent protest and widespread civil disobedience spilled over into bloodshed. A landmark attempt by James Meredith to become the first black man to enroll at the University of Mississippi required that five thousand troops be called in, and two people were killed. Medgar Evers, field secretary of the National Association for the Advancement of Colored People, was shot dead in front of his home in Jackson. Birmingham police chief "Bull" Connor turned fire hoses and dogs loose on marchers. In the same town, a black church was bombed and four young girls died. Television screens across the world showed what was happening in the "heart of democracy."

During his boxing career, Louis had never been a vocal opponent of racism. He did make a minor stand against segregation in the army during and after the war and succeeded in getting some of the rules changed, but he was always wary of offending whites. His managers had drilled into him from the start that if he once stepped out of line, it could mean the end of his fighting ambitions. He obeyed their "commandments" to the letter.

Though he resented the racism he saw all around him, he did not believe it was his role to be a spokesman for protest. Back in the 1930s and 1940s, his fellow blacks thought none the less of him for that. They were proud of what he had achieved, and his dignified behavior had helped wipe away the shame they had felt after Jack Johnson's outrageous provocations when he was at the peak of his fame. There were times when Louis expressed regret that he did not have the ability to present himself as a black leader. "Sometimes I wish I had the fire of a Jackie Robinson to speak out and tell the black man's story," he told one interviewer.

Even as the civil rights campaign led many blacks to be more outspoken, Louis preferred to keep his silence. White reporters who succeeded in dragging some comment out of him on the activities of more militant black athletes revealed him as a gradualist and an integrationist. When Cassius Clay announced his conversion to the Muslim faith and changed his name to Muhammad Ali, Louis felt sufficiently aroused to tell reporters:

> I'm against Black Muslims, and I'm against Cassius Clay being a Black Muslim. I'll never go along with the idea that all white people are devils. I've always believed that every man is my brother. I was born a Baptist and I'll die a Baptist. The way I see it, the Black Muslims want to do just what we have been fighting against for 100 years. They want to separate the races and that's a step back at a time when we're going for integration.

When some black athletes planned to boycott the 1968 Olympics, Louis showed his disapproval. He thought they could do more for racial equality by their success in the arenas than by staging demonstrations.

Four years earlier, probably feeling the pressure to be more active for civil rights, he took part in a low-key protest in the heart of Harlem. Along with entertainer Dick Gregory and local politician Jesse Gray, he celebrated "New York's Worst Fair" in contrast to the New York World's Fair then being held at Flushing Meadows, by standing on a street corner and brandishing small rubber rats labeled "souvenir of the ghetto."

In July 1964, a New York police lieutenant shot and killed a black teenager just outside Harlem. The slaying resulted in an orgy of violence, not only in Harlem but also in another black enclave, Bedford-Stuyvesant in Brooklyn. While police were clubbing protesters, stores were looted and set on fire. Despite fears of much worse, only one man was killed and thirty people were injured.

After calm was restored, Louis was among the influential black celebrities asked by city officials to listen to the people's grievances and see what could be done. In a statement, he deplored what had happened and hoped a solution could be found. He refused to back calls for the sacking of Police Commissioner Michael Murphy ("He doesn't walk the beat. He doesn't hit anyone in the head with a stick"). The various civil rights groups had a good purpose, he said, but it was a shame that hoodlums sometimes took advantage of the people's feelings.

Louis was never comfortable with calls to align himself with the civil rights campaign. In an interview with Jimmy Breslin, of the *New York Herald Tribune*, he expressed the belief that the racial problems would eventually be solved, but not by "a lot of Beatniks" who were only getting in the way of progress.

What his critics failed to acknowledge was that Louis came from a different era, when being "a good Negro" was what mattered most to many blacks as well as whites. If, back in the thirties, he had tried to act as Muhammad Ali did three decades later, the world would never have known the Joe Louis who rose to fame in the boxing ring and who made black people everywhere feel a sense of racial pride, some perhaps for the first time in their lives.

Besides, it was against his nature to be an outspoken leader of any cause. This was the man of pithy sayings like "He can run, but he can't hide" and "We'll win because we're on God's side." He could never have held a television audience spellbound for an hour as Ali frequently did. All he wanted was to be left alone to enjoy his golf, his flutters on the gambling tables, his women, and the company of his friends. In the boxing ring, he let his fists do the talking. There, few could match his eloquence.

APPENDIX I

JOE LOUIS'S

PROFESSIONAL RECORD

TOTAL CONTESTS: 67; WON: 64 (50 BY KO); LOST: 3
KEY: W = won; L = lost; D = drew; KO = knockout;
TKO = technical knockout; pts = points; disq = disqualified
*Denotes world heavyweight title fight

1934

Date	Opponent	Result	Location
July 4	Jack Kracken	W TKO 1	Chicago
July 12	Willie Davis	W TKO 3	Chicago
July 30	Larry Udell	W TKO 2	Chicago
August 13	Jack Kranz	W pts 8	Chicago
August 27	Buck Everett	W KO 2	Chicago
September 11	Alex Borchuk	W TKO 4	Detroit
September 26	Adolph Waiter	W pts 10	Chicago
October 24	Art Sykes	W KO 8	Chicago
October 31	Jack O'Dowd	W KO 2	Detroit
November 14	Stanley Poreda	W KO 1	Chicago
November 30	Charley Massera	W KO 3	Chicago
December 14	Lee Ramage	W TKO 8	Chicago

1935

January 4	Patsy Perron	W pts 10	Detroit
January 11	Hans Birkie	W TKO 10	Pittsburgh
February 21	Lee Ramage	W TKO 2	Los Angeles
March 8	Donald "Red" Barry	W TKO 3	San Francisco
March 29	Natie Brown	W pts 10	Detroit
April 12	Roy Lazer	W TKO 3	Chicago
June 25	Primo Carnera	W TKO 6	New York
August 7	King Levinsky	W TKO 1	Chicago
September 24	Max Baer	W KO 4	New York
December 13	Paolino Uzcudun	W TKO 4	New York

(Some records show wins in 1935 over Biff Bennett or Benton, Roscoe Toles, Willie Davis, and Gene Stanton, but these were billed as exhibitions.)

1936

January 17	Charlie Retzlaff	W KO 1	Chicago
June 19	Max Schmeling	L KO 12	New York
August 18	Jack Sharkey	W KO 3	New York
September 22	Al Ettore	W KO 5	Philadelphia
October 9	Jorge Brescia	W KO 3	New York
December 14	Eddie Simms	W TKO 1	Cleveland

1937

January 11	Steve Ketchell	W KO 2	Buffalo
January 29	Bob Pastor	W pts 10	New York
February 17	Natie Brown	W TKO 4	Kansas City
*June 22	James J. Braddock	W KO 8	Chicago

(Won world heavyweight title)

*August 30	Tommy Farr	W pts 15	New York

1938

*February 23	Nathan Mann	W KO 3	New York
*April 1	Harry Thomas	W KO 5	Chicago
*June 22	Max Schmeling	W KO 1	New York

1939

*January 25	John Henry Lewis	W KO 1	New York
*April 17	Jack Roper	W KO 1	Los Angeles
*June 28	Tony Galento	W TKO 4	New York

1939 (cont.)

*September 20	Bob Pastor	W KO 11	Detroit

1940

*February 9	Arturo Godoy	W pts 15	New York
*March 29	Johnny Paychek	W KO 2	New York
*June 20	Arturo Godoy	W TKO 8	New York
*December 16	Al McCoy	W TKO 6	Boston

1941

*January 31	Clarence "Red" Burman	W KO 5	New York
*February 17	Gus Dorazio	W KO 2	Philadelphia
*March 21	Abe Simon	W TKO 13	Detroit
*April 8	Tony Musto	W TKO 9	Saint Louis
*May 23	Buddy Baer	W disq 7	Washington
*June 18	Billy Conn	W KO 13	New York
*September 29	Lou Nova	W TKO 6	New York

1942

*January 9	Buddy Baer	W KO 1	New York
*March 27	Abe Simon	W KO 6	New York

1943–45

Inactive

1946

*June 19	Billy Conn	W KO 8	New York
*September 18	Tami Mauriello	W KO 1	New York

1947

*December 5	Jersey Joe Walcott	W pts 15	New York

1948

*June 25	Jersey Joe Walcott	W KO 11	New York

1949

March 1	Announced retirement as world heavyweight champion

1950

*September 27	Ezzard Charles	L pts 15	New York

(Challenge for world heavyweight title)

November 29	Cesar Brion	W pts 10	Chicago

1951

January 3	Freddie Beshore	W TKO 4	Detroit
February 7	Omelio Agramonte	W pts 10	Miami
February 23	Andy Walker	W TKO 10	San Francisco
May 2	Omelio Agramonte	W pts 10	Detroit
June 15	Lee Savold	W KO 6	New York
August 1	Cesar Brion	W pts 10	San Francisco
August 15	Jimmy Bivins	W pts 10	Baltimore
October 26	Rocky Marciano	L KO 8	New York

APPENDIX 2

MAX SCHMELING'S
PROFESSIONAL RECORD

TOTAL CONTESTS: 70; WON: 56 (37 by KO); LOST: 10; DREW: 4
KEY: W = won; L = lost; D = drew; KO = knockout;
TKO = technical knockout; pts = points; disq = disqualified
*Denotes world heavyweight title fight

1924

Date	Opponent	Result	Location
August 2	Kurt Czapp	W TKO 6	Düsseldorf
September 20	Willy Louis	W KO 1	Duisberg
September 22	Willi van der Vyver	W KO 3	Cologne
October 4	Rocky Knight	W pts 8	Cologne
October 10	Max Dieckmann	L TKO 4	Berlin
October 31	Fred Hammer	W TKO 3	Cologne
December 4	Hans Breuer	W KO 2	Cologne
December 7	Battling Marthar	W KO 3	Düsseldorf
December 17	Helmuth Hartig	W KO 1	Berlin
December 26	Jimmy Lygett	W disq 4	Cologne

1925

Date	Opponent	Result	Location
January 18	Jan Kloudts	W KO 2	Cologne
January 20	Joe Mehling	W pts 6	Berlin
March 1	Léon Randol	W KO 4	Cologne

March 15	Alf Baker	W pts 8	Cologne
April 3	Jimmy Lygett	Drew 8	Berlin
April 28	Fred Hammer	W pts 8	Bonn
May 9	Jack Taylor	L pts 10	Cologne
June 14	Léon Randol	Drew 10	Brussels
September 1	Larry Gains	L TKO 2	Cologne
November 8	René Compere	W pts 8	Cologne

1926

February 12	Max Dieckmann	Drew 8	Berlin
March 19	Willy Louis	W KO 1	Cologne
July 13	August Vongehr	W TKO 1	Berlin
August 24	Max Dieckmann	W KO 1	Berlin

(Won German light-heavyweight title)

October 1	Hermann van't Hof	W disq 8	Berlin

1927

January 13	Jack Stanley	W KO 8	Berlin
January 23	Louis Wilms	W KO 8	Breslau
February 4	Joe Mehling	W KO 3	Dresden
March 12	Léon Sebilo	W KO 2	Dortmund
April 8	Francis Charles	W TKO 8	Berlin
April 26	Stanley Glen	W KO 1	Hamburg
May 7	Robert Larsen	W pts 10	Frankfurt
May 17	Raymond Paillaux	W KO 3	Frankfurt
June 19	Fernand Delarge	W TKO 14	Dortmund

(Won European light-heavyweight title)

July 13	Jack Taylor	W pts 10	Hamburg
August 7	Willem Westbroeck	W KO 1	Essen
September 2	Robert Larsen	W KO 3	Berlin
October 2	Louis Clement	W KO 6	Dortmund
November 6	Hein Domgörgen	W KO 7	Leipzig
December 2	Gypsy Daniels	W pts 10	Berlin

1928

January 6	Michele Bonaglia	W KO 1	Berlin
February 25	Gypsy Daniels	L KO 1	Frankfurt
March 11	Ted Moore	W pts 10	Dortmund
April 4	Franz Diener	W pts 15	Berlin

(Won German heavyweight title)

1928 (cont.)

November 23	Joe Monte	W KO 8	New York

1929

January 4	Joe Sekyra	W pts 10	New York
January 22	Pietro Corri	W KO 1	New York
February 1	Johnny Risko	W TKO 9	New York
June 27	Paolino Uzcudun	W pts 15	New York

1930

*June 12	Jack Sharkey	W disq 4	New York

(Won world heavyweight title)

1931

*July 3	Young Stribling	W TKO 15	Cleveland

(Retained world heavyweight title)

1932

*June 21	Jack Sharkey	L pts 15	New York

(Lost world heavyweight title)

September 26	Mickey Walker	W TKO 8	New York

1933

June 8	Max Baer	L TKO 10	New York

1934

February 13	Steve Hamas	L pts 12	Philadelphia
May 13	Paolino Uzcudun	Drew 12	Barcelona
August 26	Walter Neusel	W TKO 9	Hamburg

1935

March 10	Steve Hamas	W KO 9	Hamburg
July 7	Paolino Uzcudun	W pts 12	Berlin

1936

June 19	Joe Louis	W KO 12	New York

1937

December 14	Harry Thomas	W TKO 8	New York

1938

January 30	Ben Foord	W pts 12	Hamburg
April 16	Steve Dudas	W TKO 5	Hamburg

*June 22   Joe Louis   L KO 1   New York
(Challenge for world heavyweight title)

1939
July 2   Adolf Heuser   W KO 1   Stuttgart
(Won European heavyweight title)

1940–46
Inactive

1947
September 28   Werner Vollmer   W KO 7   Frankfurt
December 7   Hans-Joachim   W pts 10   Hamburg
                  Drägestein

1948
May 23   Walter Neusel   L pts 10   Hamburg
October 2   Hans-Joachim   W KO 9   Kiel
                  Drägestein
October 31   Richard Vogt   L pts 10   Berlin

BIBLIOGRAPHY

Allen, David Rayvern. *Punches on the Page: A Boxing Anthology.* Edinburgh: Mainstream, 1998.

Anderson, Dave. *Ringmasters: Great Boxing Trainers Talk About Their Art.* London: Robson Books, 1991.

Andre, Sam, and Nat Fleischer. *A Pictorial History of Boxing.* London: Hamlyn, 1984.

Astor, Gerald. *Gloves Off: The Joe Louis Story.* London: Pelham Books, 1975.

Bak, Richard. *Joe Louis: The Great Black Hope.* Dallas, Texas: Da Capo Press, 1998.

Barrow, Joe Louis, Jr., and Barbara Munder. *Joe Louis: The Brown Bomber.* London: Weidenfeld and Nicolson, 1988.

Batchelor, Denzil. *Jack Johnson and His Times.* London: Phoenix Sports Books, 1956.

Bingham, Howard L., and Max Wallace. *Muhammad Ali's Greatest Fight: Cassius Clay vs. the United States of America.* New York: M. Evans, 2000.

Blewett, Bert. *The A–Z of World Boxing.* London: Robson Books, 1996.

Bromberg, Lester. *Boxing's Unforgettable Fights.* New York: Ronald Press, 1962.

Brown, Gene, ed. *The Complete Book of Boxing: A New York Times Scrapbook History.* New York: Arno Press, 1980.

Carpenter, Harry. *Masters of Boxing.* London: Heinemann, 1964.

Chandler, David, John Gill, Tania Guha, and Gilane Tawadros, eds. *Boxer: An Anthology of Writings on Boxing and Visual Culture.* Cambridge, Mass.: MIT Press, 1996.

Collings, Mark, ed. *Muhammad Ali: Through the Eyes of the World.* London: Sanctuary Publishing, 2001.

Durant, John, and Edward Rice. *Come Out Fighting.* New York: Duell, Sloan and Pearce, New York, 1946.

Fantuz, Giuliana V., Ivan Malfatto, and Gino Argentin. *My Father Primo Carnera: The Sporting Career, the Personality and the Man in Umberto and Giovanna Maria Carnera's Memories.* Milan, Italy: SEP Editrice, 2002.

Fleischer, Nat. *50 Years at Ringside.* London: Transworld Publishers, 1958.

————. *The Heavyweight Championship: An Informal History of Heavyweight Boxing from 1719 to the Present Day.* London: Putnam, 1949.

Fleischer, Nat, ed. *The Ring Record Book and Boxing Encyclopaedia.* New York: The Ring Book Shop, 1962.

Gains, Larry. *The Impossible Dream.* London: Leisure Publications, 1976.

Giller, Norman, and Neil Duncanson. *Crown of Thorns: The Bitter History of a Century's Heavyweight Championship Boxing.* London: Pan Macmillan, 1992.

Gutteridge, Reg. *The Big Punchers.* London: Century Hutchison, 1989.

Hauser, Thomas. *Muhammad Ali: His Life and Times.* New York: Simon and Schuster, 1992 (reprint edition).

Heinz, W.C., ed. *The Fireside Book of Boxing: A Collection of Pugilism's Great Literature and Art.* New York: Simon and Schuster, 2000.

Heller, Peter. *In This Corner: Forty World Champions Tell Their Stories.* New York: Dell Publishing, 1973.

Helliwell, Arthur. *The Private Lives of Famous Fighters.* Windsor: Cedric Day, 1949.

Jakoubek, Robert. *Joe Louis: Heavyweight Champion.* New York: Chelsea House, 1990.

Khan, Roger. *A Flame of Pure Fire: Jack Dempsey and the Roaring '20s.* New York: Harcourt Brace, 1999.

Leonard, Maurice. *Mae West: Empress of Sex.* New York: Carol Publishing, 1992.

Lonkhurst, Bob. *Man of Courage: The Life and Career of Tommy Farr.* Lewes, Sussex: The Book Guild, 1997.

Louis, Joe, with Edna and Art Rust Jr. *Joe Louis: My Life.* New York: Berkeley, 1980.

McNeill, Jim. *That Night in the Garden: Great Fights and Great Moments from Madison Square Garden.* London: Robson Books, 2003.

McRae, Donald. *Heroes without a Country: America's Betrayal of Joe Louis and Jesse Owens.* New York: Ecco, 2003.

Mead, Chris. *Champion: Joe Louis, Black Hero in White World.* New York: Scribner, 1985.

Miller, Margery. *Joe Louis: American.* London: Panther Books, 1952.

Mullally, Frederic. *Primo: The Story of "Man Mountain" Carnera.* London: Robson Books, 1991.

Mullan, Harry, and Peter Arnold, eds. *A Boxing Companion.* Harpenden, Herts: Lennard Books, 1992.

Myrdal, Gunnar. *An American Dilemma: The Negro Problem and Modern Democracy.* Somerset, N.J.: Transaction Publishers, 1996 (reprint edition).

Odd, Gilbert. *Great Moments in Sport: Heavyweight Boxing.* London: Pelham Books, 1973.

——— *Kings of the Ring: 100 Years of World Heavyweight Boxing.* Feltham, Middlesex: Newnes Books, 1985.

Pacheco, Ferdie, M. D. *The 12 Greatest Rounds of Boxing.* London: Robson Books, 2001.

Remnick, David. *King of the World: Muhammad Ali and the Rise of an American Hero.* New York: Random House, 1998.

Roberts, James B., and Alexander G. Skutt. *The Boxing Register: The International Boxing Hall of Fame Official Record Book.* New York: McBooks Press, 1997.

Roberts, Randy. *Papa Jack: Jack Johnson and the Era of White Hopes.* London: Robson Books, 1986.

Sammons, Jeffrey T. *Beyond the Ring: The Role of Boxing in American Society.* Urbana and Chicago: University of Illinois Press, 1988.

Schmeling, Max. *Max Schmeling: An Autobiography.* Chicago: Bonus Books, 1998 (First published in Germany by Verlag Ullstein, Berlin, 1977).

Seligmann, Dr. Matthew, Dr. John Davison, and John McDonald. *In the Shadow of the Swastika: Life in Germany Under the Nazis 1933–1945.* Staplehurst, Kent: Spellmount, 2003.

Shirer, William L. *The Rise and Fall of the Third Reich.* New York: Simon and Schuster, 1990.

Snelling, O. F. *The Ringside Book of Boxing.* London: Robson Books, 1991 (First published as *A Bedside Book of Boxing,* Pelham Books, London, 1972).

Steen, Rob. *Sonny Boy: The Life and Strife of Sonny Liston.* London: Methuen, 1993.

Stone, Norman. *Hitler.* Boston: Little, Brown, 1980.

Sugar, Bert Randolph. *The Great Fights: A Pictorial History of Boxing's Greatest Bouts.* New York: Gallery Books, 1984.

Sugar, Bert Randolph, ed. *The Ring Record Book.* New York: The Ring Publishing Corp., 1980.

Sugden, John. *Boxing and Society: An International Analysis.* Manchester: Manchester University Press, 1996.

Suster, Gerald. *Champions of the Ring: The Lives and Times of Boxing's Heavyweight Heroes.* London: Robson Books, 1992.

Weston, Stanley, ed. *The Best of* The Ring: *Recapturing 70 Years of Boxing Classics.* Chicago: Bonus Books, 1992.

Wilson, Peter. *Boxing's Greatest Prize: Twelve Legendary Fights for the Heavyweight Championship of the World.* London: Arrow Books, 1982.

———. *More Ringside Seats.* London: Stanley Paul, 1959.

Wilson, Peter. *Ringside Seat.* London: Rich and Cowan, 1949.

Wilson, Peter, ed. *The Old Holborn Book of Boxing.* London: Gallagher Ltd., 1969.

SELECT ARTICLES

Deford, Frank. "Almost a Hero." *Sports Illustrated* (December 3, 2001).

Farhood, Steve, compiler. "The Best of the Best: 100 Years of Boxing." *The Ring* (winter 1994).

Goldman, Herbert G. "A Ranking of the Top 100 Heavyweights of All Time." *Boxing Illustrated* (May 1989).

Louis, Joe, as told to George Bennett. "Inside Joe Louis." *Boxing and Wrestling* (September 1953).

O'Brian, Joseph D. "The Business of Boxing." *American Heritage* (October 1991).

The Ring editors. "The 50 Greatest Heavyweights of All Time." *The Ring* (holiday 1998).

Schmeling, Max, as told to Paul Gallico. "The Way I Beat Joe Louis." *Saturday Evening Post* (August 29 and September 5, 1936).

Shecter, Leonard. "Working Press." *New York Post* (December 6, 1960).

Silver, Mike. "The 10 Greatest Punchers of All Time." *The Ring* (September 1997).

Weisbord, Robert, and Norbert Hedderich. "Max Schmeling, Righteous Ring Warrior?" *History Today* vol. 43 (January 1993).

Weston, Stanley. "The Strange Case of Max Schmeling." *Boxing Illustrated* (June 1964).

NEWSPAPERS AND MAGAZINES

UNITED STATES

Atlanta Journal, Boxing Illustrated, Boxing International, Boxing Pictorial, Boxing and Wrestling, Boxing Yearbook, Chicago Defender, Detroit News, Life, Look, Milwaukee Journal, New York Daily News, New York Herald Tribune, New York Journal, New York Mirror, New York Sun, New York Times, Pittsburgh Courier, Pittsburgh Post-Gazette, The Ring, Washington Post.

BRITAIN AND IRELAND

Boxing News, Daily Express, Daily Mail, Daily Telegraph, Evening Herald (Dublin), *Irish Independent, The Observer, Sunday Pictorial, The Times.*

INDEX